Early Mathematical Explorations

Parents, teachers and caregivers all play a significant role in establishing a child's confidence and competence in mathematics. *Early Mathematical Explorations* shows readers how to provide young children with rich mathematical learning environments and experiences.

This book presents teachers with a sound theoretical framework for encouraging children to explore mathematical concepts and become numerate in the 21st century. It shows that mathematical learning can occur in a variety of ways, including when children explore ideas through play, problem solving and problem posing; engage in a rich variety of multimodal learning experiences; pursue self-directed activities and cooperate with others; and make connections between ideas and experiences in their everyday worlds.

Chapters include numerous practical activities for children from birth to eight years old. Written in a user-friendly style and generously illustrated with examples of activities and children's work, *Early Mathematical Explorations* is an essential resource for pre- and in-service teachers alike.

Additional resources are available online at www.cambridge.edu.au/academic/earlymaths.

Nicola Yelland is Research Professor of Education in the College of Education at Victoria University, Melbourne.

Carmel Diezmann is Professor and the Queensland Head of Education at the Australian Catholic University.

Deborah Butler is a Queensland primary teacher with over 30 years of classroom experience.

Early Mathematical Explorations

Nicola Yelland, Carmel Diezmann
and Deborah Butler

CAMBRIDGE
UNIVERSITY PRESS

CAMBRIDGE
UNIVERSITY PRESS

477 Williamstown Road, Port Melbourne, VIC 3207, Australia

Published in the United States of America by Cambridge University Press, New York

Cambridge University Press is part of the University of Cambridge.

It furthers the University's mission by disseminating knowledge in the pursuit of education, learning and research at the highest international levels of excellence.

www.cambridge.org
Information on this title: www.cambridge.org/9781107618824

First published by Pearson Publishing Solutions in 1999
First published by Cambridge University Press in 2014

Cover designed by Zo Gay
Typeset by Newgen Publishing and Data Services
Printed in Singapore by C.O.S. Printers Pte Ltd

A catalogue record for this publication is available from the British Library

A Cataloguing-in-Publication entry is available from the catalogue of the National Library of Australia at www.nla.gov.au

ISBN 978-1-107-61882-4 Paperback

Additional resources for this title are available at www.cambridge.edu.au/academic/earlymaths

To those we count on – our families

Contents

Contents

About the authors

Nicola Yelland is Research Professor of Education in the College of Education at Victoria University in Melbourne, Australia. Over the last decade her teaching and research have been related to the use of new technologies in school and community contexts. This has involved projects that have investigated the innovative learning of children as well as a broader consideration of the ways in which new technologies can impact on the pedagogies that teachers use and on school curricula. Her multi-disciplinary research focus has enabled her to work with early childhood, primary and middle school teachers to enhance the ways in which new technologies can be incorporated into learning contexts to make them more interesting and motivating for students, so that educational outcomes are improved.

Carmel Diezmann is Professor and the Head of Education (Queensland) at the Australian Catholic University in Australia. Her research and teaching interests in mathematics include the professional learning of teachers, the effectiveness of curriculum and the learning of young children, including those who struggle with mathematics or who need additional challenges. For the past decade, Carmel has been researching how visual representations (e.g. pictures, graphs, maps, number lines) are conceptual tools for thinking and communicating and how they influence understanding about mathematical situations. Visual representations can support children's learning and understanding. However, they can also mislead children or be overlooked by them. Due to the importance of visual representations in mathematics, we have incorporated various representations in the activities presented in this book to help familiarise and engage children with the activities.

Deborah Butler is a primary teacher with over 30 years of classroom experience. During this time she has taught in a variety of settings and held the position of Head of Infants at St Margaret's Anglican Girls School. She has also lectured on programming and planning in literacy and numeracy to preservice early childhood students at Queensland University of Technology. In more recent years Deborah has been involved in designing and implementing programs of support for children with specific learning needs.

Acknowledgements

We would like to thank the following people for their valuable assistance with this book:

Adele Amorson

Anne Blazak

Anne-Louise Gilbert

Brianna Shipman (photography)

Grace Choy

Helen Dunham

Irene Michaels

Jilianne Elliott

Keith Done

Leon Frainey (photography)

Lindy Sugars

Megan Dean

Samantha Hawton

staff, students and parents at Nundah State School and Eagle Junction State Preschool, both in Brisbane; and at St Margaret's Anglican School, Brisbane, in particular Angela Drysdale, Melissa Garbutt, Tamara Garvey and Jacqui Smith.

Chapter 1

Mathematics for the 21st century

On a visit to a classroom, Nicola (N), an early childhood educator, had the following conversation with Tessa (T), a Year 3 child:[1]

N: What are you doing, Tessa?

T: Another maths sheet.

N: Oh great! I love doing maths. What is this one about?

T: Adding sums [said glumly].

N: Do you like doing maths, Tessa?

T: No. It's boring and anyway why should I when my teacher hates it too?

N: Does she really hate it? How do you know that?

T: She never smiles when we do maths.

This anecdote indicates the strength of young children's perceptions of the learning environment. It also highlights the fact that some adults lack confidence in and enthusiasm for mathematics. This book is designed to support teachers, parents and caregivers in providing a rich mathematical environment for children in their early years (birth to eight years of age). Young children who have worthwhile and interesting mathematical experiences have the opportunity to acquire mathematical understandings and positive attitudes towards mathematics. This enables them to become numerate and use mathematics effectively in their daily lives.

Early childhood educators use observations and interpretations of children's abilities, needs and interests as the starting point for designing activities that will support each individual's learning. Learning occurs when children:

- *explore* ideas through play, problem solving and problem posing
- are *actively* involved in what they are doing
- *engage* in a rich variety of multimodal learning experiences
- *pursue self-directed activities* and cooperate with others
- *complete activities* or pursue ideas to a logical conclusion
- *share* their ideas with others
- *make connections* between ideas and experiences in their everyday world.

These principles resonate with a social constructivist view of learning (see Vygotsky 1978) and align with viewing pedagogies as knowledge processes, as advocated under the Learning by Design model (e.g. Kalantzis & Cope 2012; Yelland, Cope & Kalantzis 2008). They provide a guide for designing effective learning experiences that enable young children to actively construct knowledge. Parents, teachers and

[1] The sex of a child has been designated as female or male in alternating chapters throughout this book to avoid the use of the terms 'he or she' and 'his or her'.

caregivers need to find ways to promote these principles in meaningful experiences to enable mathematical understandings to flourish, so that each child can become numerate.

Mathematics and society

Mathematics is an integral part of everyday life. Therefore, to function effectively people need to develop mathematical proficiency – this is what we mean by being *numerate*. For example, going shopping requires expertise with the concepts of number and money. When children accompany adults on shopping trips and observe money being exchanged for goods and change being given, some understanding about number and money is developed. Children's understanding of number and money can extend further when they play shops and take on the role of customers and shopkeepers, who 'buy and sell' goods. However, children need a wide variety of experiences so that they are able to broaden their understandings about number and money in this context. The use of number in our society is complex. Number is used to identify a quantity (e.g. three cars), to signify order (e.g. the third car) and in labels (e.g. a car registration plate, EAB303).

The mathematics that is taught in schools is influenced by the mathematics required for everyday life. In the past, school mathematics focused on learning tables and 'doing sums'. This was understandable in an era when speed and accuracy in computation were important for jobs, such as those of a shop assistant or a clerk. However, shopkeeper arithmetic is inadequate for the 'digital era' of the 21st century in which access to information has become a valuable commodity, just like material goods. Rapid technological innovations in recent decades have had an enormous impact on everyday lives. For example, items are electronically scanned at the supermarket and shopping via the internet is an ubiquitous part of everyday lives.

With the advent of information and communication technologies (ICT), there were high hopes that it would improve children's outcomes in mathematics and justify the substantial expenditure by schools on hardware, software and internet connections. However, this did not occur because although teachers changed the mode of delivery, they did not capitalise on the technologies and use innovative approaches to learning. For example, teachers replaced number fact worksheets with number fact software that looked like worksheets. Over time, there have been 'pockets' of innovation where teachers have begun to use ICT differently and software designers have created interactive learning products to engage young learners. These include 'apps' – the games, communication media, editing features and organisational applications that are available for use on smartphones and tablets; see Chapters 3 and 5–9 for examples. These innovations by teachers and software designers have influenced thinking about the teaching and learning of mathematics in contemporary times and led to new ways of thinking about how we become numerate in the 21st century (see Yelland 2005, 2007).

A further way mathematics has changed in the technologically oriented world is in the enormous collection and generation of data. Hence, it has become important for children to learn how to represent, organise and interpret data, and to create and interpret tables and graphs. Technological advancements have also impacted on the types of problems that students are required to solve in mathematics. In a rapidly changing world, students need to acquire skills that empower them to deal with novelty. Computational skills alone are insufficient for the solution of novel (non-routine) problems. To solve novel problems, students need to have a broad mathematical knowledge base, to employ thinking skills and to have a positive attitude towards mathematics. As a consequence of new thinking about learning using ICTs, the demand for skills in data collection, analysis and representation, and the need to deal with novel mathematics situations, aspects of today's mathematics program should be vastly different to that of even a decade ago.

Teaching and learning mathematics

Figure 1.1: *Thinking and problem solving are central to mathematical development*

The need for high-quality mathematics education has been endorsed worldwide. Landmark reports in Australia (Chubb 2012), the United Kingdom (ACME 2011) and the United States (Ball 2003; National Academies 2006) have all highlighted the importance of supporting students to become mathematically proficient to ensure they can function effectively in contemporary times. However, Steen (1997) argues that mathematical proficiency is essential in everyday life because 'an innumerate citizen of today is as vulnerable as the illiterate peasant in Gutenberg's time' (p. xv). The achievement of the essential goal of mathematical proficiency requires attention to *concepts*, *processes* and *attitudes* in the teaching of mathematics.

Concepts are the 'big ideas' of mathematics. The key ones are *number, measurement, space* (i.e. geometry), and *chance* and *data*. Concepts are discussed further throughout the book.

Processes are the thinking skills that children use to work mathematically and to develop an understanding of the concepts. Problem solving is the core process in mathematics. An important goal in mathematics education is for children to become problem solvers. Reasoning, communicating, making connections and representing ideas are also important processes for the 21st century. These processes are complex and involve the use of other processes, such as describing attributes, matching, sorting or classifying, comparing, ordering, patterning, counting, calculating, estimating, measuring, explaining, validating, analysing, inferring and organising.

Attitude affects a child's learning in mathematics. If a child is motivated and confident, she is likely to persevere when faced with a challenge. Experiences need to be interesting, enjoyable and have personal relevance for the child. Adult support should be carefully matched to the child's needs. If insufficient support is provided, the child may become frustrated and give up. If too much support is provided, she may feel helpless and unable to proceed independently. A child's attitude is also influenced by the attitudes of others. If someone believes in a child's capabilities, she usually fulfils that expectation.

Beliefs about how children learn are evident from the ways in which adults interact with learners. For example, when an adult claps and smiles as a child attempts to walk, there is recognition of the importance of encouragement in the learning process. The role of an adult in supporting children's learning is underpinned by beliefs about learning. Previously, there was a widespread belief that children learnt by absorbing knowledge. From this perspective, the role of the teacher at school was to 'transmit knowledge' to children and there was a focus on drill and practice activities in the classroom. However, it is now widely accepted that children learn by actively constructing knowledge and making connections between new knowledge and prior knowledge. For example, based on her prior experiences, a young child might initially think that all dogs are brown. But when she sees a black dog in a picture book and an adult identifies this animal as a dog, her understanding of the term 'dogs' is expanded. An improved understanding of how children learn has implications for the role of adults in facilitating children's learning. The following section focuses on the ways in which young children's mathematical understandings develop.

Figure 1.2: *There are many opportunities for mathematical explorations*

Early mathematical experiences

Parents, teachers and caregivers all play a significant role in establishing a child's confidence and competence in mathematics. Mathematical understandings are enhanced when a child observes and explores an object; thinks about and tests an idea; and communicates findings or asks questions. Early mathematical experiences occur in a variety of settings that might include the home, the early childhood centre, the school, the park, the zoo, the beach, or a social occasion such as a birthday party. Planned experiences, such as weighing objects, are structured to provide opportunities promoting mathematical understandings. However, spontaneous experiences can also provide valuable opportunities for exploring mathematical ideas and enriching meaning making. For example, a child learns about *number* when an adult counts the stairs that she climbs or about *space* when she is asked to look for a grocery item in the supermarket. As adults play and work with young children, there are many opportunities to enrich mathematical understanding through explorations and interactions. Throughout this book, there are specific examples of ways in which adults can support young children's mathematical understandings. To become a successful problem solver, a child needs to understand conceptual knowledge, to establish processes for investigating a problem and to acquire a positive attitude. Therefore, a young child needs a range of early mathematical experiences to develop the necessary concepts, processes and attitudes for problem solving. During problem-solving and problem-posing experiences, a child may encounter or need to use a variety of representations. Important representations in mathematics are described in the following section.

Mathematics and representations

Representations are the ways that children experience, think about and record the ideas that they have. In mathematics, a variety of representations are used. These include real-world situations, oral and written communication, manipulatives (e.g. counters), pictures, new technologies and symbols. Table 1.1 shows the role of these representations in mathematics.

Table 1.1: *Representations in mathematics*

REPRESENTATION	DESCRIPTION	EXAMPLE/S
Real-world situations	Provide a context for understanding and interpreting mathematical concepts.	The concept of *chance* is explored in a game involving dice.
Oral and written communication	Is a fundamental aspect of early mathematical learning. The child needs to be encouraged to talk about her mathematical experiences with others. Through conversation, mathematical terms become an integral part of the child's vocabulary. The child also needs to read and write about mathematical situations.	Literature can provide a context and a rich base for mathematical explorations. A child's personal writing provides a record of an exploration. Reading a child's work provides the teacher with an insight into the child's level of understanding.
Manipulatives, such as real objects (e.g. counters) or models of real objects	Enable ideas to be physically represented and the relationship between the objects acted out.	Plastic animals or counters could be used to represent the following situation: *There are 4 dogs and 2 ran away.*
Pictures	Facilitate the link between aspects of the real world and an abstract idea. They also provide the basis for ideas to be internalised as mental images.	Through concrete experiences, a child may form an image of 5 as a row of 3 counters and a row of 2 counters. This image may be of assistance in an addition (e.g. 3 + 2) or subtraction situation (e.g. 5 – 3).
New technologies (e.g. software, learning objects, apps)	Have extended the ways people think and have the potential to enhance mathematical understandings.	Children can take digital photos or movies of what they experience and view. They can play with a large range of apps to move things around in two-dimensional space to create scenarios and images.

Table 1.1: *cont.*

REPRESENTATION	DESCRIPTION	EXAMPLE/S
Symbols, such as numerals and operation signs	Are used as efficient representations of complex ideas in mathematics. Prior to the introduction of each symbol it is essential that the child has developed the understanding associated with the symbol.	In the equation 2 + 3, the symbol '+' will be meaningless if the child does not understand the concept of addition.

Each representation is important in the development of mathematical understandings. Observing how the child functions with a particular representation provides an insight into a child's understanding of a concept, such as *number*. Teachers, parents and caregivers can facilitate the process of mathematical explorations by providing opportunities for the child to become familiar with mathematical concepts through the use of a variety of representations. We refer to this as multimodal learning (e.g. Yelland 2007) – a defining characteristic of learning in the 21st century. Multimodal learning enables the child to engage with concepts in creative and interesting ways. In the early childhood years, the child is actively engaged in exploration through playing with concepts and ideas (see Yelland 2011).

Some representations are more difficult than others for particular children. For example, if a child is asked to find the total number of cats in a story in which two cats chase three cats, it may be easier for the child to represent the situation with manipulatives (e.g. 2 counters and 3 counters) than with symbols (e.g. 2 + 3). Knowing which representations are easier for particular children is one way of supporting the development of their mathematical understanding.

Although a child may initially use particular representations in isolation, it is important for a child to be able to move fluidly from one representation to another. For example, a child may be asked a question orally (e.g. 'How many blocks are needed to build a tower as tall as the cupboard?') and the child may use manipulatives to solve the problem. This process of changing from one representation to another is referred to as *translation*. Solving a problem rarely requires the use of just one representation. To be effective problem solvers, children need to be familiar with each representation and flexible in moving between representations.

About this book

The purpose of this book is to provide ideas for teachers, parents and caregivers of young children to encourage children from birth to eight years of age to become numerate and to create contexts for the children to enrich their mathematical understandings. The book provides background information about mathematics and processes and suggests ways to encourage mathematical explorations and interactions so that children become numerate in the 21st century.

Figure 1.3: *Mathematical moments can occur in a variety of contexts*

The book is organised so that information about and activities for very young children in the preschool years are considered first. Chapters 2 and 3 address the ways in which mathematical understandings can be supported in the years before formal schooling begins (birth to approximately five years of age). Chapter 4 provides an overview of mathematics for the young child beginning school. Chapters 5–9 are designed for the first three years of school and discuss concepts such as *number, measurement, patterns* and *algebra, space,* and *chance* and *data.* Background information about the concepts is provided at the start of these chapters, followed by research-based activities. Chapter 10 suggests the context and connections for mathematical understandings when conducting investigations and exploring topics. The examples address three varying focuses. These are planning a range of mathematical activities for a topic (e.g. *Ourselves*); using everyday events to encourage mathematical understandings (e.g. *Celebrations*); and finding ways to stimulate mathematical thinking in a variety of environments (e.g. *Out and About*). Finally, Chapter 11 provides an overview of ways in which teachers can design effective teaching and learning in a mathematics program.

References

Advisory Committee on Mathematics Education, 2011, *Mathematical Needs: The Mathematical Needs of Learners*, London: ACME

Ball, D. L. (Chair), 2003, *Mathematical Proficiency for All Students: Toward a Strategic Research and Development Program in Mathematics Education*, RAND Mathematics Study Panel, Arlington and Santa Monica: RAND Education

Chubb, I., 2012, *Mathematics, Engineering and Science in the National Interest*, Canberra: Commonwealth of Australia

Kalantzis, M. and Cope, B., 2012, *New Learning: Elements of a Science of Education*, 2nd edn, Melbourne: Cambridge University Press

National Academies, 2006, *Learning to Think Spatially*, Washington, D.C.: The National Academies Press

Steen, L. A., 1997, *Why Numbers Count: Quantitative Literacy for Tomorrow's America*, New York: The College Board

Vygotsky, L. S., 1978, *Mind in Society: The Development of Higher Psychological Processes*, Cambridge, MA: Harvard University Press

Yelland, N. J., 2011, 'Reconceptualising Play and Learning in the Lives of Children', *Australasian Journal of Early Childhood*, 36(2), 4–12

——2007, *Shift to the Future: Rethinking Learning with New Technologies in Education*, New York: Routledge

——2005, 'Curriculum Practice and Pedagogies with ICT in the Information Age', in N. Yelland (ed.), *Critical Issues in Early Childhood* (pp. 224–42), Buckingham, UK: Oxford University Press

Yelland, N., Cope, W. and Kalantzis, M., 2008, 'Learning By Design: Creating Pedagogical Frameworks for Knowledge Building in the 21st Century', *Asia Pacific Journal of Teacher Education*, 36(3), 197–213

Chapter 2

Early mathematical understandings

Overview

In this chapter you will become familiar with:

- the beginning processes for early mathematical understandings – describing attributes, matching, comparing, ordering, sorting and patterning
- the mathematical concepts of number, measurement, space, and chance and data, and the ways in which these relate to the everyday experiences of young children
- the importance of language in exploring mathematics in the early years, as well as the use of children's literature to support mathematical thinking
- playful explorations as a pedagogical process to stimulate early mathematical learning.

Young children are curious from the moment they are born. They look around them, explore objects that they encounter and communicate with utterances in interactions with others. From birth to five years of age, which is generally when compulsory schooling begins, there are many different ways in which the foundations for mathematical understandings are established. The activities and experiences are usually informal and play-based, but there are also opportunities for *teachable moments* in which a teacher might consolidate particular language or highlight relationships that are fundamental to mathematical thinking and understandings. For example, when telling a child the story of *The Very Hungry Caterpillar* by Eric Carle, there are many opportunities for the adult to create contexts for understanding mathematical concepts and processes. These are shown in Table 2.1. As well as spanning the concepts of number, measurement, space, and chance and data, these opportunities provide a context for using language to communicate ideas and understandings about the various relationships that occur in the story.

Table 2.1: *Telling the story of* The Very Hungry Caterpillar

CONCEPT	EXAMPLES FROM THE STORY
Number	There are opportunities through the telling of the story to *count* the *number* of things that the caterpillar likes to eat and to realise that they are linked in a *sequence* of numbers also related to the *days* of the *week*. The caterpillar eats *one* apple on *Monday* and *two* pears on *Tuesday ...*
Measurement	The children can determine the relative *sizes* of the items in the story and collect them to *compare* these sizes. They can also *classify* the foods into categories and sort them by their various attributes – for example, the caterpillar eats fruits each day until Sunday when he eats everything! The days of the week are considered and can be used to ask the children to think about what they eat on each different day, as well as the *time* of the day that they eat their meals: breakfast, lunch, dinner and snack times. The sequence of *day and night* can also be discussed. The children can think about what they eat for breakfast, lunch or dinner and make a list (*count*) of their favourite foods.
Space	The caterpillar starts out as an egg that has been laid *on* a leaf. He then hatches *out* from *inside* the egg and starts on a journey. The children might relate this to a journey they make, such as going to school. The children can also study the *symmetry* of patterns, such as those on a butterfly, and shapes in our environment.
Chance and data	The children can *collect data* about favourite foods and record their findings on a *graph*.

Using language is an integral part of understanding and communicating mathematical ideas and children's literature is a rich source of opportunities for talking about and exploring concepts. In this chapter we introduce the essential beginning *processes* and *concepts* of mathematics. We define the most important terms and suggest ways in which teachers and parents can stimulate interest in processes and concepts by asking questions and providing contexts for exploring ideas. In the next chapter we provide more detailed activities that promote mathematical understanding in the first five years of life before school. Throughout this book we will provide examples of suitable children's books that you can share and read with young children to support their understandings about mathematical ideas. We will also list iPad apps that can support engagement and learning in mathematics and the use of effective language.

Figure 2.1: *'This is my house ...'*

To start with, we need to consider the mathematical processes that provide ways for children to explore the mathematical concepts.

The beginning processes

The beginning processes are the early thinking skills that require specific language to enable young learners to describe and communicate their ideas about their world. They are *describing attributes, matching, comparing, ordering, sorting* and *patterning*. Each of these processes is described in turn and illustrated with reference to everyday activities and examples of possible interactions that will help the children to use the processes and acquire the relevant language.

Describing attributes

An *attribute* is a particular characteristic or feature that helps to identify a person, animal, place or object. For example, in the story of *Goldilocks and the Three Bears, size* is an important attribute. Father Bear is *large*. Mother Bear is *middle-sized* and Baby Bear is *small*. We can encourage children to describe attributes when they are talking about themselves, their homes and their toys. Teachers and adults can support children in this process by modelling appropriate language.

Jake has brown hair and blue eyes. He lives in a small house with a white fence. His favourite toy is a ball with yellow stripes.

Encourage children to use all their senses when describing attributes. How does it look, feel, taste, smell or sound? Additionally, ask questions about people, events and things that require the child to consider the various attributes associated with them.

What is Sophia wearing today? What was the weather like when we went on our visit to the zoo? I am thinking of a soft, furry object that I take to bed with me every night. What could it be?

Being able to identify and describe attributes is important in the other beginning processes.

Figure 2.2: *'My garden has lots of flowers ...'*

Matching

Matching involves identifying objects that have a common attribute. In *Goldilocks,* there is a *large* bed for the *large* bear and a *small* bed for the *small* bear. Objects are matched when a child puts a red peg in the red bucket or finds a pair of shoes. Pictures are matched in card games such as Snap, Fish and Memory, and when doing puzzles.

Figure 2.3: *Matching with puzzles*

An object can also be matched to a picture or an outline of an object. For example, cookie cutters can be matched to their outlines. Trace around the outlines of different objects, such as wooden blocks, to help children return materials to their correct place. Ask questions such as:

I am holding a shoe – which shoe on the carpet matches this shoe?

Can you show me another cupcake that is exactly the same as this one?

Comparing

Comparing involves two items and is the process of determining whether items have *more* or *less* of a particular attribute. Goldilocks was *heavier* than Baby Bear so when she sat on his chair she broke it. Initially, children may use opposites when discussing the attributes of two items.

The tree is tall but the plant is small.

Encourage children to compare these items by modelling 'er' language.

The tree is taller than the plant.

Some young children are natural comparers.

My tower is taller than your tower. My dad can run faster than your dad. I am older than you.

Comparing objects by sight can sometimes be misleading. For example, a pillow is *larger* than a bag of potatoes but is *lighter* than the potatoes. Provide opportunities for a variety of comparing experiences to encourage children to use each of their senses. For example, ask:

Is an orange sweeter than a lemon?

Figure 2.4: *'The polar bear is taller than me ...'*

Ordering

Ordering is an extension of comparing and involves sequencing three or more items or events according to a specific attribute. In *Goldilocks,* three bears, bowls, chairs and beds can be ordered according to size. The emphasis in ordering is on 'est' language. Father Bear is the *largest* bear. This language can be modelled in everyday situations. Sam is tall. Sue is taller. Sally is the *tallest.* As children become proficient with ordering three items or events, gradually more objects or events can be ordered. Provide opportunities for children to order a variety of attributes, such as texture (rough to smooth), preference (best to worst), width (narrow to wide), colour (light to dark or bright to dull), height (tall to short), smell (strong to faint) and number (least to most). Ask questions such as:

Which person is the tallest? Which colour is the darkest? Which instrument is the noisiest?

Sorting

Sorting involves grouping items on the basis of one or more attributes and provides an opportunity for children to analyse the attributes of an object. In *Goldilocks*, the bears' clothes could be sorted according to size. Sorting occurs with cutlery when knives, forks and spoons are placed in separate compartments in the cutlery drawer and when the groceries are put in the correct place in the pantry after a shopping trip. There are many everyday opportunities for young children to engage in sorting. Pegs can be sorted according to colour. Blocks can be sorted according to type. Shoes can be sorted according to size. Sorting by two attributes is more complex than sorting by one attribute. For example, it is more challenging to sort buttons by colour and size than simply by colour. It is important to provide opportunities for children to make decisions about how items should be sorted and to *explain* their sorting rules. Items can be sorted on the basis of attributes related to each of the senses, including taste, texture and smell.

Figure 2.5: *Sorting by colour and matching shapes*

Patterning

Patterning is fundamental to mathematics and involves the repetition of a sequence of items or events. A child may make a patterned necklace by threading red, yellow and blue beads in order repeatedly. A game may involve a clapping pattern, such as loud clap, soft clap, loud clap, soft clap and so on. Patterns may be visual, auditory, tactile or involve movement. Visual patterns include horizontal, vertical, diagonal and circular patterns. Patterns also occur in language. The pattern of 'large, middle-sized, small' occurs throughout the story of *Goldilocks*. Patterning activities include looking for patterns, copying a pattern, making a pattern, extending a pattern and finding the missing element in a pattern. In Chapter 6 we explore activities that support understanding and building patterns for young children in school-based contexts.

The importance of the beginning processes should not be underestimated. Although a young child can carry out these processes, they continue to be important in the early years at school. For example, a child who is *sorting* pens by colour in kindergarten may later be expected to sort numbers into odds and evens. They lay the foundation for later work in mathematics.

The next section provides an overview of mathematical concepts and suggests ways in which they can be introduced to young children informally in various contexts in the years before school. Examples of ways in which conceptual understandings are provided in the first three years of school are provided in Chapters 6–10. Chapter 11 explores ways that mathematical concepts can be used in our everyday lives and investigations.

Mathematical concepts

The mathematical concepts of number, measurement, space, and chance and data are part of the everyday experiences of young children. For example, when a baby watches a mobile of differently shaped objects that is hanging above his cot, his experience includes number and space (e.g. shape). When a toddler's mother takes him to the clinic to be measured and tells him that they are taking raincoats in case it rains, his experience includes measurement, and chance and data. Although mathematical concepts are not formally introduced until a child goes to school, experiences in these early years provide the foundation for understanding mathematical concepts later in life. An overview of the four mathematical concepts in the preschool years follows. Specific ideas for activities and resources that support the development of children's understanding of these concepts are provided in Chapter 3.

Number

Young children encounter numbers in their environment, in songs, rhymes and books. They are often fascinated by numbers and enjoy counting. Initially, a young child may not count rationally. Adults can support children's early attempts at counting by encouraging and modelling counting. In order to be able to count accurately, the young child needs to:

- recognise that individual items *can* be counted
- use the unique *number name* for each item in a group (one-to-one principle)
- say the number names in a stable or consistent *order*

- know that the last number name represents *how many* items are in the group
- know that the order in which objects are counted does not matter in determining how many items are in a group – the important thing is to count *all* the items once only.

In the preschool years, children begin to use number and recognise number names and numerals. For example, in play situations a child might have a pretend party for four friends, or need three additional blocks to complete a tower that he is constructing. He might build a street and make a letter box with the numeral 25 written on it. Children's interest in number can be fostered by highlighting the use of numbers in daily life and by including numbers in conversations with children. For example:

Jon's sister is two. Tim, how old is your sister?
What is the number of your house?
How many days are there in a week?

These are all important prerequisite experiences which will help children to extend their concept of number as they enter school for the first time, at five or six years of age.

Figure 2.6: *Counting dinosaur prints*

Measurement

The measurement of *length, mass, volume, temperature, time* and *area* has many real-world applications. Measurement represents opportunities to use numbers in everyday lives and to link mathematical concepts in practical ways. In the preschool years, children's understanding of measurement can be supported by providing opportunities for them to identify the attribute to be measured, and to use non-standard units for measuring it. For example, a child may determine how much water a jug can hold by counting the number of cupfuls that are needed to fill the jug. These are wonderful opportunities to use number in playful ways. Many measurement opportunities are provided in water, sand and block play.

Space

Spatial understandings develop as children acquire an awareness of shapes in their environment. When babies explore objects, they are acquiring a sense of shapes and how they exist and function in the world. As children move around, they have many experiences with shape and space. An understanding of space can be fostered through activities including jigsaws, puzzles, mazes, construction, painting and drawing. Spatial understandings are also nurtured when children look at the world from different viewpoints. Most young children like to peek out from behind a door, to look up from under the table or to be carried high on someone's shoulders. As children become more active, they may like to climb playground equipment or swing very high! To develop mathematical vocabulary, parents and caregivers can talk to children about any location that they find themselves in.

My car is *at* the traffic lights.
The bird is sitting *on* the tree branch.
The sand pit is *under* the shade cloth.
The door is at the *front* of the house.

These types of statements represent opportunities to link to positional and relational terms, presented later in this chapter, in everyday contexts. Parents and caregivers can stimulate the use of appropriate vocabulary by asking questions about space in everyday conversations.

Where do we keep the baking tins?
Who is sitting next to you (as you are eating dinner)?
Where does Dora the dog sleep at night?

The importance of language in mathematical understanding is discussed later in this chapter.

Figure 2.7: *'My car is at the traffic lights'*

Chance and data

An early understanding of chance and data can be developed through interaction with children and in play situations. Use chance terms in conversation, such as *lucky*, *might* and *possible*.

Remember to bring a jacket because it *might* get cold.

Games provide opportunities to explore chance and data. Encourage children to look closely at a die to see what numbers are on it and to talk about why they think certain numbers are lucky.

Collecting information, or data, provides a context for using the language of mathematics in everyday activities. We often ask children which month their birthday is in, whether they have pets or what their favourite foods are. All these require the collection of data from the group which can then be represented in a map or diagram and used as the basis for mathematical discussions. For example:

How many children were born in May?
Which month has the highest number of birthdays?
How many more children were born in December than in June?

Language, using literature and mathematics

In the years before school, young children learn to communicate and most of them will acquire an extensive vocabulary. Language activities that incorporate stories, poems and rhymes provide a rich context for the development of mathematical concepts. For example, in the *Goldilocks* story you can explore not only the mathematical concepts of number, measurement, space, and chance and data, but also the specific and useful mathematical language used in the story. Table 2.2 shows how parts of the story correspond to each of the mathematical concepts. The mathematical language is shown in italics.

Table 2.2: Goldilocks *and mathematical concepts*

CONCEPT	RELEVANT PART OF THE STORY
Number	There are *three* bears, *three* chairs, *three* bowls and *three* beds.
Measurement	The bears are different *sizes*. Father Bear is *large*. Mother Bear is *middle-sized*. Baby Bear is *small*. The *size* of each bear corresponds to the relative *size* of the chair, bowl and bed. Father Bear is the *largest* bear and has the *largest* chair, bowl and bed. The bears go for a walk to give the porridge *time* to cool. Goldilocks is *too heavy* for Baby Bear's chair and when she sits on the chair it breaks. One bowl of porridge is *too hot* for Goldilocks, another is *too cold*, but Baby Bear's porridge is the right *temperature*. Goldilocks eats *all* of Baby Bear's porridge.
Space	The bears go *out* of the house and *into* the woods. Goldilocks comes *into* the house and goes *up* the stairs.
Chance and data	Goldilocks is hungry. *Luckily*, she finds a bowl of porridge that is just right for eating.

During storytelling and while reading books, encourage children to interact with you or their peers. Talking provides an opportunity for a young child to think about objects, experiences and ideas, and to increase his vocabulary. Questions encourage interactions and can be used to explore a child's thinking out loud. For example, we might interact with a very young child by playing a pointing game and asking:

Where is your nose? Where is your teddy?

Figure 2.8: *'Where is teddy?'*

Explore children's thinking with questions that ask them to recall details or provide an explanation.

Why did the three bears go for a walk?
Why did Goldilocks run away from the house?

Questions can be structured to suit each of the concepts by varying the first few words. For example:

How many bears went for a walk? (number)
When did Baby Bear's chair break? (measurement – time)
Where were the three bears when Goldilocks woke up? (space)
What might have happened if Goldilocks had not woken up? (chance and data)

Creating contexts for mathematical language

Questions can also be used to facilitate the development of mathematical language. For example, the response to the question 'Where did Goldilocks fall asleep?' requires the use of a positional term in the answer: 'Goldilocks is asleep *on* Baby

Bear's bed'. Positional words describe location. Relational terms are also important in mathematics and are used for comparing and ordering.

Father Bear's bed was *hard* but Mother Bear's bed was *soft*.

Examples of positional and relational terms are shown in the following table. They are very important for being able to describe locations and additionally form the basis for understanding the mathematical concepts that are included in school mathematics curricula.

POSITIONAL TERMS		RELATIONAL TERMS	
above/below	centre/corner	above/below	thick/thin
before/after	inside/outside	after/before	deep/shallow
back/front	down/up	behind/in front	hard/soft
behind/in front	edge	far/near	same/different
left/right	up/down	high/low	narrow/wide
on/off	over/under	centre/edge	big/little
below/above	high/higher/highest	over/under	full/empty
beside/next to	low/lower/lowest	slow/fast	young/old
between	first	top/bottom	new/old
top/bottom	second	hot/cold	long/short
near/far	third	warm/cool	long/longer/longest

Figure 2.9: *'Let me look in your ear'*

Some books provide particularly rich contexts for the use of positional and relational terms. Favourite books that have interesting stories and illustrations include all the *Spot* books (Eric Hill); *Each Peach Pear Plum* and *The Jolly Postman* (Janet and Allan Ahlberg); *Mister Magnolia* (Quentin Blake); and *The Lighthouse Keeper's Lunch* (Ronda and David Armitage). Positional or relational terms can be included in questions about the story. For example, as you discuss *The Jolly Postman*, ask:

Which house did the postman go to *first/ last*?
What does it say *at the top* of the letter?
Who is *next to* the bicycle?
Who is *under* the tree?

Modalities: new technologies

During this early learning period in young children's lives it is important to consider the *modalities* of learning. The work of Yelland et al. (2008) has highlighted the ways in which new technologies have enriched the ways in which we can learn in the 21st century. People communicate and make meaning in different modes (linguistic, visual, aural, gestural and spatial). Today's children are growing up in a world saturated with multimedia which impact on what they can do and understand. This means that they can express themselves in written or spoken modes, but they might also draw a picture or make up a dance to convey their feelings. Similarly, they can experience concepts and ideas in different modes with new technologies. This has become increasingly important in the early years when, for example, they can read books and e-books, play in a sandpit in the centre and play a game in an electronic sandpit, and see Dora and Elmo on TV, in a book or in a game. All these experiences enable them to understand how things exist, and how they can simultaneously exist and be represented in different forms. Engaging with new technologies has become an integral part of play, and an essential part of learning in the 21st century.

There are wonderful e-books available as apps, which not only enable the children to read good stories, but also, through their interactive nature, allow the children to explore the various elements included on each page. In one example, *What Does My Teddy Bear Do All Day?* by Bruno Hächler, there are many opportunities for adults to ask children interesting questions about the story, as well as the items in the various rooms with the teddy bear. Many parts of the picture can become animated, including doors and windows, cupboards full of toys, rugs on the floor and pictures on the wall. All these things encourage conversation and using language in a stimulating way. Other e-book apps that are useful for extending mathematical understandings are:

A Special Delivery: A Thomas and Friends Adventure (HiT Entertainment)

Peppa Pig: Fun at the Fair (Me Books)

Teddy's Night (Stories Alive)

The Cat in the Hat (Oceanhouse Media)

The Heart and the Bottle (Oliver Jeffers)

The Very Cranky Bear (We Are Wheelbarrow)

The Wrong Book (We Are Wheelbarrow).

Additionally, there is an increasingly growing market in electronic toys that have possibilities for new types of learning. The LeapFrog company has a wide range of pre-reading and early reading materials that also offer the opportunity for multimodal learning since they incorporate visual, aural, linguistic and kinaesthetic features. Very young children can play with letter names and sounds in various contexts.

They are able to read books with their parents or caregivers, or use a device called a Tag Junior to have the story read to them.

The preschool years are a period of rapid language acquisition. Encouraging children to discover and use mathematical language in interactions and with stories, poems and rhymes is an important element in their learning at this time.

Playful explorations

Quality learning environments support children's learning with a rich variety of materials that enable them to explore and make discoveries. In the preschool years, it is generally thought that young children learn best through play. Parents and caregivers can foster this play by interacting with children and providing interesting toys and objects for them to explore. Teachers observe children and, based on their professional judgements and by talking with parents, design and cater for children's learning needs. They are also able to intervene while children are investigating to ask questions, share ideas and extend the potential of the activity as well. The teacher takes on the role of facilitator or enabler of learning. This will occur not only by providing children with resources but also with the introduction or follow-up of ideas and questions. Drake (2005) has suggested that such adult support might include:

- stimulating children's interest in the activity
- providing high-quality resources
- listening and responding to children's talk
- questioning children in order to extend learning
- working alongside children, modelling skills and the use of key vocabulary
- encouraging, reassuring and praising children
- valuing and celebrating children's achievements (pp. 60–1).

Through these actions it becomes apparent that learning through *play* should involve more than teachers providing materials and time for young children to choose what they want to do. Teachers should consider a wide range of pedagogical factors (such as the ones suggested by Drake) so that young children are afforded experiences and opportunities for *playful explorations* (Yelland 2011) that are both spontaneous and planned, and linked to learning outcomes in relevant and dynamic ways. *Playful explorations* are initiated by the child(ren) or the teacher and can be extended in multiple directions. They incorporate the use of new technologies. They are structured yet flexible. In many instances they can be linked to specified learning outcomes, while in others they might make a contribution to more global aims for learning, such as fostering creative thinking by enabling the children to generate diverse solutions. They can extend beyond the preschool years into the early years of schooling.

There are pedagogical challenges to consider in order to support such playful explorations. The fact that teachers can, and should, design playful explorations in the first instance, or intervene to suggest new directions, might not align with the views of those who regard play as being initiated by the child, self-selected and voluntary, but the change in nomenclature from *play* to *playful explorations* is a deliberate one. It suggests a shift in emphasis with regard to being able to articulate learning outcomes as the result of creating these types of learning scenarios (playful explorations) and incorporating adult participation and scaffolding in this process.

Rethinking play as playful explorations in which experimentations and meaning making is scaffolded and extended by a teacher has the potential to provide enriched learning environments for young children. Further, the use of new technologies and the opportunities they create for meaning making, extending communications and interactions, are vital to such explorations.

Many young children come to preschool with a broad range of experiences and a high level of interest in using a variety of technologies, including computers, digital cameras, MP3 players, mobile phones and many hand-held digital devices. They have had time for playful explorations with these technologies in the years before they participate in educational settings and learn how to use them specifically for a variety of purposes. In this way, new technologies become resources for children to be creators and share their creations with audiences beyond those in their immediate physical space.

Making new technologies available alongside traditional materials (e.g. blocks) enables and extends playful explorations. Further, they can be used to document learning stories that describe the types of learning that have occurred (Carr & Lee 2001) and also can be shared with parents. Children can play with iPad apps such as Play School Art Maker to create scenes from a location (e.g. farm, beach, land and moon) or just a plain background. Once they have chosen which characters from Play School they want to include in their scene, they can touch the video recorder option and make a one-minute movie. They can then play back the movie to all their friends and family.

Figure 2.10: *Play School Art Maker, farm scene*
© 2012 Australian Broadcasting Corporation

Yelland (2007) has suggested that the challenge for parents and educators is to maintain a balance between the real and virtual worlds that young children experience. Both are relevant to the lives of young children and can support learning in structured and unstructured ways. Parents have often expressed the concern that if they let their children play with computers and other new technologies, this will take away from their 'real-world' experiences and opportunities to socialise with others. It is up to parents, teachers and caregivers to ensure that this does not occur. Children should be given opportunities to self-select activities, but parents and other adults should be able to encourage diverse contexts for playful explorations that give young people a range of learning opportunities with a variety of materials. Often it would seem that parents think that because they have purchased a toy or software, their child will spontaneously want to play with it without adult intervention. This might be the case, but it is also evident that the new toy can be a shared learning context in which parents or other adults can interact with the child, with a variety of positive outcomes emanating from the conversations. For example, an adult can provide the context to broaden the language/vocabulary base of the child by asking probing questions which will facilitate the learning of specific concepts and hopefully enable the child to make the appropriate abstractions that lead to higher levels of thinking and knowing.

Summary

This chapter has provided a background to the mathematical concepts, processes and language that are appropriate in the years before school. It has also considered the contexts of learning. The notion of playful explorations has been introduced to characterise the ways in which adults can enrich learning in the first five years of life before children enter formal schooling. Such informal opportunities for learning enable young children to experience mathematical concepts and processes in various contexts. These early experiences lay the foundation for children becoming numerate by effectively using mathematics in their everyday lives and the formal work of school.

In Chapter 3, specific activities and experiences for preschool-aged children that support this type of learning are presented.

References

Carr, M. and Lee, W., 2001, *Learning Stories: Constructing Learner Identities in Early Education*, London: Sage

Drake, J., 2005, *Planning Children's Play and Learning in the Foundation Stage*, London: David Fulton

Yelland, N. J., 2011, 'Reconceptualising Play and Learning in the Lives of Children', *Australasian Journal of Early Childhood*, 36(2), 4–12

——2007, *Shift to the Future: Rethinking Learning with New Technologies in Education*, New York: Routledge

Yelland, N. J., O'Rourke, M. E., Lee, L. and Harrison, C., 2008, *Rethinking Learning in Early Childhood Education*, Buckingham, UK: Oxford University Press

Chapter 3

Mathematical learning in the first five years of life

Overview

In this chapter you will become familiar with:

- activities suitable to encourage the use of the *beginning processes* for young children in the first five years of life
- the importance of using *language*, *children's literature* and *playful explorations* as sources for mathematical experiences in the early years. This includes traditional materials such as books and manipulatives as well as new technologies.

From the time a baby is born, she uses her five senses (taste, touch, smell, sight and hearing) to investigate the world. In the years from birth to five, there is a dramatic change in her physical growth, capabilities and skills. It is exciting when a baby says her first word or takes her first steps. It is equally wondrous when she successfully makes a tower of blocks or completes a puzzle independently. Building with blocks and puzzle making are two examples of early experiences that facilitate the development of mathematical thinking. Increasingly, from the age of two, young children are also experiencing using new technologies in a range of activities. Tablet technologies can support early multimodal learning which, when supported by parents, caregivers and teachers, not only enables children to link the two-dimensional experience of using these technologies with 'real-world' activities and contexts, but also enriches language acquisition. Encouragement from adults and conversations about activities will help children to connect the mathematical understandings that are relevant to their everyday lives. During these early years, parents, caregivers and teachers play an important role in creating contexts for using mathematical language and supporting the use of the beginning processes and concepts of mathematics that children will encounter in a wide variety of situations. These early experiences are fundamental to enabling the young child to feel confident and competent about doing mathematics in school and being numerate in the 21st century.

The first three years

In the first three years of life, a child may spend time in a variety of settings. These include the family home, family day care or a childcare centre. There are many opportunities to lay the foundations for mathematical thinking as the child engages in playful explorations and participates in routines and teacher-designed experiences. Table 3.1 gives examples of activities related to the child's physical capabilities in the first year of her life.

Table 3.1: *Major milestones and supporting activities for the first year*

AGE		PHYSICAL	ACTIVITIES AND MATERIALS
1 month		Turns head to light/sound Watches faces/objects Smiles	Mobiles above cot (musical and colour) Beads across cot Tape recorder for music/songs Rattles Picture books

Table 3.1: *(cont.)*

AGE		PHYSICAL	ACTIVITIES AND MATERIALS
1–3 months		Lifts head Increasing awareness of objects Smiles Moves limbs when excited	Singing songs/rhymes Musical toys Picture books Rattles/toy keys/ clutch items Recognising your voice during routines, e.g. feeding/bathing/ resting
3–6 months		Lying on tummy Rolls over Grasping objects More alert/greater concentration	Lying on rug with toys Colourful balls, rattles for grasping Plastic bucket with coloured objects Picture books
6–9 months		Reaches for toys Focuses on objects Starts to sit Starts to crawl Points to people and objects	Kitchen cupboard items Building towers Making sounds and music Picture books and rhymes Personal games, e.g. 'Where is your …?'

AGE		PHYSICAL	ACTIVITIES AND MATERIALS
9–12 months		May stand/walk Show what they want through sound and action	Push/pull toys Balls, bricks for stacking Drums/musical toys Sorting/stacking toys Picture books

Babies should have opportunities to interact with others, listen to language and be stimulated by people and interesting objects. There are a variety of ways to establish the foundations of mathematical language and thinking. At first, a baby cannot hold an object so she needs to have mobiles and pictures hanging above the cot or stroller to have something to look at and wonder about! It is useful to change these items to maintain her interest. As she grows, she will reach out to an object, finally grabbing it and taking it to her mouth to taste! Obviously, it is important to have materials that are suitable for sucking. Objects that make noises and can be squeezed are important for sense stimulation. Ensure that the objects vary in sound, texture, colour or shape. As the child explores an object it is important to interact with her in this play. Adults can talk to the child about the object, saying things such as:

> This is a purple box with flowers on it, and it has a lid that opens. Inside the box are different toys. There is a red star, a blue moon and a yellow sun. They are all made out of wood. Can you see the yellow star? I am holding the blue moon.

Such conversations, while they might seem to be 'one-sided', enable the baby to hear the nuances of a conversation and link words to actions and objects. They also provide opportunities for babies to listen to the sounds that are made if the objects make a noise.

Once a baby can sit, a whole new world opens up for her. This new perspective seems to encourage exploration and experimentation. She will throw objects to see how they are affected and will attempt to put objects together.

Again, providing the baby with a variety of materials is essential. These need not be expensive commercial materials, but naturally health and safety are of paramount importance. Materials such as balls and blocks and clutching toys such as rattles are useful. Access to kitchen cupboards may be appropriate once the baby can crawl. At around 9–12 months of age, there seems to be nothing more satisfying than banging a saucepan with a wooden spoon. Interaction with others is important in developing language skills, but it is equally important to give the baby time for independent play (carefully supervised). Again at this time adults will talk with the child about what is happening as they play and make noises. They will make statements such as:

I can see you are banging the spoon on the lid and making a lot of noise! What are you playing with? What sound does that rattle make? It sounds just like a bell chiming!

Daily routines, such as meal- and bath times, can provide a focus for early mathematical language development. Talking about the number of objects in the bath or the amount of juice in a cup provides starting points for understanding number and volume. Rhymes and songs are also rich in mathematical opportunities. For example, reciting 'Twinkle, Twinkle Little Star' allows the child to develop an understanding of the positional word 'up' and the shape of a 'diamond'. Colourful picture books also provide many opportunities for adults and children to engage in mathematical talk.

Figure 3.1: *Bath time can be mathematics time*

Toddlers

Table 3.2: *Major milestones and supporting activities for toddlers*

AGE	PHYSICAL	ACTIVITIES AND MATERIALS
12–18 months	Walking Busy and curious Improved coordination	Plastic household objects/pots and pans Different-sized objects for sorting Containers with lids Stacking toys/ pegboards/ posting boxes/pull-along toys Picture books Water and sand play Songs and rhymes
18–24 months	Walking Carrying objects Increased vocabulary	Cart for putting toys on/pulling Building blocks/ nesting toys Large wooden beads for threading (closely supervised) Books – trips to library Outdoor equipment/ sandpit/water play

Once the child is walking, there is much greater potential for exploring the world. Her newly acquired skill allows her to investigate different locations. For example, she delights in peering at you through the laundry basket, hiding under the table and emptying the contents of the cupboards. The toddler also has a fascination for creating things and taking them apart. She likes to fill containers and empty them, build towers and knock them down, put pegs in holes and take them out, push and pull toys and thread large beads.

Figure 3.2: *Building a tower*

Outside, there are different opportunities for playful explorations. The child is developing an awareness of space as she slides down the slide, swings high or climbs up a ladder. Filling and emptying containers with water or sand is not only enjoyable but provides first-hand experiences in measuring.

As the active toddler continues to explore, her understanding of the concept of *space* develops. An adult can foster a child's exploration through conversation. Ask the child to put herself and objects in different positions, such as *above* or *below*, *in* or *out* and *between*. This interaction can occur as the child participates in daily routines.

You are *on* the bed.
Please put the cup *next* to the plate.
We are walking *along* the path.

Picture books provide another opportunity to discuss location. As a book is read, ask questions about the location of characters and objects in the story (e.g. 'Where is Goldilocks sleeping?'). Games are also appropriate for the development of mathematical language.

At this time activities such as the three that follow can provide rich opportunities for using and extending mathematical language, and laying the foundation for mathematical thinking.

Tell me about Teddy

Aim: Developing mathematical language through playful explorations
Materials: Teddy bear
Activity: Put a teddy (or your child's favourite toy) on the sofa and ask:

Where is Teddy sitting? Teddy is *on* the sofa.

Keep playing the game by putting the toy in different locations. Ask the child to put the toy somewhere different and discuss its location. This game might be extended to a hide-and-seek option where you take turns hiding and finding Teddy in different places.

Figure 3.3: *'Tell me about Teddy'*

Follow the leader

Aim: Using mathematical language in a traditional game
Materials: A suitable setting (e.g. in a child's house or garden, or in a centre)
Activity: Say 'Let's play follow the leader' and move around the house or garden talking about where you are. Extend this to use a variety of positional terms.

We are playing *outside*.

We are *next to* the sandpit.

We are *on* the deck.

We are *in* the shed.

We are at the *top of* the stairs.

Figure 3.4: *'We are playing outside'*

Let's join in

Aim: Using mathematical language in songs and rhymes

Materials: None

Activity: Many songs and rhymes can help facilitate mathematical learning – for example, 'Incy Wincy Spider' and 'Hickory Dickory Dock'.

Incy wincy spider
Crawled *up* the water spout.
Down came the rain and washed poor incy out.
Out came the sun and dried up all the rain,
Now incy wincy spider climbs *up* the spout again.

Hickory dickory dock,
The mouse ran *up* the clock.
The clock struck one,
The mouse ran *down,*
Hickory dickory dock.

Using new technologies

When their children are around two years of age, many parents use tablets and smartphones for early learning, or simply to occupy their children's curiosity while the family is engaged in specific tasks, such as shopping or travelling. This has been called 'the pass back effect' (Chiong & Schuler 2010), defined as when a parent or adult passes their own mobile device to a child, usually for entertainment for short (15-minute) sessions.

Talking and playing

Aim: Extending mathematical language with new technologies

Materials: iPad, smartphone or laptop computer

Activity: There are a number of apps that can support early learning and language acquisition during this age range:

Alpha Tots (Spinlight Studio)

Angelina Ballerina Bubble Pop (HiT Entertainment)

Animal Shape Puzzle (Puzzlingapps)

Balloonimals (IDEO)

Farm Flip (Salvijs Bilinskis)

Kids Vehicles: City Trucks and Buses (Yaycom)

Singing Fingers (Beginner's Mind).

Play the app with the child and ask her questions as she plays, as well as commenting on what other features are included in the app that may not necessarily be a planned part of the game. For example, ask:

What is Angelina Ballerina wearing in this game? What colour are her ballet shoes? Do you think that Angelina's favourite colour is purple? What is your favourite colour?

Children's storybooks

Aim: Using positional and relational terms with a storybook stimulus

Materials: *Spot's First Walk* (or any suitable storybook/picture book)

Most of the children's books for very young children are picture books and/or have minimal text. They can be a catalyst for using language that links to the beginning processes and the concepts of number, measurement, space, and chance and data. Useful books include:

Ahlberg, J. and Ahlberg, A., A Baby's Catalogue, Puffin

Ahlberg, J. and Ahlberg, A., Each Peach Pear Plum, Puffin

Hill, E., Spot's First Walk, Penguin

Hutchins, P., Rosie's Walk, Red Fox

Rosen, M. and Oxenbury, H., We're Going on a Bear Hunt, Little Simon

Simmons, J., Come Along, Daisy! Little, Brown

Activity: Read the book and ask questions such as:

What is Spot chasing on the cover of the book? *(a butterfly)*

Who is taking Spot on the walk? *(his mum)*

Who did Spot see when he went through the fence? *(his friend the snail)*

Who was hiding in the vegetable patch? *(a rabbit)*

What was he eating? *(carrots)*

Where was the last place Spot visited on his walk? *(the pond)*

How many chicks did the hen have? *(six)*

The preschool years (three to five years of age)

At age three, a child may benefit from attending playgroups or early childhood programs where she has the opportunity to interact with other children and play with a broader range of materials. This might be the same setting she has attended earlier or a new setting. If children attend a community kindergarten or preschool, there would usually be an educator who has an early childhood teaching qualification. Early childhood programs for children aged three to five years are traditionally designed to support the child's cognitive, physical, social and emotional development. They are generally characterised by activity- or event-based programs with a focus on learning through play. They usually have physical spaces set up to encourage different types of activities. In the first instance the spaces are either indoors or outdoors and allocated times are set so that play can be supervised in the various areas. Outside, there might be a sandpit, places for painting and playing with water, climbing equipment and space to run. Indoors, there might be tables set up for activities that require sitting (e.g. model building and collage); a carpet area for listening to stories; a book corner; a home corner which might have a stove, or an area for sitting and having tea parties; a 'dress-up' area with various costumes and outfits for playing in; and a block area with large wooden blocks and an adjacent free space for building constructions. These settings now might contain various new technologies for children to explore and use.

Figure 3.5: *Playing together*

Effective programs are based on children's interests and needs. Planned and spontaneous activities are a catalyst for the development of mathematical understanding. These programs build on the mathematical foundations that were laid in the first three years of life by using a variety of materials and providing opportunities for the development of mathematical language.

The beginning processes

As outlined in Chapter 2, the beginning processes are describing attributes, matching, comparing, ordering, sorting and patterning. Examples of activities for each of the beginning processes for preschool children follow, accompanied by a list of suggested children's books and iPad apps at the end of each section where possible.

Describing attributes

Vocabulary development is important for describing attributes. Encourage children to use their senses when talking about people, animals, places, events and pictures. Make a note of each child's vocabulary in different contexts and model more advanced vocabulary as appropriate. The following lists provide some examples of vocabulary that is related to each of the five senses.

SIGHT	TOUCH	SOUND	TASTE	SMELL
red/blue *(colour)*	hot/cold	loud/soft	sweet/sour	strong/weak
big/small *(size)*	rough/smooth	noisy/quiet	delicious	sweet
circle/square *(shape)*	slimy	high/low	salty	fragrant

About me!

Aim: Using language for describing attributes

Materials: None

Activity: Ask children questions about themselves and their families. Encourage them to expand on their answers.

Q: What do you look like?

A: I am … a girl/boy; tall/short; with (*blue/brown*) colour of eyes and (*curly/short*) hair; wearing red shoes.

Q: What do you like doing best?

A: Playing with blocks/drawing/swimming/painting.

Q: What is your favourite …?

A: (*food*) Juice/bananas.

A: (*game*) Chasing, dress-ups.

A: (*animal*) Dog/cat.

Q: Tell me about your family.

A: (*how many in the family*)

A: (*description of family members*)

A: (*likes and dislikes of family members*)

Figure 3.6: *'Mum and me' (Phoebe 3.5 years)*

Conversations

Aim: Describing attributes in play contexts

Materials: An object that a child may be using in a play setting

Activity: In the sandpit, ask the child to describe the bucket that she is using.

Can you tell me about this bucket? What colour is it? What is it made of?

Variation: Children can describe attributes from pictures and photographs.

Tell me about the horse you have drawn.

Figure 3.7: *'The horse is playing in the field'*

Matching

The language developed in describing attributes provides the basis for matching.

Home corner

Aim: Matching items in the home corner

Materials: Everyday objects found in cupboards and drawers

Activity: Match items in cupboards (e.g. socks) and in the kitchen (e.g. pots and lids). Say:

Can you find the matching socks so that they are in pairs?

Which lid goes on this pot?

Home with family

Aim: Matching colours

Materials: Coloured pegs

Activity: While you are hanging out the clothes, put matching coloured pegs on items. Tell the child:

Put two red pegs on the red shirt and two blue pegs on the blue shorts.

Comparing

Comparing involves two items or people and uses 'er' language. The following two activities provide children with opportunities to compare similar and different objects.

Block hunt

Aim: Comparing similar objects

Materials: Different-sized blocks

Activity: Give a block to the child. Ask her to find a larger block and a smaller block. Emphasise the 'er' language. For example:

This block is bigger than this one. This block is shorter than this one. This block is wider.

Take two

Aim: Comparing different objects

Materials: Different everyday objects

Activity: Ask the child to select two different objects and hold one object in each hand. She needs to compare the objects using 'er' words.

The book is heavier than the teddy. The teddy is softer than the book.

Ordering

Ordering involves organising three or more items or people on the basis of an attribute. The following activities use 'est' language in addition to 'er' language (e.g. big, bigger, biggest).

Fitting in

Aim: Ordering people

Materials: Children in an early childhood setting

Activity: Ask three children to stand in front of the group and ask:

Who is the shortest? Who is the tallest? Who is in the middle? Let's put them in order from tallest to shortest.

Select a fourth child and ask:

Where should this person stand? Who is the tallest now? Who is the shortest now?

Variation: Ask the children to work in groups of three and arrange themselves in order. Have them describe their ordering rule (e.g. shortest to tallest, oldest to youngest).

Which is?

Aim: Ordering objects

Materials: A collection of objects (e.g. balls, toys, bottles, blocks) that vary by a particular attribute (e.g. size, mass, texture or shade of colour)

Activity: Ask the child to choose three items (e.g. bottles) and to put them in order. Point to one of their bottles and ask:

Can you find another bottle that is taller (shorter) than this bottle? Where should the new bottle go in the line of bottles?

Discuss the order of the bottles using the words 'tall', 'taller' and 'tallest'. Repeat the process with different items.

Planting a seed

Aim: Sequencing the planting of a seed

Materials: Seeds, potting soil and suitable containers

Activity: Purchase some seeds and help the children plant them in containers. Record the sequence of events. For example:

'Our Bean Plants'

1. I got a pot and put some soil in it.
2. I put the seed in very carefully.
3. I added more soil and patted it down.
4. I gave the plant some water.
5. I put my pot in the sun on the window ledge.

Figure 3.8: *Planting seeds*

Sorting

Sorting involves grouping items on the basis of an attribute or function. While children are sorting, ask them to explain how they have sorted. For example, if they have sorted on the basis of colour they might say:

I put the red ones here, the blue ones there and the yellow ones over there because my sorting is colours!

Fruit and vegetables sort

Aim: Sorting foods

Materials: Different fruits and vegetables

Activity: Show the children a range of fruit and vegetables and ask:

What do I have here? What are they called? Can we put them into groups? How? What shall we call each group?

Children may sort by colour (green or not green); texture (hard skins or soft skins); taste (like or dislike); or place grown (on a tree or in the ground).

Figure 3.9: *Sorting fruit*

Mystery sorting

Aim: Guessing the sorting rule

Materials: A collection of objects (e.g. buttons)

Activity: Start to sort the buttons on the basis of some attribute (e.g. colour) and ask the children to guess what your rule is. Have the children give the group a name.

Variation: Choose a child to start the sorting and have the other children guess her rule.

Suitcase sorting

Aim: Collecting like items in a group

Materials: A suitcase or bag, and different types of clothing from the home corner

Activity: Ask the children to look at the collection of clothes in the home corner and say:

If I was going on a holiday to the beach, what clothes would I put in my suitcase?

Have the children sort them into clothes for the beach and other clothes. Pack the suitcase.

Variation: Pose this problem:

If you were going on a trip on a plane and could only take one favourite thing in the bag, what would it be?

Ask the children to draw the item. Sort the children's suggestions into groups (e.g. clothes, toys, books).

Patterning

When children are making patterns, have them chant the pattern (e.g. 'red block, yellow block, red block, yellow block') to emphasise the repetitive nature of their creation. Encourage the making of linear and circular patterns.

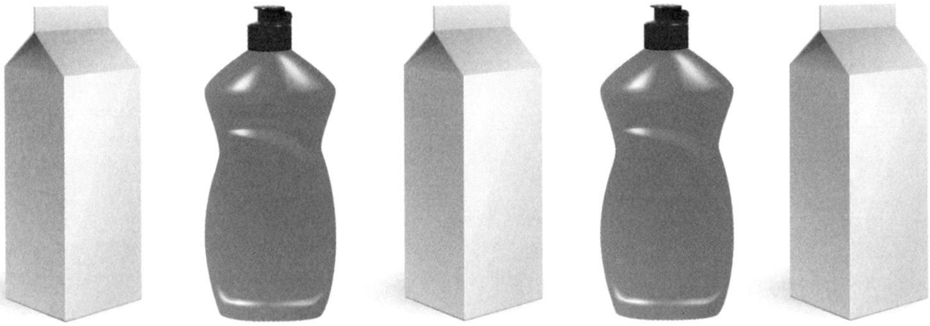

Figure 3.10: *Patterns with everyday objects*

Pattern hunt

Aim: Identifying everyday patterns

Materials: A variety of materials, such as clothes and tiles

Activity: Encourage the children to look for and describe patterns on clothes, wallpaper, gift paper or tiles. Hunt for patterns in the home, street, shop or park. Ask the children to explain the pattern to you. They might say:

The pattern is stars all in a row!

The pattern is red, blue and white, red, blue and white!

Figure 3.11: *Patterns on clothes*

People patterns

Aim: Making patterns with children

Materials: Children in an early years setting

Activity: Use the children to make patterns. Ask one child to stand and another to curl into a ball on the carpet. Continue the pattern with about 10 children. Ask for suggestions for different body positions. Again, encourage the children to identify the pattern.

Make a shoe pattern

Aim: Using everyday items for patterning

Materials: Everyday items, such as shoes or socks

Activity: Ask the children to take off their shoes and think about different ways they can use the shoes to create a pattern. Before patterning, the children could sort the shoes into sports shoes and sandals or left feet and right feet. After patterning, the children can find the matching shoes.

Variation: Create a circular pattern with the shoes and ask the children to explain the pattern.

Figure 3.12: *Shoe patterns*

Object patterns

Aim: Creating patterns

Materials: Wooden beads, pattern blocks or buttons

Activity: Use these materials to create patterns. While children are making patterns, ask:

Why is this a pattern? Where does the pattern start or finish? What comes next in the pattern?

Variation: The children may draw a copy of their patterns with crayons or paints.

Copy clap

Aim: Making sound patterns

Materials: None

Activity: Clap a pattern with your hands. Encourage the children to join in. Bring an action into the clapping pattern, such as nodding your head on every second clap. Ask the children to suggest other actions that could be used instead of nodding and try their ideas.

Pattern-making centre

Aim: Making a variety of patterns

Materials: Coloured paper, paper strips, shapes, stamps, pattern blocks, small items (e.g. buttons, bottle tops, pegs, coloured pasta, dyed iceblock sticks, small toys, Lego blocks, cotton reels, fruits and vegetables)

Activity: Using a variety of materials, make patterns for the children to copy. Start a pattern and ask the children to finish it. Encourage children to make their own patterns. Leave out essential elements of a pattern and ask what is missing.

Variations: Decorate the room for a party or a special occasion with patterned items (e.g. paper chains, table cloths, napkins, hats or crowns to wear). Make printing blocks with sponges, wood or cork. Vary the type of paper used for printing on (e.g. different coloured paper, newspapers, absorbent paper).

Figure 3.13: *Missing elements in a pattern*

Auditory patterns

Aim: Applying and using patterns based on sounds and rhythms

Materials: Use patterns that occur in songs, music, rhymes and in literature (e.g. 'The Three Billy Goats Gruff', 'The Three Little Pigs'). Engage children in singing songs and rhymes that repeat phrases or words.

Activity: Chanting song

Lead: I don't know what I've been told.
Group: I don't know what I've been told.
Lead: Australia's streets are made of gold.
Group: Australia's streets are made of gold.
Lead: Sound off!
Group: Sound off!
Lead: 1, 2, 3, 4.
Group: 1, 2, 3, 4.

Variations: There are some rhymes or raps that are fun because of their rhythm. They seldom make sense but the children enjoy the chanting. A good example is 'Doctor Knickerbocker'.

Doctor Knickerbocker, Knickerbocker, number nine
Loves to dance to the rhyme of time
Now let's get the rhythm of the hands
(clap, clap)
Now we've got the rhythm of the hands
(clap, clap)
Now let's get the rhythm of the feet
(stamp, stamp)
Now we've got the rhythm of the feet
(stamp, stamp)
Now let's get the rhythm of the eyes
(blink, blink)
Now we've got the rhythm of the eyes
(blink, blink)
Now let's get the rhythm of the dance
(wiggle bottom)
Now we've got the rhythm of the dance
(wiggle bottom)
Now let's get the rhythm of the number nine
One, two, three, four, five, six, seven, eight, nine

Repeat the rhyme as many times as the children want to.

Integrating the beginning processes

Once the children encounter and use the beginning processes, these can be integrated with and applied to everyday activities. We can help facilitate this in many ways. Some teachers use a theme or topic or a particular child's book to develop a set of related activities for the beginning processes. For example, Megan Dean, a preservice early childhood teacher, created the following activities around the topic of fairies:

- *describing attributes* of different fairies, elves and wizards
- *matching* fairies of different colours to a wand of the same colour
- *comparing* the size of different fairies and wizards with their possessions (e.g. hats, wands and toadstools)
- *ordering* fairy clothes, wands, crowns, wings and wands
- *sorting* stars and fairies by colour and pattern
- *patterning* with fairy flowers and stars.

Figure 3.14: *Ordering fairy clothes*

Another preservice teacher, Helen Dunham, used a book called *The Secret of the Sneezing Pillow* by Simon McLean to create contexts for using the beginning processes. In this book, a possum and his friends have an adventure in a rainforest. The activities that she created were:

- *describing attributes* of animals (e.g. Prank the possum)
- *comparing* the different toothbrushes belonging to Gus the goanna
- *matching* items and animals from the book with cut-out pictures
- *comparing* Prank's ears with another animal's ears
- *ordering* the animals according to the size of their bodies and their eyes
- *sorting* the animals' possessions (e.g. clothes)
- *patterning* using items from the forest to create a necklace.

Books for the beginning processes

The following books are ideal for exploring the beginning processes with young children. They act as a catalyst for conversations around different topics and enable teachers to ask the children focused questions, so that they are able to consider and practise the various beginning process in different and complementary ways.

Chocolate, D. and Aronoff, C. E., *Kente Colors*, Walker & Co

Dodds, D. A. and Lacome, J., *The Shape of Things*, Candlewick Press

Ganly, H., *Jyoti's Journey*, Andre Deutsch

Grossman, V. and Long, S., *Ten Little Rabbits*, Chronicle Books

Martin, B. Jr, Archambault, J. and Ehlert, L., *Chicka Chicka Boom Boom*, Simon & Schuster

Turpin, L., *The Sultan's Snakes*, Child's Play International

Apps for the beginning processes

The apps listed here are all available from iTunes and are compatible for use on the iPad. They enable young children to use the processes in active and interesting ways. Parents and educators need to choose apps thoughtfully because there are a huge number of apps available but many do not encourage exploration and they can be prescriptive in allowing what can be done within the app. Open-ended apps are very useful for creating contexts to apply the beginning processes. The apps listed below enable young children to use the processes in active and interesting ways and afford the opportunity for playful explorations.

Angelina Ballerina Bubble Pop (HiT Entertainment)

Fireman Sam (P2 Games Limited)

LEGO® Creationary (The Lego Group)

Monkey Lunchbox (THUP Games)

My Scene (MyFirstApp.com)

Play School Art Maker (Australian Broadcasting Corporation)

Playful Minds (Gameloft)

Tally Tots™ (Spinlight Studio)

Figure 3.15: *Play School Art Maker, underwater scene*
© 2012 Australian Broadcasting Corporation

As previously noted in Chapter 2 with regards to the Play School Art Maker app (illustrated in Figure 2.10), children can choose different scenes (such as the underwater scene shown in Figure 3.15) and place their favourite *Play School* characters into the scene. They are then able to animate and record the scene with the video record facility.

Concepts

There are four ways in which mathematical concepts can be grouped. These are number, measurement, space, and chance and data.

Number

Sophia just had her fourth birthday and had an ear infection that required antibiotics.

Mum: Sophia, if you are a good girl and take your medicine you can have two jelly beans afterwards! Then, when you take your medicine tonight after your bath, you can have two more jelly beans for being such a good girl!

Sophia: I like jelly beans, Mummy!

Later, after the bath and medicine, her mum gives her three jelly beans instead of two.

Sophia: Mummy, you are so nice! You gave me five jelly beans instead of four!

There are many ways to encourage children to count and recognise numbers. For example, count as you put away the cutlery, or create a number scrapbook with favourite photographs so that children can count familiar items. Outdoors, incorporate counting into games. Play a target game and count how many bean bags land on the target. Help the children with counting by emphasising the last number word in a counting sequence. For example:

One, two, *three*. There are *three* dogs in the park.

Figure 3.16: *There are three dogs in the park*

Encourage children to learn numbers that have personal relevance, such as their age, their clothing size, their house number and their telephone number. Point out numerals in books, on birthday cards, in elevators, on car number plates, on advertising boards, on televisions and videos, and on calendars. Matching games, dot to dots, sewing cards and simple board games provide opportunities for children to learn to recognise numerals. The following activities will provide children with the vital early experiences that are built on by number activities in the early years of school (these are explored in Chapter 5).

A counting rhyme

Aim: To learn a rhyme that uses a sequence of numbers

Materials: The rhyme 'Five Little Ducks'

Five little ducks went swimming one day,
Over the pond and far away.
Mother Duck said, 'Quack, Quack, Quack, Quack!'
But only four little ducks came back.

Four little ducks went swimming one day,
Over the pond and far away.
Mother Duck said, 'Quack, Quack, Quack, Quack!'
But only three little ducks came back.

Activity: Say the rhyme with the children. Ask the children:
How many ducks did we start with? How many were left at the end of the day?

A number poem

Aim: To use a poem to generate number stories and a lesson on counting

Materials: The poem 'Band-Aids' by Shel Silverstein is an excellent stimulus for thinking about 'How many?'

'Band-Aids'
I have a Band-Aid on my finger,
One on my knee, and one on my nose,
One on my heel, and two on my shoulder,
Three on my elbow, and nine on my toes.
Two on my wrist, and one on my ankle,
One on my chin, and one on my thigh,
Four on my belly, and five on my bottom,
One on my forehead, and one on my eye.
One on my neck, and in case I might need 'em

I have a box full of thirty-five more.
But oh! I do think it's sort of a pity
I don't have a cut or a sore!

Activity: Draw a large cut-out picture of a child, paint it and decorate the picture with Band-Aids to illustrate the poem. When all the Band-Aids have been placed on the painting, ask questions about the number and location of Band-Aids on specific parts of the body.

How many Band-Aids were on my shoulder? How many were on my thigh and ankle?

Counting cows

Aim: Counting to 5

Materials: A shoe box, various plastic animals (e.g. cows, pigs, sheep, horses)

Activity: Put the animals in the box and ask the children to estimate and then count how many cows are in the field (box) by taking them out one by one.

Variation: Have numeral cards and ask the children to match the number to how many of each animal they have each time.

Skittles

Aim: Counting to 9

Materials: Plastic drink containers filled with sand

Activity: Set the skittles up in a triangular shape and knock them down with a ball. Count how many you have knocked down. Keep score for a challenge.

Pace off!

Aim: Counting the number of paces (steps) to a given place

Activity: Ask the children to estimate how many paces there are to a particular place. Have them count the number of paces it takes.

Number steps

Aim: Recognising numerals and following the sequence of numbers

Materials: Large cards with numerals 1–9 printed on them

Activity: Place the cards on the floor. Ask the children to step on each card in sequence from 1 to 9.

Variation: Place the cards in close proximity on the floor. Ask the children to put different body parts on specific numerals (e.g. 'Put your right hand on 5').

Number hunt

Aim: Matching numerals

Materials: Two sets of cards with large numerals printed on them

Activity: Separate one set of numeral cards and place them around the room – for example, on a bookshelf. Give each child a card from the second set of numerals and ask them to hunt for the matching card.

There are a large number of books that can support counting and using numerals. Even in picture books very young children can count items and use them to create number stories. For example:

I can see 2 trees on the hill.

There are 4 windows on this house and 6 windows on the house next to it. That means I can see 10 windows!

Further resources – number and counting

Books

Adams, P., *There Were Ten in the Bed*, Playspace

Anno, M., *Anno's Counting Book*, Harper and Row

Barber, L., *Twelve Days of Christmas*, Northern Times

Burningham, J., *The Shopping Basket*, Crowell Junior Books

Carle, E., *The Rooster Who Set Out to See the World*, Hodder & Stoughton

Flack, M., *The Story about Ping*, Puffin

Gag, W., *Millions of Cats*, Puffin

Hughes, S., *Lucy and Tom's 1, 2, 3*, Gollanz

Keats, E. J., *Over in the Meadow*, Scholastic

Kitamura, S., *When Sheep Cannot Sleep*, A & C Black

Owen, A., *Annie's One to Ten*, Orchard Books

Pomerantz, C., *One Duck, Another Duck*, Greenwillow

Winer, Y., *Mr Brown's Magnificent Apple Tree*, Ashton

Wood, A. J., *Animal Counting (Jungle Hideaways)*, Macmillan

Apps

Angelina Ballerina Bubble Pop (HiT Entertainment)

Animal Shape Puzzle (Puzzlingapps)

Bugs and Buttons (Little Bit Studio)

Bugs and Numbers (Little Bit Studio)

Counting (by fishdog.net)

Fireman Sam (P2 Games Limited)

Monkey Lunchbox (THUP Games)

My Scene (MyFirstApp.com)

Playful Minds (Gameloft)

Tally Tots™ (Spinlight Studio).

Measurement

The concept of measurement includes understandings about volume, time, temperature, mass, money, length and area. As with the other suggestions thus far, it is important to interact with children as they engage with the activities in order to acquire an insight into their understandings about what they are doing and thinking. For example, in the following conversation four-year-old Sophie's understanding of distance (length) and time was explored. The conversation occurred while Sophie was travelling in the car on a holiday in Queensland. It reveals that she has begun to think about words that describe various aspects of our lives that involve measurement.

Sophie: Why is everything in Queensland long?

Nicola: What do you mean long?

Sophie: Well, everywhere we have been is long.

Nicola: You mean it takes a long time to get there?

Sophie: Yes. In Kalgoorlie, everything is short except Perth.

We were at Caloundra and on our way to Mooloolaba and she asked:

Sophie: Is it long to Mooloolaba?

Nicola: No, only 15 minutes or so.

Sophie: Is 15 minutes long?

Figure 3.17: *'Everything in Queensland is long!'*

During playful explorations and in everyday events there are many opportunities to enhance children's understanding of the various components of measurement. For example, children learn about *temperature* when they make daily weather charts or participate in cooking activities. They gain greater insights into the concept of *time* if you tell them the time when they are doing different activities. They will understand *volume* as the space inside containers in their water play and in cooking activities. When they are out shopping they will figure out how much *money* they need to buy different items. They will also wonder about the *weight (mass)* of the various food items that they might buy and determine the size of the *area* of shops as being big and small.

Volume

Figure 3.18: *Exploring volume*

Exploring volume

Aim: Exploring how much a container can hold

Materials: Hoops, funnel or sieve, a variety of containers that hold water – for example, bottles, bowls, cups, jugs and jars

Activity: Ask the children to sort the containers into the ones that hold water and the ones that will not hold water. Have the children choose one container that holds water (e.g. a bottle) and identify containers that hold more, less or the same volume as their first container. Place items that hold the same amount in the same hoop. Ask:

Which container would hold the most water? In which container would you mix a cake? Can you find a container that holds three cupfuls of water?

Variation: Use sand or coloured rice instead of water.

Baths and boats

Aim: Using books to talk about volume

Materials: Books and a tub of water

Activity: Stories about volume include *Mr Archimedes' Bath* and *Who Sank the Boat?*, both by Pamela Allen. These books can be used with children of a wide range of ages. Explore the ideas contained in the books. For example, the children can conduct experiments about floating and sinking. Children can draw the results of their experiments.

Further resources – volume

Books

Comber, B., *Dad's Diet*, Ashton

Cowley, J., *The Biggest Cake in the World*, Nelson

Furchgott, T. and Dawson, L., *Phoebe and the Hot Water Bottle*, Collins

Gretz, S., *Teddybears Go Shopping*, Ashton

Lord, J. V., *The Giant Jam Sandwich*, Piccolo

Wild, M., *Something Absolutely Enormous*, Picture Lions

Apps

Where's My Water? (Disney Productions)

Time

Fun with funnels

Aim: Exploring time

Activity: Show the children some different-sized funnels. Ask them to predict which funnel will let the water through the quickest/slowest. After the children have experimented with the funnels, ask them to order the funnels from fastest to slowest.

Variation: Use sand instead of water.

When I was small

Aim: Reflecting on growth

Activity: Ask the children to bring photographs of themselves at three different stages of their lives (e.g. as a baby, a toddler and now) and put the photographs in order. Make a wall display of the growth of each child.

Birthdays

Aim: Ordering events

Materials: This could be done with paper and coloured pens or on the computer/tablet.

Activity: Talk about birthdays and other special days, and make a chart to record the month they are in.

What's the time, Mr Wolf?

Aim: Sequencing the days of the week and the hours in a day according to events

Materials: *Mr Wolf's Week* by Colin Hawkins (Mammoth)

Activity: Read the book to the children. Collect pictures of clocks and discuss the events in *Mr Wolf's Week*. Relate time to seasons and the weather. The story can provide a starting point for discussions about the various aspects of time, including the week, day, month and the seasons.

Further resources – time

Books

Blackburn, C., *Waiting for Sunday*, Ashton

Campbell, R., *My Day*, Picture Lion

Carle, E., *The Bad-Tempered Ladybird*, Puffin

Harper, A. and Hellard, S., *Just a Minute*, Puffin

Hawkins, C., *Mr Wolf's Week*, Heinemann

Hill, E., *Spot Tells the Time*, Heinemann

Hughes, S., *Lucy and Tom's Day*, Gollanz

Hutchins, P., *Clocks and More Clocks*, Puffin

Ormerod, J., *Moonlight*, Puffin

Oxenbury, H., *The Birthday Party*, Walker

Pienkowski, J., *Time*, Puffin

Shields, G., *When the World Is Ready for Bed*, Bloomsbury

Apps

Tell Time – Little Matchups (Grasshopper)

Temperature

Let's make a cake

Aim: To consider the everyday use of temperature

Materials: A cooking session with utensils and appropriate recipe

Activity: During a cooking experience, talk about what you are doing, the coldness of the refrigerator ('Does a fridge keep things hot or cold?') and the need for heat in the cooking process ('Why do you need to put the cake in the oven before you are able to eat it?'). Warn children of the dangers of touching hot objects.

What is hot and what is not

Aim: To think about classifying temperature into categories (e.g. hot, cold, warm)

Materials: Paper to make a chart, old magazines for children to cut up pictures from to add to the chart

Activity: Prepare a chart of things that are hot, cold and warm. Ask the children to add their own pictures and drawings to the chart.

Figure 3.19: *What's hot and what's not*

Today it is?

Aim: Observing and recording weather patterns

Materials: A book or chart created on a computer

Activity: Make a weather book for each child. Observe the weather on a daily basis and ask the children to draw a picture in their weather books. The pictures can be used to talk about the weather and the temperature.

Variation: The group could take it in turns to draw the weather pictures on a class weather chart. Children could draw people dressed appropriately for the weather.

Further resources – temperature

Books

Bruna, D., *Miffy in the Snow*, Methuen

Burningham, J., *Seasons*, Cape

Carle, E., *Spot Looks at the Weather*, Heinemann

Carle, E., *The Tiny Seed*, Picture Knight

Hunt, N., *Rain, Hail or Shine*, Collins

Pienkowski, J., *Weather*, Puffin

Vaughn, M., *Where Does the Wind Go?* Ashton

Wolde, G., *Thomas Bakes a Cake*, Hodder & Stoughton

Apps

Blue's Clues, 'Stormy Weather' (TV show, Nickelodeon)
Equator (Tigerface Games)

Weight (mass)

Scales

Aim: Balancing objects to compare weight (mass)

Materials: A balance scale and a variety of objects which can be weighed and compared

Activity: Using the balance scale, compare the mass of different objects (e.g. a crayon and a pair of scissors). Ask:

Why do you think one side of the balance scale is hanging lower/higher?

Can you find a way to make this side change its position? Can you find something that will make this side go up/down?

Before placing items on the scale, ask:

What do you think the balance scale will look like when I put this crayon on this side and the scissors on the other?

Variation: Use the balance scale to find out how many blocks are needed to balance a heavier object (e.g. a book). Ask the children to use the blocks to balance a range of different objects (e.g. a toy, a lunch box).

Figure 3.20: *A balance scale*

Feel it!

Aim: Ordering mass

Materials: Containers of different masses

Activity: Ask the children to estimate the order of three containers from lightest to heaviest. They should check the order by lifting each container.

Variation: Choose another container and ask the children which containers are heavier or lighter or the same mass as the new container. Ask them to put the four containers in order.

Further resources – mass

Books

Comber, B., *Dad's Diet*, Ashton

Cowley, J., *The Biggest Cake in the World*, Nelson

Gretz, S., *Teddybears Go Shopping*, Ashton

Lord, J. V., *The Giant Jam Sandwich*, Piccolo

Money

Shopping time!

Aim: Playing shops with money in order to understand the use and structure of money

Materials: Shop corner with associated items, including play/real money

Activity: Encourage the children to set up different kinds of shops (e.g. supermarket, shoe shop) in their dramatic play. The children can collect goods (e.g. empty packets), make signs and prepare money to use in their shops.

On board!

Aim: Using money appropriately

Materials: Set up the play corner as a train or bus. Provide play money and bags and other assorted items so that the children can take a train/bus ride.

Activity: The children can set up a play train or bus and take people or toys for a ride. One person is the conductor and collects fares from the passengers. Everyone will need to buy a ticket!

Hot cross buns

Aim: Linking money and goods

Activity: Tell the rhyme 'Hot Cross Buns' to the children.

Hot cross buns!
Hot cross buns!
One a penny, two a penny,
Hot cross buns.

Variation: Ask the children to substitute new products and prices.

Big juicy pears!
Big juicy pears!
One costs 10 cents, two cost 20 cents,
Big juicy pears!

Further resources – money

Books

Burningham, J., *The Shopping Basket*, Picture Lion

Gordon, M., *Wilberforce Goes Shopping*, Puffin

Hutchins, P., *Don't Forget the Bacon*, Picture Lion

Linbolm, S., *Let's Go Shopping*, Golden Books

Snow, A., *Busy Bear's Shopping Day*, Victoria House

Viorst, J., *Alexander Who Used to Be Rich Last Sunday*, Bluegum

Wolff, M., *Let's Go to the Store*, Budget

Wolff, M., *Me Shopping*, Abelard

Apps

My Cake Shop (Lai Systems)

Length

My hand is ...

Aim: Using arbitrary lengths (e.g. handspans) to measure objects and areas

Materials: Paper/pens and assorted items for measuring length

Activity: The children draw around one of their hands and cut the shapes out. Ask them to find things that are smaller or larger than their hand cut-outs. The children can also measure objects with their hand cut-outs. Record the results pictorially and in words. For example:

The table is six handspans long.

The book is one and a bit of my handspans.

Block play

Aim: Comparing length

Materials: The block corner

Activity: When the children are playing with blocks, give them these instructions:

Build a structure that is taller/shorter than you.

Build something that is wider/narrower than you can stretch.

Build something that is longer/shorter than your arm.

Figure 3.21: *Block play*

Plant growth

Aim: Observing how the attribute of height/length can change over time

Materials: Seeds/seedlings, flower pots, soil, gardening implements and a watering can

Activity: Plant a seed and monitor the height of the plant over a period of time. There are different ways to do this. For example, use iceblock sticks in the soil and mark the height each week with a felt pen, or measure the height of the plant with a piece of string and glue the string onto a chart with a label (e.g. Week 1, Week 2).

Variation: Keep a pictorial record of other major events (e.g. new leaves).

Further resources – length

Books

Dodd, L., *The Smallest Turtle*, Nelson

Pigdon, K., *How Far Can You Jump?* Macmillan

Smyth, G., *A Pet for Mrs Arbuckle*, Ashton

Wild, M., *Something Absolutely Enormous*, Picture Lions

Wood, G. W., *Angus Thought He Was Big*, ERA Publications

Apps

Measurement HD (Emantras)

Small Street (Glu Games)

Area

Tiling the floor

Aim: Using the concept of area as covering a space (e.g. the floor)

Materials: Pattern blocks

Activity: Ask the children to use large pattern blocks or tiles to make a new floor for the home corner.

Filling space

Aim: Covering an area with blocks

Materials: Blocks and masking tape

Activity: Define an area with masking tape and ask the children to use the blocks to make a structure that fills the whole area. (Take a photo of the area when you have finished to compare all the various possibilities of filling the space.)

Further resources – area/measurement

Books

Hinchcliffe, J., *The Hilton Hen House*, Ashton Scholastic

Wild, M., *Something Absolutely Enormous*, Picture Lions

Apps

Measurement HD (Emantras)

Toy Tangram (TabTale)

Space

The development of *spatial sense* occurs from infancy as children investigate the world around them through their senses, gradually master control of their bodies and view the world from different perspectives – underneath the table, on Dad's shoulders and so on. This informal learning is complemented by opportunities in early learning settings to learn about space through block play, puzzles, collage and construction, and even tidying up when putting objects back into the spaces where they belong. Children also experiment with ways of representing two- and three-dimensional shapes and space through painting, playdough and picture making. If the children have attended an early education setting with a Froebel philosophy, they will have encountered a set of 'play gifts' which are heavily oriented towards geometry. For example, Gift 2 is a set of three solids (sphere, cylinder and cube) that can be suspended from a frame, while Gift 3 is a 'divided cube' composed of smaller cubes. By the time these young children commence school, they will have had many and varied spatial experiences.

Gift 2: Sphere, cylinder and cube

Gift 3: Divided cube

All around me!

Aim: Discussing items and places in the world

Materials: As appropriate

Activity: One of the best places to explore space and shape is outdoors. Ask the child:

What can you see in the sky?

Which way do you want to go next?

What do you think will be around this bend?

What is over on the other side of the river?

Activities that involve motor skills are important in the development of spatial awareness. Young children love to run, jump, hop, skip, crawl and dance. Games that involve these kinds of experiences include musical statues, musical chairs, chasing games and hide and seek.

Obstacle course

Aim: Moving through space

Materials: Outdoor equipment

Activity: Set up an obstacle course so the children have to climb up and down and pass through different equipment. This can be done indoors or out. Use positional language to describe where children are.

You are *at the top* of the ladder.

Variation: Hide some items in the course and give the children clues about their location so that they may search for them. Ask a child to hide an object and make up a clue for its location.

Figure 3.22: *Puzzle photographs*

Puzzles

Aim: Fitting shapes together

Materials: Any jigsaw puzzles

Activity: Make a two- or three-piece puzzle by cutting up a photograph of a child or a favourite animal. Have another child complete the puzzle.

Variation: There are various iPad apps (e.g. Jigsaw Box by Sparkle Apps) that enable you to use your own photos to make jigsaws. These are lots of fun for preschool children who love to see their faces and those of their friends and family on personalised jigsaws.

Making shapes

Aim: Creating different shapes

Materials: A sandpit

Activity: Make handprint or footprint patterns in the sand.

Variation: Fill containers with wet sand and turn them out to see what shapes are created. Make jellies, muffins, cakes and ice cubes of different shapes. Bake cookies and pastry shapes and use them to create a pattern. Cut up fruit and arrange the pieces on a plate.

Block it out

Aim: Exploring space with blocks

Materials: Various types of building blocks

Activity: Children love to create shapes, buildings and even cities with large blocks. Encourage them to add new materials to their block constructions to create a scene that can be the venue for a dramatic play experience. While children are engaged in the construction, observe the shapes that are used. Engage children in conversation about the shape, size, quantity and location of the blocks.

Variation: Use smaller construction sets, such as Duplo and Lego, which allow children to form new shapes.

Further resources – space

Books

Bernstein, S. and Bernstein, J., *Inside, Outside, Upside Down*, Collins

Bruna, D., *I Know about Shapes*, Methuen

Campbell, R., *Shapes*, Blackie Books

Dodd, L., *Hairy Maclary's Bone*, Puffin

Fox, M., *The Straight Line Wonder*, Ashton

Hill, E., *Spot Looks at Shape*, Heinemann

Hill, E., *Where's Spot?* Puffin

Seymour, P., *Busy Bears*, Collins

Apps

Angry Birds Space (Rovio Entertainment)

Equator Puzzle (Tigerface Games)

Sandbox (Bulkypix)

Toy Tangram (TabTale)

Chance and data

In the early years of primary school, children will encounter the concepts of chance and data (see Chapter 9 for more detail). The ideas behind *chance* relate to the notion of randomness of events and features that may occur in our daily lives. For example, we might consider the chances of the weather being favourable for a school excursion, or we might think about what the chances are of us throwing a die and getting a six. *Data* relates to collecting, organising, representing and interpreting any type of information. In the first five years of life the teacher and child might collect information and record it in some way, so that it becomes possible to talk about ways we come to school, our favourite foods, what types of pet we all have, and which month our birthdays are in. This data might be represented in a variety of ways (e.g. graphs, pictures or other types of chart) and can form the basis of discussions much in the same way that a picture book can be a stimulus for language in the first five years of life. We live in a world full of data that can be read and interpreted. It is imperative that we think about this concept in the early years.

Roll the die

Aim: Exploring chance

Materials: A die

Activity: Prepare a die with different-coloured spots. Sort the children into colour groups. Use the die to determine which group performs a simple action – for example, 'Red, stand up. Blue, clap hands'. Record the number of times each colour is rolled.

Animal sightings

Aim: Collecting data and organising it into groups

Material: Chart paper, pens and pictures/drawings of animals

Activity: Ask the children to look for animals in different locations and, when they have made a sighting, to draw a picture or find a photo of the animal. Discuss what animals were seen. Record the animals and their location pictorially. After the pictorial recording has been completed, ask questions about the data:

Where did David see a cat?

Who saw a dog in the park?

Figure 3.23: *Animal sightings*

Further resources – chance and data

Books

Anno, M., *Anno's Magic Hat Tricks*, Philomel Books

Geringer, L. A., *A Three Hat Day*, Harper & Row

Summary

This chapter has outlined activities for educators and parents to try with a young child in the first years of her life. The activities can be used in formal (e.g. centre) and informal learning (e.g. home) contexts. They are designed to be spontaneous or planned, to promote early learning in the use of the foundational processes and concepts of mathematics, and will assist the child with her school mathematics as she enters the first years of compulsory schooling. Being mathematical is part of our everyday lives and by establishing beginning processes and early conceptual understandings of number, measurement, space, and chance and data in these first five years of life, the young child will become fluent in their use and application in real-world contexts. This will in turn support her later understandings and enable her to feel confident about school mathematics.

References

Chiong, C. and Shuler, C., 2010, *Learning: Is There an App for That? Investigations of Young Children's Usage and Learning with Mobile Devices and Apps*, New York: The Joan Ganz Cooney Center at Sesame Workshop

Chapter 4

The young child at school

Overview

In this chapter you will become familiar with:

- the key concept areas in mathematics for young learners – number, measurement, space, chance and data, and patterns and algebra – and the way they relate to the 'Big Ideas' in mathematics
- the mathematical processes that form the basis of the mathematics curriculum in schools
- the importance of fostering positive attitudes towards mathematics, particularly through the careful selection and design of tasks
- the substantial variation in children's understanding and performance in mathematics and the need for responsive teaching.

In the years before starting school, the young child has had many experiences that provide the foundation for mathematical understandings. A child stacking pots and pans begins to learn about ordering. When Dad counts with Sam, or Mum reads *The Three Little Pigs* to Simon, they are helping their children to develop an understanding of numbers. Children also develop an understanding of mathematics through everyday activities. At the shops, seeing people buying groceries provides some understanding of the value of coins and how we exchange coins for goods. Children enjoy acting out everyday mathematical situations that they have seen, such as 'playing shops'. When children play together they have an opportunity to learn from each other and to use mathematical language, such as 'price', 'money', 'how much' or 'change'. When the young child goes to school, he will continue to build on these foundations of mathematical learning.

This chapter is concerned with the work involved in supporting mathematical learning in school. It commences with an overview of being a mathematical learner. It then describes the concepts and processes of mathematics that relate to learning in the early years and the characteristics of tasks that support mathematical learning, including the role of materials in tasks. Here, we use the term *tasks* in discussions of the literature on mathematical experiences. Throughout the book we suggest *activities* that can be used to promote learning about particular mathematical concepts and processes. Tasks form a broad category that can comprise different levels and numbers of activities. The chapter concludes with a discussion of exceptional mathematical learners and the importance of positive attitudes for mathematical learning.

The mathematical learner

Within any group of young children at the start of the school year, there will be variation in the proficiencies of these learners. Some of the differences will be due to the inherent capability of each child because we each vary in our potential across the spectrum of academic domains. However, much of the difference can be attributed to children's preschool experiences at home and in early learning settings, and whether or not their learning was encouraged and supported. Due to the impact of the learning environment on young children's learning, the teacher needs to endeavour to create a rich learning environment for every child in the class. This environment will include a variety of interesting and worthwhile tasks that accommodate each child's existing mathematical proficiency. The tasks need to be appropriately challenging for the individual if they are to have learning value for him. In tandem, the child needs adequate support and guidance so that he is not overwhelmed by the challenge presented by the tasks. Subsequent chapters of this book provide a variety of tasks that relate to the different concept areas in mathematics. We now provide an overview of the key concept areas in mathematics for young learners.

Mathematical concepts

The concepts of number, measurement, space, and chance and data were discussed with reference to the preschool years in Chapters 2 and 3. In our consideration of the school-aged child, we add to this list *patterns* and *algebra*. Many activities that are appropriate for the preschool years may still be appropriate in the first years of school. *Number* activities can include singing number songs and playing hopscotch. Moulding shapes with clay and constructing with boxes helps children to understand *space*. *Measurement* is the focus in discussions of the date and month of children's birthdays. Predicting tomorrow's weather provides children with everyday experiences in *chance* and *data*. As the child's proficiency with mathematics develops, he should engage in more challenging activities to enhance mathematical understanding. Of particular importance in designing learning experiences at this time is attention to the 'Big Ideas' in mathematics (Randall 2005): 'A *Big Idea* is a statement of an idea that is central to the learning of mathematics, one that links numerous mathematical understandings into a coherent whole' (p. 10; emphasis in original). The Big Ideas provide a unifying focus for mathematics throughout the school years. This section provides an overview of the concepts typically covered in early childhood mathematics curricula and, where appropriate, introduces the relevant Big Ideas. Particular attention is given to space and data due to their increased emphasis in recent years. Further Big Ideas will be introduced to children later in their schooling.

Number

Knowledge of number empowers children to understand quantitative mathematical situations and, consequently, is fundamental to mathematics learning. However, number is quite complex for most young learners because proficiency requires an understanding of mathematics as a language that uses symbols and has various rules for calculation (e.g. + – x /). Table 4.1 shows some important Big Ideas in *number* with reference to early years mathematics. Many early years mathematical activities will be designed to help children understand these Big Ideas through a variety of tasks. Chapter 5 presents a large selection of mathematical tasks relating to number.

Table 4.1: *Big Ideas relevant to early mathematical learning*

BIG IDEAS IN NUMBER	EARLY YEARS MATHEMATICS
Numbers: 'The set of real numbers is infinite, and each real number can be associated with a unique point on the number line' (Randall 2005, p. 12).	Whole numbers, including zero and fractions.

Table 4.1: (*cont.*)

BIG IDEAS IN NUMBER	EARLY YEARS MATHEMATICS
The Base 10 Numeration System: 'The base ten numeration system is a scheme for recording numbers using digits 0–9, groups of ten, and place value' (Randall 2005, p. 13).	There are only 10 numerals. Hence, to show numbers greater than 9, the placement of a digit becomes important (9, 90, 900). The placement of a digit changes its value by a magnitude of 10. Digits that are moved to the left become 10 times greater (90, 900) and those moved to the right become 10 times smaller (90, 9). The value of a number is understood by the combination of the digits in each place. (99 = 90 + 9)
Equivalence: 'Any number, measure, numerical expression, algebraic expression, or equation can be represented in an infinite number of ways that have the same value' (Randall 2005, p. 14).	Numbers can be broken down into smaller numbers that are equivalent to the original number. (10 = 6 + 4)
Comparison: 'Numbers, expressions, and measures can be compared by their relative values' (Randall 2005, p. 14).	Numbers can be compared using the terms *greater than, equal to* or *less than.*
Operation meanings and relationships: 'The same number sentence (e.g. 12 – 4 = 8) can be associated with different concrete or real-world situations, AND different number sentences can be associated with the same concrete or real-world situation' (Randall 2005, p. 15).	Numbers can be joined (+ x) or separated (– ÷), increasing or decreasing their value. (6 + 3 = 9; 6 x 3 = 18; 6 – 3 = 3; 6 ÷ 3 = 2)
Estimation: 'Numerical calculations can be approximated by replacing numbers with other numbers that are close and easy to compute with mentally' (Randall 2005, p. 17).	Estimation is useful for approximating a calculation and determining the reasonableness of a calculation.

Patterns and algebra

Mathematics can be defined as the study of patterns and relationships. Hence, building the foundations for patterning in the early years is important. Patterning involves children being able to recognise, describe, copy, extend and create patterns. The pattern can be numerical or non-numerical (e.g. colour, shape, position, sound, movement). Hence, there are many opportunities to engage children in patterning throughout the day. There are three general types of patterns. *Repeating patterns* have a core element that repeats, such as AB AB AB. There are also *growing patterns,* which are built from a core element – for example, 12, 123, 1234, 12345. *Relationship patterns* focus on the relationship between two groups. For example, 1 table has 4 chairs, so 2 tables have 8 chairs. The Big Idea with *patterns* may be expressed as follows: 'Relationships can be described and generalizations made for mathematical situations that have numbers or objects that repeat in predictable ways' (Randall 2005, p. 17). An example of this idea is skip counting where 2 is added repeatedly to create the pattern 2, 4, 6, 8, 10, 12.

Algebra has been identified as a domain for study throughout schooling commencing with the early years due to its mathematics power: 'Algebra is foundational in all areas of mathematics because it provides the tools (i.e. the language and structure) for representing and analyzing quantitative relationships, for modeling situations, for solving problems, and for stating and proving generalizations' (Ball 2003, p. xx). Underpinning algebra is the Big Idea of *variable*: 'Mathematical situations and structures can be translated and represented abstractly using variables, expressions, and equations' (Randall 2005, p. 18). In the skip counting example above, the core element was +2. Hence, in algebraic terms, this pattern could be described as '$\boxed{x} + 2$', where x is an unknown. Teachers can foster the link between patterns and algebra by encouraging children to identify the rule (+2). This rule (+2) changes the value of the initial number into a new number. This rule can also be expressed in words: 'If I increase 4 by 2, what is my new number (6)?' The process can also be reversed: 'If my number has been increased by 2 and I have 6 now, what was my original number (4)?' This type of thinking is referred to as functional thinking where the focus is on the mathematical change that occurred. For example: 'How can 4 be changed into 6?' The activities in Chapter 6 provide ways to engage children in learning about patterns and algebra.

Measurement

The Big Idea in *measurement* is that 'Some attributes of objects are measurable and can be quantified using unit amounts' (Randall 2005, p. 20). Some of these attributes can be measured directly, such as length, height, mass, volume and capacity of objects. However, other attributes, such as temperature, time and money, are measured indirectly. Temperature is measured by a thermometer; time is measured on clocks and calendars; and value is measured by money. Initially, children are encouraged to measure objects directly using familiar units. For example, they might measure the length of a table using a book and find that the table is 6 books long and 4 books wide. The use of non-standard or arbitrary units for measuring provides opportunities for children to learn how to measure. They need to choose an appropriate unit for measurement (a book), place objects (same-sized books) end to end without overlap or gaps on the item to be measured (the table), and count the number of units needed to cover it. If the books do not cover the table exactly, the children need to decide how to deal with the leftover part. They might ignore it, state that it was 6 books and a bit long, state that it was nearly 7 books long or include a fraction, such as six and a half.

The other approach they can take is to use a smaller measuring unit such as a pencil as the unit of measurement. Using non-standard units or referents, such as a pencil, relates to the Big Idea in measurement that 'Measurements can be approximated using known referents as the unit in the measurement process' (Randall 2005, p. 17). While measuring with non-standard units provides an understanding of the measuring process, accuracy is limited because non-standard units, such as a pencil, vary in length. Hence, it is more practical to use standard units of measure – for example, metres and centimetres for length.

Because so many different attributes of objects can be measured, children need to become familiar with the standard units for length and height, area, volume and capacity, mass (weight), time, temperature and money. Over time the standards for measuring units have changed, with the majority of the world using the metric system (e.g. metre, kilogram, litre, Celsius). The United States is one exception, using US customary units (e.g. foot, pound, pint, Fahrenheit) that originated with English units. Time is measured in both systems using seconds.

Space

Space, more formally known as *geometry*, is the strand of mathematics that focuses on the properties, measurement and relationships of points, lines, angles, surfaces and solids. As a field of study, geometry has a long history dating back to thousands of years before the Common Era, with famous geometers including Pythagoras, Euclid and Archimedes. In the third millennium, geometry has increased in importance. This is manifested in everyday technological applications of geometry, such as graphical user interfaces on computers, and global positioning systems (GPS); the myriad of virtual worlds to traverse or create in computer games; mobile technologies; and the creation of new careers due to medical advances, including sophisticated medical imaging.

There are three Big Ideas in mathematics related to space. The Big Idea about *shape and solids* is that 'Two- and three-dimensional objects with or without curved surfaces can be described, classified, and analyzed by their attributes' (Randall 2005, p. 19). Thus, at school, children's interest and curiosity about two- and three-dimensional shapes is encouraged, and opportunities are provided for them to progress from describing the everyday characteristics of a shape to observing its critical attributes. For example, a cube might be yellow and wooden, but those everyday characteristics don't distinguish it as a cube. The distinguishing aspects of a cube are its geometric properties – its six *square faces*, sometimes referred to as sides, and its 12 *edges* that meet each other at *right angles*. Number has a role in classifying three-dimensional shapes because the faces, edges and angles of different shapes vary in quantity. Based on their descriptions of geometric shapes, children can classify and reclassify groups of shapes by different attributes and analyse a new shape to determine its classification.

An object's shape can be changed in many ways without losing the integrity of the shape. It can be moved from one location to another, rotated or reflected. It can also be enlarged or reduced, or split in half with one part folding exactly onto the other due to line symmetry. These ideas are captured in the Big Idea of *transformation*: 'Objects in space can be transformed in an infinite number of ways, and those transformations can be described and analyzed mathematically' (Randall 2005, p. 20).

Shapes exist in space whether in two or three dimensions. Hence, children need to be able to recognise shapes in various orientations. This brings in the Big Idea of *orientation and location*: 'Objects in space can be oriented in an infinite number of ways, and an object's location in space can be described quantitatively' (Randall 2005, p. 19). An important learning for children is that though a change in viewpoint might alter what they see, it does not actually alter the attributes of a shape. For example, a four-legged table still has four legs even though they might not be visible from a *bird's-eye view*. The other key learning associated with this Big Idea is that the location of objects in space can be described mathematically. For example, a location on a map or grid can be described using coordinates.

The importance of space (geometry) in a technological society has been strongly advocated by the (US) National academies (2006), which consider spatial thinking to be a fundamental 21st-century skill and promote 'learning to think spatially' as a key goal of education across school curricula. The Academies' description of spatial thinking involves knowing about *space*, *representation* and *reasoning*. This awareness of space is referred to as *spatial sense*. Ideas for developing knowledge of space, including spatial sense, are presented in Chapter 8.

Chance and data

Chance and *data* are relatively new concept areas in early years mathematics classrooms. However, they are relevant in the everyday lives of children and provide the foundations for later work in probability and statistics.

Chance focuses on the likelihood of an event occurring, such as it raining tomorrow or rolling a six on a die. In everyday situations, we communicate the chance of various events using relative terms, ranging from 'impossible' to 'certain', with terms in between including 'possible', and 'likely' and 'unlikely'. The following table shows the chance of various events occurring when a four-part Spinner is spun and the relevant everyday language. In later years, the approximation of everyday language in mathematical situations is replaced by precise calculations of mathematical probability.

Table 4.2: *Chance with a spinner*

THE CHANCE OF: 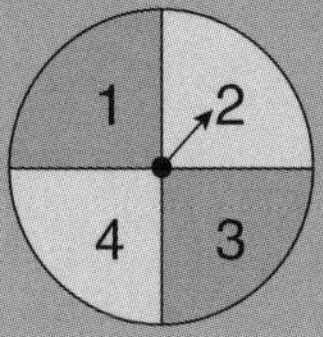	*SPINNING A 5*	*SPINNING A NUMBER HIGHER THAN 3 (4)*	*SPINNING A 2 OR A 3*	*SPINNING A NUMBER LOWER THAN 4 (1, 2, 3)*	*SPINNING A NUMBER LESS THAN 5 (1, 2, 3, 4)*
CHANCE (everyday language)	Impossible	Unlikely	Possible	Likely	Certain
PROBABILITY (calculation)	0 in 4 chance (0)	1 in 4 chance (.25)	2 in 4 chance (.5)	3 in 4 chance (.75)	4 in 4 chance (1)

Children's learnings about chance in the early years provide the foundation for their later understanding of the Big Idea that 'The chance of an event occurring can be described numerically by a number between 0 [impossible] and 1 [certain] inclusive and used to make predictions about other events' (Randall 2005, p. 21; terms added). Hence, chance vocabulary is an important stepping stone in mathematical understanding. The numerical calculations of chance are taught in later school years.

Data focuses on collecting, organising and representing information. During the implementation of these processes, children will learn about a variety of visual formats, including tallies, lists, tables, picture graphs and bar graphs. In addition to using various visual representations, children need to be able to interpret these representations and make inferences from them. For example, a survey can be used to collect data about children's favourite colours, which is then organised on a table and represented with a bar graph. However, someone else looking at the graph needs to be able to interpret the embedded mathematical information to answer questions, such as 'What is the girls' most popular colour?' or 'Is the same colour popular with girls and boys?' Hence, data involves children undertaking the dual roles of creator and interpreter of information.

The data processes referred to above involve two Big Ideas reflecting the importance of data in the 21st century. The Big Idea in *data collection* is that 'Some questions can be answered by collecting and analyzing data, and the question to be answered determines the data that needs to be collected and how best to collect it' (Randall 2005, p. 21). The Big Idea in *data representation* is that 'Data can be represented visually using tables, charts, and graphs. The type of data determines the best choice of visual representation' (Randall 2005, p. 21).

Figure 4.1: *The young child at school*

Although chance and data are each unique concepts, they are both underpinned by the two central ideas of *variation* and *expectation*:

> The most fundamental idea is that of *variation* … Variation is the raison d'être for statistics. Variation in people's feet means that shoe manufacturers have to make different sizes of shoes and hence have a great interest in knowing the distribution of sizes across ages in the population … Intuitively variation is 'everywhere' in all data handling contexts … *Expectation*, on the other hand, can be more difficult to describe across contexts. Expectation may arise from a data-collecting situation, for example the expected height of a student … In a chance context, however, expectation may be the starting point; for example when tossing a coin many times there is likely to be the initial expectation that half of the outcomes will be heads and half tails (Watson 2007, pp. 5–6; emphasis added).

Figure 4.2: *Teaching measuring to the young child at school*

Hence, exploring variation and expectation should be integral to chance and data activities for young children. See Chapter 9 for activities on chance and data.

As shown above, the range of content in mathematics in the early years is vast. Clearly, the Big Ideas can provide useful reference points for how the small concepts in mathematics contribute to building mathematical understanding.

Mathematical processes

Mathematical processes are the thinking skills that help children learn about mathematical concepts. There are four groups of such processes. The *beginning processes* are the skills that children began developing before school, such as describing attributes, matching, sorting, comparing, ordering and patterning. The *logical mathematical processes* include counting, sequencing, calculating, estimating and measuring. The *visual spatial processes* include being able to use diagrams and pictures to represent mathematical information holistically, to visualise images from different positions in space, and to manipulate or transform these images. The *general processes* are the skills that are important across the curriculum. These include explaining, validating, analysing, inferring, organising and representing. A child may use a variety of processes in order to understand a concept, such as 'six'. For example, he may *count* six objects, *represent* (draw) six ducks, or *explain* that three and three equals six. As the child develops the processes needed to work mathematically and develops an understanding of the concepts of mathematics, he is becoming 'numerate'. Numeracy is the ability to function in everyday mathematical situations. Because teachers cannot anticipate all the mathematics that a child might require in his life, particular attention needs to be given to problem solving. Problem solving is knowing what to do when you encounter a challenge or an obstacle to a goal.

Problem solving and problem posing are key focuses in mathematics education. Initially, problem solving might involve finding the answer to a simple operation. For example, although Jim (eight years) may quickly know the answer to 6 and 6 because he has learnt his number facts, Jon (seven years) may not know the answer. Jon needs to be encouraged to use the processes to work out the answer. He could *represent* the situation with blocks and then *count* how many he has. When children are learning the operations, word problems are appropriate. For example, if there are six children and each child has two balloons, how many balloons are there altogether? As the children's mathematical understanding develops, the problems need to become more challenging or they are not providing children with opportunities for problem solving! Examples of problems related to each of the four concepts are included in Chapters 5–8. These problems should be supplemented by a range of other problems and puzzles. Problems that require long-term engagement are ideal for those children who need to be challenged. In problem posing, children assume more responsibility as they work towards understanding a mathematical situation. For example, a family might be visiting and everyone agrees that they will order pizza for dinner. A question posed spontaneously by a young child – 'How many pizzas will be ordered?' – provides a rich mathematical moment. A response of 'How will we find out?' encourages the child to investigate this authentic situation. For example, the child might respond, 'We could ask how many people are having pizza' or 'What type of pizza do they like?' or 'How many people will one pizza feed?' Each one of these questions is relevant to ordering pizza and shows the relevance of mathematical investigations in everyday life.

Positive attitudes and mathematical learning

Figure 4.3: *Two schoolboys*

Attitudes are important for learning. Children need to develop confidence and a positive attitude towards mathematics. Sometimes the actions or words of teachers or parents have a negative effect on children's attitudes. Consider what a child might think about mathematics, for example, if it is used as a 'punishment' for the class being too talkative. Also think about how a child might feel about himself, as a mathematical learner, if he hears a parent saying 'Well, I was never any good at mathematics'. Teachers need to plan for the development of positive attitudes just as they plan for concept and process development. Quality tasks including mathematical puzzles and games provide opportunities to enhance children's attitudes towards mathematics.

Tasks for mathematical learning

Typically, tasks in early years classrooms have been relatively small and discrete. However, for learning to occur, the tasks need to have learning value – that is, they need to challenge children beyond their current capabilities. The learning value can be achieved in two ways.

First, tasks can be carefully sequenced to build on prior knowledge. During the preschool years, the mathematical activities are characterised by spontaneous and informal activities. However, as the child encounters more complex mathematics, careful consideration should be given to sequencing the content. For example, calculating with one-digit numbers (0–9) should precede calculating with two-digit numbers (i.e. 10–99). A child's understanding of numbers determines what is appropriate in other concept areas. For example, a child will have difficulty understanding a measurement of 250 millilitres if he is only familiar with two-digit numbers. The difficulty level of many activities can be adjusted by varying the size of the numbers that are involved. Guidance in sequencing mathematical content is provided in most curriculum documents.

Second, the tasks can be made more challenging by making one or more of the four crucial aspects of mathematics multidimensional rather than unidimensional: (1) using mathematical concepts and processes; (2) applying mathematical knowledge; (3) opportunities for exploration; and (4) learning outcomes (Yelland 2005). Unidimensional tasks are 'simple sequences of activity that usually had a single outcome' (Yelland 2005, p. 233). In these tasks there are minimal opportunities for exploration and usually only one way to solve them. In contrast, multidimensional mathematical tasks are 'integrated investigations in which skills and concepts are used in innovative ways to solve authentic problems' (p. 233). They extend the foundational mathematical skills and concepts, providing children with multiple opportunities for exploration. The descriptors on Yelland's (2005) Mathematics Task Continuum enable teachers to benchmark aspects of a particular task, as closer to unidimensional or multidimensional, and through these descriptors identify ways to increase task complexity – see Figure 4.4.

1. *Using mathematical concepts and processes*

STRUCTURED USE	OPEN-ENDED USE
• The task requires a single outcome and usually only one way is accepted to achieve it.	• The task allows for problem-solving and problem-posing opportunities in open-ended investigations.
• The teacher has structured the task for the learner to use and practise a particular process or concept.	• The children share strategies and have input into the direction of their learning.
• The children complete the task requirement(s) and do not deviate from set goal(s).	• Children are motivated and inspired to investigate and trial ideas.
• Children are not challenged to go beyond the single outcome or level achieved.	• There are opportunities for the children to experience challenges.
• Traditional media are used (pencil, paper).	• The children and teacher integrate various media, including ICT.

2. *Applying mathematical knowledge*

FOCUSED APPLICATION	EXTENDED APPLICATION
• Specific mathematical concepts and processes are introduced via structured tasks.	• A range of mathematical concepts and processes are applied by the children.
• The application/use is not integrated with other knowledge.	• Application of knowledge is integrated.
• There are few connections made between the task and the children's prior understandings.	• Connections are made and encouraged between the task and the children's prior understandings.
	• The children use their own initiative and draw on a broad range of knowledge and processes to complete the task.

3. *Opportunities for exploration*

MINIMAL OPPORTUNITIES	MULTIPLE OPPORTUNITIES
• Children are mostly taught in large groups (whole-class instruction).	• Children have ample time in large and small groups and on their own to conceptualise, plan and reflect.
• The task is mostly teacher-directed and completed individually.	• The children engage and lead discussion about their learning.

MINIMAL OPPORTUNITIES	MULTIPLE OPPORTUNITIES
• The children are encouraged not to deviate from the predetermined instructional plan.	• Tasks are initiated and/or extended by the child.
• Children respond with yes/no answers or closed/fixed answers.	• The structure of the session is flexible.
• The child mainly learns the process/concept in isolation.	• Children can approach the task in different ways.
• The children may not show interest in the task if the concept is already known and the solution is mechanical application of skill.	• The children can learn additional complementary processes and mathematical concepts in task solution.
	• Collaborative and cooperative learning is encouraged.
	• The children find the task meaningful and are interested.

4. *Learning outcomes*

LIMITED LEARNING OUTCOME(S)	VARIED LEARNING OUTCOMES
• The children's work looks the same.	• The children choose different media to represent and communicate their ideas and knowledge.
• The learning processes are specific to the task.	• The children's learning processes are varied.
• There are right and wrong answers and particular processes to follow.	• There are multiple solutions and outcome levels.
• Opportunity to use initiative is limited.	• The children develop confidence in their own learning initiatives.
• The children's own interpretations and learning extensions are not recognised as valid.	• The children's additional learning is recognised as valid or important.
• Communication of findings is not valued as a learning outcome.	• The children communicate their findings to others.

Unidimensional ⟵⟶ Multidimensional

Figure 4.4: *Mathematics Task Continuum*
Source: Yelland 2005, p. 234

Using materials in mathematics

To support children's learning of mathematics in tasks or activities, a wide range of materials can be used. These materials include everyday objects (e.g. buttons, plastic lids, scales, clocks), environmental items (e.g. seed pods, pine cones) and manipulatives (e.g. counters, unifix cubes). Manipulatives are important in mathematics because they enable children to represent and act out mathematical situations. For example, small planes could be used to enact the following airport story about subtraction.

> There are five planes on the runway. If one takes off, how many planes are left on the runway?

As the children become more familiar with the operation, context-specific manipulatives, such as planes, are replaced with more general manipulatives. General manipulatives, such as counters or unifix cubes, can represent any object, person or animal.

Figure 4.5: *Two schoolgirls and their tablets*

The use of a particular manipulative depends on the mathematical concept being explored. For example, iceblock sticks can be used to develop an understanding of length and two-digit numbers. To measure the length of the table, the iceblock sticks are laid end-to-end and counted. To determine how many iceblock sticks there are in a pile, the sticks are bundled together with a rubber band in groups of 10. First, the bundles of 10 are counted – 10, 20, 30. Then, the loose sticks are counted – 31, 32, 33, 34. Because bundles of 10 iceblock sticks correspond to the base 10 structure of our mathematics system, they are particularly useful in representing two-digit numbers and in two-digit addition and subtraction. When iceblock sticks are used to represent two-digit numbers, the bundles of 10 are placed to the left and the loose sticks are placed to the right to correspond to the positions of the 10's and ones in the written symbol. So 2 bundles of 10 sticks and 3 loose sticks would be represented as 23. Larger numbers can be represented with base 10 blocks. A set of blocks comprises ones, tens, hundreds and thousands. The role of a manipulative is to support mathematical understanding. Hence, it is not necessary for a child to use a manipulative once he has developed the appropriate understanding of a particular topic.

In addition to planned uses of materials, teachers can capitalise on situations where materials can support mathematical understanding. For example, in the following picture the young boy has created a basket full of flowers. The mathematics in this picture can be revealed through questioning:

How many flowers are in the basket altogether? How many different colours are there? What colour is the smallest flower?

Figure 4.6: *A boy and his artwork*

Exceptional learners in mathematics

Even though a teacher has planned quality tasks and scaffolded the learning, there will be some children who struggle with mathematics more than others. There are three perspectives on why children might experience learning difficulties: (1) the deficit model, (2) the inefficient learner model and (3) the environmental factors model (Twomey 2006; and see further Table 4.3). However, rather than consider these perspectives in isolation, they can be used together to optimise the child's learning experience. Initially, the teacher can ensure that the child is engaged in a rich learning environment suited to his needs (environmental factors). Children who have had limited experience with a particular mathematical topic should benefit from engaging in a rich diversity of experiences to build their knowledge base. Teachers can also take time to establish what these children can do and try to pinpoint the source of their difficulty (inefficient learner). This knowledge will enable the teacher to respond to the learner's needs and support his mathematical learning. For example, if a child is using finger counting rather than number facts in addition calculations, there needs to be a concerted effort to support the child to learn number facts. If these approaches do not result in improved learning, specialist investigation is needed to establish the source of the learner's difficulties because the underlying cause might be physical or intellectual. Once the difficulty is identified, the teacher will need to work with a specialist to provide the most effective support possible for that child.

Table 4.3: *Models and causes of learning difficulties*

MODEL	CAUSES
Deficit	Below average intelligence, lack of automaticity in basic academic skills, attentional difficulties, motivational difficulties, visual and auditory processing difficulties, poor memory capacity, language and literacy difficulties, dyscalculia.
Inefficient learner	Inaccurate or inefficient cognitive strategies, slow and error-prone retrieval of content, non-awareness of intelligent learner behaviours.
Environmental factors	Insufficient or inappropriate instruction, little or no differentiation of learning activities, inappropriate assessment tasks.

Just as there will be children who struggle with mathematics in most classrooms, there will also be gifted children who are capable of high-level mathematical performance. These children are distinguished by their exceptional reasoning ability and exhibit some other characteristics (House 1987; and see further Table 4.4). Due to gifted children's different capabilities in logico-mathematical and/or spatial tasks, there are three distinct types of mathematically gifted children: analytic thinkers, geometric thinkers and harmonic thinkers (Kruteskii 1976). *Harmonic thinkers* have high logico-mathematical ability and high spatial ability and, hence, should perform well on all mathematics tasks for their grade level. *Analytic thinkers* have high logico-mathematical ability and weaker spatial ability. These children should perform well on tasks and tests that involve number work and logical thinking. However, they will do less well on spatially oriented tasks. A third group of gifted children are the *geometric thinkers*. These children have high spatial ability and weaker logico-mathematical ability. Hence, they may struggle on tasks involving the recall of number facts or mathematical calculations. However, these children should excel when they engage in visual spatial tasks, such as identifying the characteristics of shapes. Care needs to be taken that this latter group do not disengage from mathematics in the early years of schooling due to a curriculum emphasis on number work.

Thus, gifted children can vary substantively in their interest and achievement in particular types of mathematical tasks. To address these children's mathematical needs, tasks need to be adequately challenging to foster their capability and to avert boredom and a loss of engagement. These children may need extension or enrichment work beyond what is provided to other children in the class. For more about exceptional learners, see Diezmann, Stevenson and Fox (2012).

Table 4.4: *Characteristics of a mathematically gifted student*

• Has exceptional reasoning ability and memory.
• Has a tendency to choose to do mathematics when presented with a choice of activities.
• Masters typical content more quickly and at an earlier age than his or her classmates.
• Often skips steps in problem solving and may solve problems in unexpected ways.
• Is more willingly and capable of doing problems abstractly: often prefers not to use concrete aids.
• Enjoys and is successful in looking for patterns and relationships, and attempts to explain them.
• Concentrates for long periods of time on a problem that he or she finds interesting.
• Is more likely to see relationships between a new problem and problems previously solved; enjoys posing original problems.
• Is capable of more independent, self-directed activities.
• Enjoys the challenge of mathematical puzzles and games.

Source: House 1987, pp. 51–2

Summary

Throughout this chapter, there has been a focus on how to support school-aged children in their mathematical learning. This learning involves building their understandings of mathematical concepts – that is, number, measurement, space, chance and data, and patterns and algebra – some of which provide the foundations for the Big Ideas of mathematics. The chapter has also highlighted how mathematical learning is encouraged through positive attitudes and mathematical processes, particularly problem solving and problem posing. The chapter has described how tasks can provide challenges through sequencing from simple to complex activities and through attention to emphasising more multidimensional than unidimensional aspects of mathematics. To accommodate these challenges, supportive materials are often used. The chapter concludes with a discussion of exceptional learners whose learning needs can differ substantively from their peers.

In the following five chapters, a range of mathematical activities are suggested for the early school years. These activities have been planned to interest and engage young learners and to provide scope for mathematical learning. Teachers are encouraged to select or adapt these activities to suit individual children and to supplement these activities with ideas from other sources.

References

Ball, D. L. (Chair), 2003, *Mathematical Proficiency for All Students: Toward a Strategic Research and Development Program in Mathematics Education*, RAND Mathematics Study Panel, Arlington and Santa Monica: RAND Education

Diezmann, C. M., Stevenson, M. K. and Fox, J. L., 2012, 'Supporting Exceptional Students to Thrive Mathematically', in B. Perry et al. (eds), *Research in Mathematics Education in Australasia: 2008–2011* (pp. 89–109), Rotterdam: Sense Publishers

House, P. (ed.), 1987, *Providing Opportunities for the Mathematically Gifted K–12*, Reston, VA: NCTM

Kruteskii, V. A., 1976, *Psychology of Mathematical Abilities in School Children*, Chicago, IL: Chicago University Press

National Academies, 2006, *Learning to Think Spatially*, The National Academies Press: Washington, D.C.

Randall, C. I., 2005, 'Big Ideas and Understandings as the Foundation for Elementary and Middle School Mathematics', *NCSM Journal of Mathematics Education Leadership*, 8(1), 9–24

Twomey, E., 2006, 'Linking Learning Theories and Learning Difficulties', *Australian Journal of Learning Disabilities*, 11(2), 93–8

Watson, J., 2007, 'The Foundations of Chance and Data', *Australian Primary Mathematics Classroom*, 12(1), 4–7

Yelland, N. J., 2005, 'Curriculum, Pedagogies and Practice with ICT in the Information Age', in N. Yelland (ed.), *Critical issues in Early Childhood Education* (pp. 224–48), Milton Keynes: Open University Press

Chapter 5

Number

Overview

In this chapter you will become familiar with:

- ways to represent quantity using physical items, words and numerals
- activities to encourage children to count, compare and order numbers
- ways to foster conceptual understanding of place value in the base 10 number system
- how mathematical operations on a quantity increase or decrease its value.

Number knowledge is fundamental to understanding mathematical situations in the everyday world. To develop this understanding, young children need a range of experiences, such as counting, recognising and writing numerals, composing and decomposing numbers, and simple operations. Children's understandings can be supported by the use of physical materials and tools that aid thinking. For example, the calculator is a useful tool when children are learning to count by twos and fives because children can check what they are saying with what the visual display of the calculator is showing. It is also useful for checking answers when children have completed an operation. Throughout their school years, children are expected to acquire increasingly complex understandings of number. Hence, it is important for children to master simple concepts and gradually build their proficiency with number.

Number experiences

Recognising and writing numerals. Just as young children need to learn to recognise and write letters, they also need to learn how to recognise and write numerals. Initially, some children may reverse numerals when they write them, but with practice the majority of children quickly learn how to form the numerals correctly.

Counting. Many young children enjoy counting. When children begin learning to count they may confuse the order of the number names or leave out certain numbers. They may also have difficulty with one-to-one correspondence. For example, a child may say '1, 2, 3, 4, 5' when counting three toys. The goal is for children to become rational counters. Rational counters say the numbers in the correct order without leaving any numbers out and they only say one number name for each object. They also say the last number name in a counting sequence when they are asked how many objects there are in a group. Children need to be able to count forwards and backwards. They also need to be able count by twos, fives and 10's. Skip counting is more efficient than counting by ones.

Subitising. The term 'subitising' means to recognise how many items are in a group without counting each item individually. It can be encouraged by providing children with opportunities to become familiar with particular representations of quantity, such as the way dots are arranged on a die. Children's recall of images of a particular number can help them with calculations when two numbers are added together, such as 3 and 2. Subitising can also assist children with questions when they have a particular number of objects and are trying to reach a particular goal. For example: 'If I start with 6 counters, how many more counters do I need to make 9?' Knowing that 6 is made up of two rows of 3 and that 9 needs three rows of 3, children can readily identify that 3 more counters are needed.

Numbers to 10. When children begin to learn about numbers, the focus is on understanding quantities up to 10, such as 3 pigs or 7 dogs. This helps children associate the idea of numbers with different quantities and with the question 'how many?'.

Larger numbers. After children have become proficient with quantities to 10, they are introduced to larger numbers. To understand these numbers, children need to develop an understanding of the base 10 system and place value. Instead of counting every object in a large group, they are shown how to group the objects in 10's and to count first by 10's and then count any leftover objects separately. After grouping some objects, a child might say '*10, 20, 30*, 31, 32, 33, 34'. When children are familiar with grouping in 10's, 100's are introduced as 10 groups of 10. Children also need experiences working with larger numbers. These experiences should include opportunities to identify odd and even numbers, the numbers before and after a given number, and ordinal numbers. A similar approach is used to introduce children to thousands.

Operations. Gradually the children learn about the four operations: addition, subtraction, multiplication and division. Children are introduced to the concept of each operation in a meaningful context that incorporates specific language and manipulatives (e.g. plastic farm animals). Then number facts are developed through thinking strategies (e.g. doubling). Finally, the children are introduced to the standard algorithm (procedure and setting out) for the operation.

Fractions and decimals. Young children will encounter mathematical situations where parts of an item are involved, such as half a cookie, a quarter of an orange or an eighth of a chocolate bar. Encourage students to talk about how many parts are needed to make the whole item (e.g. 'Four quarters make a whole orange').

Calculators. Adults use calculators to perform tedious or lengthy calculations quickly and accurately. However, a calculator is also a valuable tool for exploring numbers and learning about mathematics. For example, a young child who is counting aloud can use the calculator to see what certain numbers look like.

The following pages present a range of activities designed to enhance young children's understanding of number.

Counting

The beehive

Aim: Counting to 5

Activity: 'Here is the Beehive' is one of several well-known rhymes used to teach children counting.

Here is the beehive,
[*Clasp hands together.*]
Where are the bees?
Hidden away where nobody sees.
Soon they come creeping out of the hive,
[*Slowly bring thumb out of clasped hands.*]
One, two, three, four, five!
[*Bring out other fingers as you count.*]

The rhyme can be adapted for other numbers. For example:

Soon they come creeping out of the tree [*three*]
Soon they come creeping out of the door [*four*]
Soon they come creeping out to play tricks [*six*]

Variation: The children could use counters or cut-outs of bees on a magnetic board.

The tapping song

Aim: Counting to 5

Amy taps with one finger,
One finger, one finger;
[*Tap lightly with one finger or hold up numeral card 1.*]
Amy taps with one finger,
All join in.
Amy taps with two fingers,
[*Tap lightly with two fingers or hold up numeral card 2.*]

Repeat the song for 3, 4 and 5.

Amy goes to sleep now,
Sleep now, sleep now;
[*Place palms of hands together, and rest head on hands.*]
Amy goes to sleep now,
Let's rest too.

Variation: Children tap with their feet or place counters on a storyboard to represent the number of taps.

Ten ducks

Aim: Counting to 10

Activity: Pretend to draw a pool in the middle of the floor. Ten children crouch like ducks around the edge. With each number word, a 'duck' jumps into the pool and pretends to swim. When the 10 are in, they spread their wings, waddle out and return to their places in a single file.

> One duck, two ducks splashing in a pool.
> Three ducks, four ducks find the water cool.
> Five ducks, six ducks want to stay and play.
> Seven ducks, eight ducks love a rainy day.
> Nine ducks, ten ducks, all with wings outspread,
> Shake their glossy feathers and waddle off to bed.

Variation: Use the rhyme as a finger play. The appropriate number of fingers is held up as the number words are mentioned. After 10, shake the hands and walk the fingers to the lap.

Number line counting

Aim: Counting to 10

Materials: A number line on the ground

Activity: Draw a number line on the ground. Children count as they hop, skip, jump or walk along the line. As a variation, challenge the children to count and move backwards.

A number line can also be used to identify numbers. For example:

Stand on numeral 3. What number comes after 6?

Figure 5.1: *Number line*

One rock, two rocks

Aim: Counting to 10

Activity: This counting game is an adaptation of an old favourite. Children stand in a circle and hold out their hands in a fist. Choose a leader who begins counting off each fist while the group chants the rhyme. The child whose fist is being counted, when the group says 'no more' and 'out the door', must place her fist behind her back. Repeat the rhyme until one fist is left. That child is the winner and becomes the new leader.

> One rock, two rocks,
> Three rocks, four.
> Five rocks, six rocks,
> Seven rocks, no more!
> Eight rocks, nine rocks
> Ten is out the door!

Extension: For 'buzz counting', have the children stand in a circle. Start at one and count around the circle until they get to 10. The child whose turn it is to say 10 says 'buzz' instead and sits down. The next child commences again at one and so the game continues until there is one child, the winner, left standing. This game can also be played to a larger number or used to count backwards or in twos, fives and 10's.

Circle counting

Aim: Counting to 20

Materials: Numeral cards for 1–20

Activity: Children form a circle. Give each child a numeral card from 1 to 20. Choose a child to call out her number while doing an action, such as clicking or tapping. The children then count on in turn from that number, performing the same action. When 20 is reached, the next child holds up her numeral card and the activity is repeated. Try counting backwards. As an alternative, have a child say her number and the child holding each successive number calls out their number.

Extension: Challenge the children to use a template and make a dot-to-dot drawing, incorporating the numerals 1–10. Hand the dot-to-dot to a friend to complete.

Body-part counting

Aim: Counting by twos, fives and 10's

Materials: Paper, glue, pencils and strips of cardboard

Activity: Count by fives using fingers and hands. Children draw around their hands, cut out the shapes and glue them onto a strip of card. Number the prints to help them count in fives, then in 10's. This activity could also be repeated using feet and toes.

Variations: Stand a group of children in a row at the front of the room and play the game 'How Many?'

How many eyes on 1 person? How many eyes on 2 people? How many eyes on 3 people? (and so on)

Cut out sets of eyes from magazines to count by twos. Have the children suggest other things to count by twos (feet, shoes, ears, arms, knees).

Figure 5.2: *Body-part counting*

Recognising numerals

Twister

Aim: Recognising numerals to 5

Materials: Large numeral cards 0–5, and tape

Activity: Scatter and tape large numeral cards 0–5 (no more than half a metre apart) on the floor. The children direct a volunteer to place body parts on different numerals. For example:

Place your right foot on 5. Place your left hand on 1. Place your right elbow on 0.

When the volunteer falls down, it is the next person's turn.

Variation: Hide numeral cards around the room. Children have to find the numeral cards and arrange them in the correct order.

I wrote four letters

Aim: Recognising numerals to 5

Materials: Old envelopes and cards, and enough numeral cards (0–5) for every child to receive a card

Activity: Children sit in a circle. The envelopes are scattered around the outside of the circle. The numeral cards are passed, face down, around the circle while the children say the following poem:

> I wrote four letters to my friend,
> And on the way I lost them.
> A busy postman picked them up,
> And took them to his office.

At the end of the poem, the children turn over the numeral card in front of them. If they have the numeral card mentioned in the poem (e.g. 4), they leave the circle to collect the corresponding number of letters and then return to their places. At the end of the game, the children talk about how many letters they have.

Millie Mouse

Aim: Recognising numerals to 6

Materials: Paper, pencils, a die and plastic cup

Activity: Play with two to six players. Draw a mouse body and head on a piece of paper. Take it in turns to throw the die and draw in the parts shown by the score. If the score shows parts already drawn in, then that turn is missed. If a six is thrown, any body part can be drawn. The first player to finish Millie Mouse is the winner.

Figure 5.3: *Millie Mouse*

Numeral necklace

Aim: Recognising numerals to 10

Materials: Make numeral necklaces by attaching numeral cards to pieces of string

Activity: Each child is given a numeral necklace to wear around her neck. The children respond according to the direction given.

All children with a 7 do 7 star jumps. All children with a 4 hop on one foot. (and so on)

Have the children switch cards after a few directions.

Variation: The children sit in a circle. Place a numeral card, face down, in front of each child. Pass the cards by sliding them along the floor to the next child. When the passing stops, the child looks at her card and must perform a specified task. For example:

If you have numeral 7, skip around the circle and back to your position.

Figure 5.4: *Numeral necklace*

Musical numerals

Aim: Recognising numerals to 10

Materials: A set of numeral cards and some recorded music

Activity: Children dance around while music is playing. When the music stops, the teacher holds up a numeral card and the children must form groups corresponding to the number on the card. Alternatively, when the music stops, the children balance on the number of body parts that correspond with the numeral on the card. For '3', you might balance on your elbow, hand and foot. Change the numeral cards to word form rather than digit form.

Variation: Peg a secret numeral card to a child's back so the rest of the group can see it. The child asks questions of the class: for example, 'Is the number more than 5?' Only 'yes' or 'no' answers are permitted. (It helps to write the numerals to 10 on the board so the eliminated numerals can be erased.)

Sandpaper numerals

Aim: Identifying numerals to 10

Material: Numeral cards made of sandpaper

Activity: The child is blindfolded and chooses a card. She feels the numeral and identifies it without looking at the card.

Variation: Cover a sandpaper numeral with a piece of paper. Make a guessing game of rubbing over the numeral with a wax crayon to see what number appears.

Figure 5.5: *Sandpaper numerals*

Number monster

Aim: Recognising numerals to 10

Materials: Construction material such as boxes and cardboard cylinders, playdough and clay

Activity: Explore a specific number, such as 5, by making a monster with 5 of everything – for example, 5 arms, 5 eyes. Draw the monster or make it out of playdough, clay or construction material.

Variation: Make a group mural depicting paintings or drawings about a certain number – for example, a table with 4 legs, a car with 4 tyres.

Figure 5.6: *Number monster*

A story with numbers

Aim: Recognising numerals

Activity: Tell a story that makes frequent use of number words. Every time you say a number word in the story, the child should hold up a corresponding numeral card or, as her skills develop, print the appropriate numeral on her paper.

Number diaries

Aim: Identifying numerals in the environment

Activity: The children create individual diaries. Each night for one week they enter a new number fact about themselves and report it back to the class the next day.

Monday – My phone number is 38427509.

Tuesday – I have 3 goldfish and 2 dogs.

Wednesday – My birthday is the 28th of April.

Thursday – Our house number is 16.

Friday – There are 7 photos in my room.

Variation: A booklet of personal numbers can be made. Phone numbers, birth dates, ages and addresses are only a few possibilities. Make a slide show of personal numbers to share with the group.

Extension: Search for numbers in the classroom, around the school and in the neighbourhood. Create a list of these numbers as they are observed.

Writing numerals

Numeral printing centre

Aim: Forming numerals to 10

Materials: Set up numeral printing centres to allow children to practise forming the numerals:

- in trays of sand or salt
- on the board with paintbrushes and water
- on large sheets of paper with markers
- on the chalkboard with chalk
- with finger-paint or shaving cream
- out of plasticine or playdough
- on the cement with a paintbrush and water
- with blocks, stamps, stickers
- with coloured wool or string
- with seeds
- by bending pipecleaners
- on the whiteboard
- with lego.

Demonstrate how to form the numerals one at a time. Invite the children to write the numerals in the air and on their palms. Always display models of the numerals. Children require experiences involving the tracing and copying of numerals before they form the numerals freely.

Variation: Guess a mystery numeral a friend traces on your back.

Figure 5.7: *Printing centres*

Sparkles

Aim: Writing numerals to 10

Materials: White paper, clear or white glue and glitter

Activity: Children are asked to write their favourite number in glue on the white paper. It magically appears when sprinkled with glitter.

Variation: Use sand, parsley flakes or cinnamon to sprinkle over the glue.

Rainbow numerals

Aim: Writing numerals to 10

Materials: Large sheets of paper, a black marker and paints of various colours

Activity: A child selects a numeral and it is written in black marker on a large sheet of paper. She then traces around the outline of the numeral with different coloured paints to create a rainbow effect.

Variation: Have each child incorporate the numeral of her choice into a picture. Display the drawings and challenge the others to identify the numeral.

Playdough numerals

Aim: Making numerals to 10

Materials: Playdough of various colours, large numeral cards

Activity: Roll the playdough into thin strips. Make the shape of the number by placing the strips of playdough on the numeral card.

Variation: A friend is blindfolded and asked to guess the number by tracing her finger around the playdough shape. Alternatively, bend pipecleaners to the shape of the number.

Figure 5.8: *Playdough numerals*

Invisible numerals

Aim: Writing and recognising numerals to 10

Materials: White paper, white crayons and a coloured wash made up of paint and water. (The darker paint colours such as blue or green are more effective.)

Activity: Write a numeral in white crayon on the white piece of paper. The numeral is invisible until after it has been submerged in coloured water.

Variation: Give several clues so the children can guess the numeral before it is submerged in the water. For example:

This numeral is larger than 5. It is an even number.

Children can make up their own clues.

Starry numerals

Aim: Forming numerals to 10

Materials: Construction paper, felt pens and toothpicks

Activity: Write a numeral on a piece of construction paper. The child sits on the carpet and uses a toothpick to poke holes through the paper along the outline of the numeral. When she holds the paper up to the light, she will see tiny 'stars' in the shape of her numeral.

Hidden numerals

Aim: Writing numerals to 10

Materials: Large sheets of paper or card, felt pens, paint and collage material

Activity: Ask each child to print her favourite numeral on a large sheet of paper. Encourage the child to create a creature out of the numeral. Challenge the others to guess the numeral.

Figure 5.9: *Hidden numerals*

Numbers to 10

Number headbands

Aim: Understanding numbers to 10

Materials: Paper strips and construction material

Activity: Choose a labelled paper strip and use construction material to make a number headband.

Variation: Make a specified number of fingerprints. Turn the fingerprints into creatures by adding tails and whiskers, etc.

Figure 5.10: *Number headbands*

Moving with numbers

Aim: Exploring numbers to 10

Activity: In an open space, give instructions that require children to work with numbers:

In groups of 3, make yourselves into a sun.

Make a shape with 6 children.

Move 2 body parts. Move 4 body parts, etc.

Arrangements

Aim: Exploring conservation of numbers to 10

Materials: Sheets of card and a variety of materials, such as toothpicks, iceblock sticks, buttons, coloured shapes, cubes and bottle tops

Activity: Place a variety of materials at work centres. Select a certain number for the day and challenge the children to make many different arrangements of that number using the materials provided. They can record their arrangements by gluing the materials on sheets of card or by tracing around the objects and colouring.

Figure 5.11: *Arrangements*

Choc chip cookies

Aim: Exploring quantities to 10

Materials: Paper plates and plasticine or playdough

Activity: Each child has a paper plate in front of her and some plasticine. Explain that the plate is a cookie and that she is going to make choc chips for her cookie out of plasticine. Specify the number of choc chips to place on the cookie and have the children add choc chips one at a time until a set is created. Repeat this procedure several times using different numbers. Encourage her to clear her plate by taking off one choc chip at a time.

Variation: This activity can be adapted for use when working with addition or subtraction. For example:

Make 6 choc chips for your cookie.

Add 1 more choc chip. How many choc chips are there now?

6 and 1 more makes 7.

Or:

Make 4 choc chips for your cookie.

Take 1 choc chip away. There are 3 choc chips left.

4 take away 1 leaves 3.

You may wish to substitute counters or buttons for plasticine.

Each child can create her own number story and tell it to a friend.

Try making some real choc chip cookies.

Figure 5.12: *Choc chip cookies*

Dragon spots (Today's number is ...)

Aim: Representing numbers to 10

Materials: A large picture of a dragon for the wall, large dragon spots

Activity: Select a number for the day. Find as many ways of representing that number as possible. Write the number stories on the spots and pin them on the dragon – for example, six, 3 + 3, two groups of three.

Figure 5.13: *Dragon spots*

Mystery bag

Aim: Exploring combinations to 10

Materials: Drawstring bag and 10 flat marbles

Activity: Work in pairs. One child places an amount of marbles into the bag. The second child counts the marbles by feeling them and says the number. Empty the bag to see if the answer was correct. Decide how many marbles have been left out of the bag. Ask:

How many marbles are needed to make 10?

Make 10

Aim: Learning combinations that make 10

Materials: Ten frames, counters

Activity: Provide each child with a blank ten frame. Discuss how many squares there are altogether. Ask her to place seven counters on the frame. Discuss how many squares are empty. Discuss how many counters are needed to fill the frame. Encourage her to provide a number story about the frame – for example, that '7 and 3 make 10'.

Variations: Place 10 counters on the ten frame. Take away two counters and ask:

How many are gone? How many are left?

Encourage the child to provide a number story about the frame – for example, that '10 take away 2 leaves 8'. Use double-sided (green/red) counters. Place 10 counters, green side up, on the ten frame. Encourage the child to turn over different numbers of counters and recite a number story.

6 green counters and 4 red counters make 10.

5 green counters and 5 red counters make 10.

Figure 5.14: *Counting with a ten frame*

Subitising

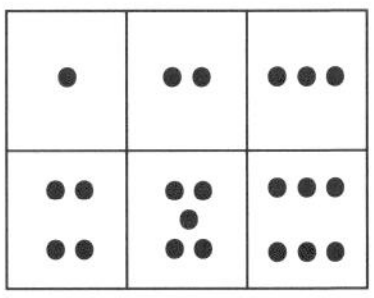

Figure 5.15: *Dot cards 1–6*

Make a train

Aim: Recognising the number of items in a group without counting

Materials: Dot cards 1–6

Activity: Children are asked to arrange their dot cards in order from 1 to 6. The teacher says a number or holds up a numeral card and the child is asked to find the matching dot card.

Dot pattern creature

Aim: Recognising the number of items in a group without counting

Materials: Die, coloured buttons, subitising picture made by using the outline of an animal divided into dot patterns

Activity: Give each child an outline divided into dot patterns. Take it in turns to throw the die. Place a button on the dot pattern outline that matches the dot pattern on the die. First one to fill her animal outline is the winner.

Variation: The teacher holds up a numeral card and the child has to place a counter on her corresponding dot pattern outline. First one to fill her card with markers is the winner.

Figure 5.16: *Dot pattern creature*

Dot card match

Aim: Recognising the number of items in a group without counting

Materials: Dot cards, paper plates, counters

Activity: Teacher holds up a dot card and asks the children to make the same pattern on their plate using counters.

Variation: Place two empty plates down with a dot card in the centre. Ask the children to make a set that is one less than the dot card on one plate and one more than the dot card on the other. Repeat the activity using numeral cards.

Dot number target

Aim: Recognising the number of items in a group without counting

Materials: A set of dot cards and numeral cards

Activity: The teacher holds up a numeral card. The children are asked to find two dot cards that combined will have the total number of dots named by the numeral card. Encourage them to find more than one combination.

Add them up

Aim: Recognising the number of items in a group without counting

Materials: Two sets of dot cards

Activity: Play with a partner. Each child turns over her top dot card. The child who correctly calls the total amount of both cards gets to keep both cards. Alternatively, each child is asked to turn over two dot cards and call out the total of her two cards. The child with the biggest total gets to keep all four cards.

Variations: *Concentration* – Place two sets of dot cards face down. Children turn over two cards at a time to try to find a matching pair. *Snap* – Work in pairs. Both children flip over their top dot card. If the dot patterns show the same amount they say 'snap'. The student who says snap first gets both cards.

Figure 5.17: *Add them up*

Ordinal position

Which cup?

Aim: Exploring ordinal numbers to fifth

Materials: Five styrofoam cups and a coloured counter

Activity: Children work in pairs. One child closes her eyes while the other places the cups in a straight row and hides the counter under one of the cups. The partner must then open her eyes and guess where the counter is hidden. The child is to respond by describing the ordinal position – for example:

I think the counter is under the third cup.

Figure 5.18: *Which cup?*

Build a tower

Aim: Exploring ordinal numbers to 10th

Materials: Five interlocking cubes of different colours

Activity: Provide each child with five interlocking cubes of different colours. Build a tower as instructions are given, such as 'Make the first floor green, the second floor blue'. Each child gives similar instructions to a friend. Extend to 10 cubes.

Musical chairs

Aim: Exploring ordinal numbers to 10th

Materials: 10 chairs, ordinal number labels to 10th

Activity: Play musical chairs. Label each chair with an ordinal number. Discuss where individual children are sitting after each turn.

Decimal numbers

Decimal number line

Aim: Understanding decimal numbers

Materials: Decimal number cards between 3 and 4

Activity: Create a line starting at 3 and finishing at 4. Give each child a card depicting a decimal number between 3 and 4. Discuss where each card would be placed on the line – for example:

Where would 3.5 be placed on the number line? Would 3.2 be before or after 3.5?

Peg each card on a line across the room.

Record that number

Aim: Working with decimal numbers

Materials: Stopwatch, measuring tape and bathroom scale

Activity: Record personal measurements that include decimal numbers (e.g. height, weight or how fast you can run 100 metres). Discuss the decimal point and what it means in each measurement. Order or group the measurements according to a set criterion. For example:

Numbers less than 50, times close to 10 minutes, children taller than 1.5 metres.

Fractional numbers

Magic halving machine

Aim: Exploring 'half'

Materials: A large cardboard box (the magic machine), pictures of objects such as a pizza, an orange or a cake and a collection of objects such as counters, small animals or blocks

Activity: One or more children sit inside the box. Place different objects or collections inside the 'magic machine' and ask the children to halve whatever is put in the machine (e.g. 4 blocks becomes 2 blocks).

Variation: Create puzzles where the children have to find the matching half.

Equal portions

Aim: Understanding that an equal portion means 'half'

Materials: Blocks, counters and iceblock sticks

Activity: Children work in pairs with a variety of materials. Ask each child to share her material with her partner and to ask 'How do you know there is an equal share?' Encourage one-to-one correspondence to check that there is an equal share. Emphasise the term 'half' when referring to equal portions. Read the picture book *Give Me Half!* by Stuart J. Murphy (HarperCollins), which explores halving and fractional notation.

Extension: Explore different ways, other than counting, to divide a quantity of iceblock sticks into halves. This could involve spreading out the iceblock sticks on two pieces of identical card (area), using a balance scale (mass), making identical trains of iceblock sticks (length), or placing iceblock sticks in two identical containers (volume).

Mad Hatter's party

Aim: Working with fractions – half, quarter, sixth, eighths

Materials: Collage materials for making a 'Mad Hatter's' hat, fairy bread (slices of bread and butter sprinkled with 'hundreds and thousands'), pizza, cake and fruit juice

Activity: Make a party hat where 'half' the hat is decorated one way and the other 'half' is decorated a different way. Ask 'half' the children to sit on one side of the party table. When preparing the food for the party, discuss portions.

How many different ways can we cut the fairy bread? Halves (2 triangles or 2 rectangles), quarters (4 squares or 4 triangles).

Divide the pizza or cake into portions and discuss (halves, quarters, sixths, eighths). Talk about half a cup of fruit juice or sharing a jug of juice between 4 people.

Figure 5.19: *Mad Hatter's party*

Find the parts

Aim: Dividing into halves, quarters and eighths

Material: Strips of equal length

Activity: Cut a strip of paper into two equal lengths or half. Then halve the halves and name the four equal parts as quarters. Repeat this exercise for eighths. Ask:

What is happening to the number of parts? What is happening to the length of each part?

Pet care

Aim: Exploring equal portions

Activity: Pose the following or similar problem to be solved by the group.

I have four guinea pigs in four different cages. I have a bottle of water, a bag of sawdust for the bottom of the cage and 6 sticks of celery. How do I share these items to make sure each guinea pig gets an equal portion?

Paddocks

Aim: Exploring parts of a surface area

Materials: 4 x 4 grids that have been partly shaded.

Activity: Provide each child with a range of 4 x 4 grids (paddocks) that have been partly shaded. Identify the grids where 'half' the area has been shaded. Use blank grids and ask the children to explore ways of shading half the area.

Extension: Provide each child with a 10 x 10 grid to represent a farmer's block of land. Explore different ways of dividing the land into five paddocks of equal area. Discuss the fact that paddocks of equal area do not have to 'look' the same.

Understanding larger numbers: place value

How many 10's?

Aim: Making groups of 10

Activity: Provide a variety of materials so that the children have many opportunities to make bundles of 10. This could include:

- logs represented by bundles of 10 iceblock sticks or straws fastened with rubber bands
- gardens represented by 10 coloured toothpicks stuck in playdough
- towers of 10 interlocking cubes
- necklaces of 10 threaded beads
- plastic bags containing 10 buttons.

Variation: Children work in pairs and grab as many iceblock sticks as possible in one handful. Count the sticks in groups of 10 to determine who has the most sticks.

Base 10 game

Aim: Using place value to count collections

Materials: Iceblock sticks, rubber bands, a die, and a tens board for each group

Activity: Take it in turns to throw the die and collect the corresponding number of iceblock sticks. Place the sticks in the ones column on the tens board. Keep in mind that there must be no more than nine in the ones column. Once there are 10 sticks in the ones column, they must be fastened with a rubber band and placed in the 10's column. The child with the largest number of sticks at the end of the game is the winner.

Variation: Record what is happening in words or numerals. Try two dice and vary the type of dice (e.g. a numeral die or a dot die). Using a numeral die and a dot die encourages the child to count on. When the total reaches the 90's, try subtracting the totals on the die.

Figure 5.20: *Base 10 game*

Hit the target

Aim: Using place value to count collections

Materials: A hoop or bucket and nine beanbags for each group

Activity: Take it in turns to toss a beanbag into a target. The beanbags that land inside the circle are worth 10 and those that land outside the circle are worth one. After all the beanbags have been tossed, have the children count the points scored and record the total. Compare scores and try to improve on previous attempts.

Figure 5.21: *Hit the target*

Crossword

Aim: Partitioning numbers using place value

Activity: Make a crossword puzzle using numbers to 99. Read the expanded notation clues and print the number in the puzzle (e.g. 'Across: 40 + 3'). Make up a puzzle for classmates to solve.

Working with larger numbers

Odds and evens

Aim: Exploring odd and even numbers and adding two numbers

Materials: Two dice

Activity: Work in pairs and take it in turns throwing the dice. One player scores a point if the sum of the dice is an even number – 2, 4, 6, 8, 10. The other player scores if the sum is an odd number – 3, 5, 7, 9 or 11. A double six means the player gets to double her score. Play until one player has scored 10 points.

Make a 50's board

Aim: Exploring numbers to 50

Materials: (For two players) two blank grids (five by 10 squares), two grids numbered 1–50 and cut into strips five squares long

Activity: Place the number strips face down in the middle and give each player a blank grid. Players take it in turns to choose a number strip and place it on their grids. If the child already has the strip, she puts it back and misses a turn. The game continues until someone has covered her whole grid.

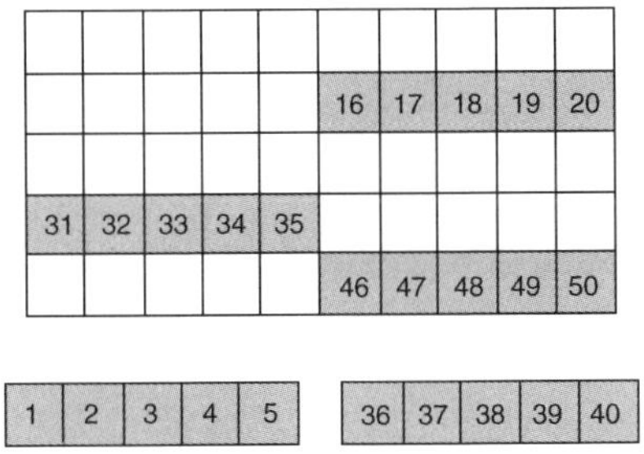

Make a 50's board

Figure 5.22: *Make a 50's board*

100 days of school

Aim: Exploring 100

Materials: Iceblock sticks and a 100's board

Activity: Start at the beginning of the year and use iceblock sticks to count and mark each day until you reach 100 days at school. Look at the 100's chart to see what the new number of the day will be (e.g. 'Today's number is 42'). Group the iceblock sticks into bundles of 10's and ones and label the groups. On the 100th day of school, celebrate all things 100 by:

- building 100 block towers
- estimating and measuring 100 steps from the classroom
- estimating and counting how many rolls of a die it will take to reach 100
- filling a snap-lock bag with 100 items from home (e.g. cotton buds, leaves)
- participating in a '100 party' that involves a 100 cake and the making of a 100 hat (e.g. 10 strips of paper with 10 dots on each strip).

Read the book *I'll Teach My Dog 100 Words* by Michael Frith (Random House).

(This activity was suggested by Tamara Garvey.)

Figure 5.23: *100 days of school*

Hide the numbers

Aim: Exploring numbers to 100 using a hundreds board

Materials: A hundreds board, counters and paper

Activity: Provide each pair of children with a hundreds board, counters and paper. One child takes 10 counters, covers 10 numbers with the counters and asks her partner to identify the covered numbers. The partner records the numbers on a piece of paper and then checks by removing the counters.

Variations: Provide each child with a copy of a hundreds board. Following a pattern you have prepared, give directions as to how she must shade in the squares. For example:

Shade the number that comes after 18.

Shade the number that comes before 26.

Shade the number that is made up of six 10's and two ones.

Shade the first even number after 80.

Children can make up their own pattern and describe it to a friend. Alternatively, take a hundreds chart and cut along the lines to make a jigsaw puzzle with three or more numbers in each piece. A child may piece together her own puzzle or trade with a partner.

Figure 5.24: *Hide the number*

Find my number

Aim: Exploring numbers to 100

Materials: Hoops, and cards with numbers to 100

Activity: Take the class outside to the basketball court. Place hoops around the court and label them with different numbers. Call out instructions such as:

Run to an even number. Find a number that is greater than 16. Find a number that has six 10's.

Variation: Work in pairs. The first child writes down a number between 0 and 99. The second child has to guess the number by asking questions such as:

Is it greater than 57? Is it an even number?

Use a hundreds board to help eliminate numbers. See how many questions it takes for the number to be guessed correctly.

Partitions for 100

Aim: Using place value to explore numbers to 100

Materials: Centimetre grid paper

Activity: Take the centimetre grid paper and draw a line to partition a 100-square grid into two parts: e.g. 36 and 64, or 22 and 78. Extend this activity using a 1000-square grid. Encourage children to discuss how they can see, at a glance, how many 100's, 10's and ones are in each partition.

Read a story about numbers

Aim: Exploring larger numbers

Activity: Share a variety of picture books that explore number (there are several listed at the end of this chapter). A good starting point is *Minnie's Diner: A Multiplying Menu* by Dayle and Ann Dodds (Candlewick). In this book a family of brothers reveal the power of multiplication as they order from the menu at Minnie's Diner. Starting with the smallest brother, who orders one of everything, the doubling sequence of 1, 2, 4, 8, 16, 32 is illustrated with humour and rhyming verse.

Number challenge

Aim: Working with numbers to 1000

Material: Squared paper that is three squares wide and a die

Activity: Children are asked to roll the die three times and record the numbers rolled. They then choose which square to enter each digit in to make the *largest* or *smallest* number possible. Challenge the children to make other numbers – for example:

The closest number to 400, a number less than 500.

Number plate hunt

Aim: Working with numbers to 1000

Materials: A clipboard, paper and a pen

Activity: Work in pairs and record the number plates of cars passing the school. Sort the numbers and give reasons for the groupings. Promote a discussion about why number plates are used.

Extension: Explore the possible arrangements of three given numbers on a number plate.

Which day of the year?

Aim: Working with large numbers

Materials: Calculators and a calendar

Activity: Ask the children to calculate which day of the year it is by using their knowledge of how many days are in each month and a calculator (e.g. 243rd day). Children can then calculate how many days there are, for example, until New Year's Eve. They can check the correctness of their answers by adding the two numbers together. The two answers should total 365, except in a leap year when the total will be 366. Discuss the different ways of working out how many days are left in a year.

Variation: The children list all the special days of the year (e.g. Christmas Day, Easter, their birthday) and calculate which day of the year they are in a regular year and in a leap year.

Figure 5.25: *Which day of the year?*

Operations

Count the bottle tops

Aim: Creating addition number stories

Materials: A cup and 10 bottle tops

Activity: Choose a quantity of bottle tops and place them in a cup. Shake the cup and empty its contents. Record a number story to describe how many bottle tops landed face up and how many landed face down.

Variation: Encourage the children to represent addition number stories in a variety of ways, such as:

- coloured iceblock sticks stuck in playdough
- threaded beads of different colours
- paper chains of different colours
- a number line on the floor or desk
- a digital presentation.

Skyscraper city

Aim: Creating addition number stories

Materials: Game board covered with addition number stories, interlocking cubes

Activity: Each child needs a game board covered with sums and some interlocking cubes. Make a skyscraper city by placing cubes on each square of the game board to match the sum. Alternatively, give each child a blank game board and ask her to fill it with sums, and then create her own city. Another suggestion would be to have the children fill a blank game board with number facts relating to a specified number.

Target 21

Aim: Adding with a calculator

Materials: Calculators

Activity: One child enters a 1, 2 or 3 on the calculator. She then passes the calculator to her partner who adds either a 1, 2 or 3. The game continues until one child reaches 21.

Baker's shop

Aim: Reinforcing subtraction

Activity: Use this popular rhyme to reinforce subtraction.

> Ten brown buns in the baker's shop,
> Big and brown with sugar on top,
> [*Name of child*] came in with one dollar to pay,
> She bought one bun and took it away.
> Nine brown buns in the baker's shop …

Take 2 or 3 away depending on the level of the group.

Variation: Provide each child with an egg carton cut to a specified number of sections. The sections act as place holders and help the child remember the initial set. Place a counter in each section and state how many counters there are. Remove some counters and describe the subtraction story.

Number cover

Aim: Creating subtraction number stories

Materials: Die or spinner, plastic container, and counters

Activity: Roll the die or spin a spinner and select the corresponding number of counters. Place a container over some of the counters and encourage the group to guess how many counters are covered. For example:

There were 5 counters. 2 are uncovered so there must be 3 counters covered.

Figure 5.26: *Number cover*

Skittles

Aim: Creating subtraction number stories

Materials: Six plastic bottles with sand in the bottom and a ball

Activity: Take it in turns to roll the ball and try to knock over the skittles. Create subtraction stories for six, such as:

I had 6 skittles. I knocked down 2 skittles. There are 4 skittles left. 6 take away 2 is 4.

Variation: Children record the number of skittles they knock down on each turn. Scores are added at the end. The child with the highest score wins.

Number story station

Aim: Creating and solving number stories

Materials: Paper and containers of various materials (e.g. cubes, shells, beads and pencils)

Activity: At work stations, the children make number stories using materials such as shells or beads. The number stories are recorded and left at the work station. The materials are returned to the containers. The children move to the next work station where they represent the previous group's number stories with materials.

Figure 5.27: *Number story station*

Stretch the wombat

Aim: Reinforcing number facts

Materials: Cardboard wombats cut in half and sets of cards with number facts on them (e.g. 10 + 2; 2 x 5).

Activity: Each child starts with the head and body of a wombat. They take it in turns to pick up a number fact card from the centre pile. If the child's answer is correct, the card is placed between the two halves of her wombat. If the answer is incorrect, the card is put back on the pile. The object of the game is to see who can create the longest wombat.

Variation: Play addition or subtraction bingo where the number fact must match the numeral on the bingo card.

Figure 5.28: *Stretch the wombat*

Mirror image

Aim: Creating double addition facts

Materials: A mirror and 10 counters

Activity: Create the double addition facts by placing a set of up to 10 items in front of a mirror and seeing it doubled. Keep a record of the number sentences created.

Figure 5.29: *Mirror image*

Number spin

Aim: Reinforcing addition and subtraction to 20

Materials: Addition and subtraction spinner, and two dice

Activity: Work in pairs. Take it in turns to roll one die and record the number rolled. Then spin the spinner to determine the operation and roll again. Add or subtract the second number rolled. If the number cannot be subtracted, miss a turn. The pair continues to spin, roll and record each turn until someone reaches 20.

Fill the envelope

Aim: Calculating the missing addend

Materials: Envelopes and small squares

Activity: Label envelopes with a numeral from 1 to 10. In each envelope, place a set of squares less than or equal to the numeral recorded on the envelope. The child selects an envelope, counts the contents and fills the envelope to the correct amount. Record the results.

What's my group?

Aim: Exploring multiplication

Materials: Paper and pens

Activity: Present activities that involve building and investigating equivalent sets – for example, birds in nests, candles on cakes, apples on trees, lollies in bags, spots on dogs or biscuits on plates. Draw a picture and label the set.

Variation: Invite a small group of children to sit in a circle. Provide each child with paper plates and counters. Explain that you are going to tell some stories for them to represent using the plates and counters. To maintain interest, make sure the counters and plates represent different things:

4 plates with 5 cookies on each plate

3 flying saucers with 2 aliens in each saucer

5 baskets with 3 puppies in each basket

Children can make up their own stories and label them.

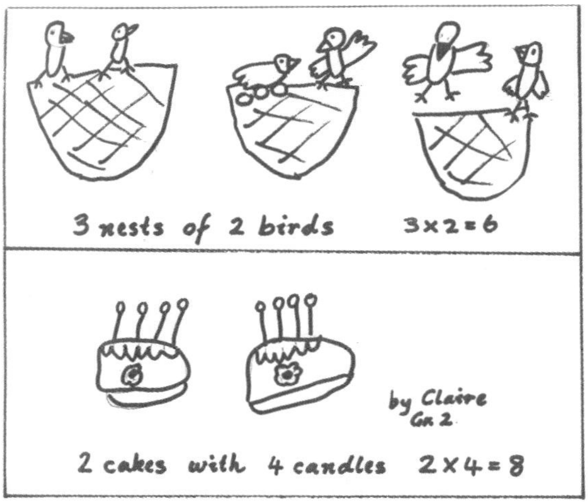

Figure 5.30: *What's my group?*

What's my number?

Aim: Adding, subtracting and multiplying numbers

Activity: Work in pairs. Both players hold one hand behind their back. While their hand is behind their back, they choose a number from 1 to 5 and hold that number of fingers open. At an agreed time, they both reveal their hidden hand and write down the total number of fingers. Discuss whether the number is *odd* or *even* or find *the difference* between the two numbers. Try two hands. Try multiplying the two numbers. What interesting rules can be discovered? For example, when we multiply two odd numbers the answer is always odd.

Calculator search

Aim: Making number stories with addition and multiplication

Materials: Calculators

Activity: Using the numbers 3, 4 and 6 and the +, x and = signs on the calculator, make as many different number sentences as possible that are less than 30 (e.g. 3 x 4 + 6 = 18). Vary the activity by using other numbers or signs, or specify a target number.

Share around

Aim: Exploring division

Materials: An egg carton and 20 counters

Activity: Provide each child with an egg carton and 20 counters. Ask them to make groups of two in the egg carton compartments.

How many counters did you start with? How many did you put in each compartment? How many compartments did you fill?

Repeat this process with four or five counters in the egg carton compartments. Repeat this activity, starting with different numbers of counters.

Variation: Explore different ways of packaging 20 cookies. For example, they could be boxed in twos, fours, fives, 10's, or one box of 20. Record the results with diagrams and numbers.

Problem solving using numbers

Fun with number squares

Aim: Solving problems with numbers

Materials: Squared paper

Activity: Look at the number squares (see Figure 5.31). Add each row and record the answer. Do the same for the columns and then record the corner square. Now finish the number squares.

Variation: Make your own addition squares. Each number in the square must be different.

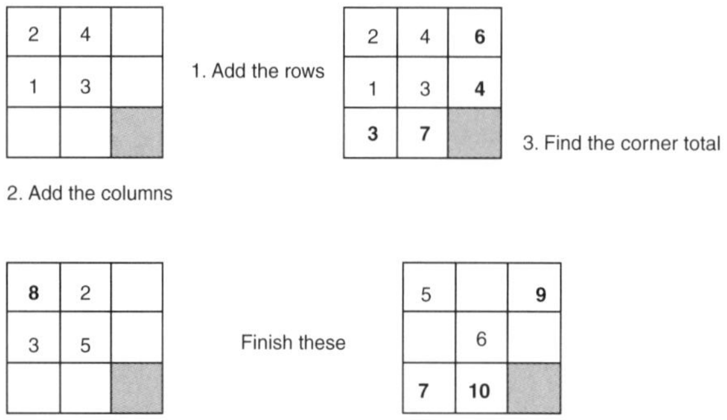

Figure 5.31: *Fun with number squares*

Post bags

Aim: Solving problems with numbers

Activity: After four postal workers lost one parcel from their bags, the total of the numbers on the remaining parcels was the same in each bag. Find out which parcel each person lost.

Figure 5.32: *Post bags*

How many people on a page?

Aim: Solving problems with number

Materials: Calculator and pages of the phone book

Activity: Discuss with the children ways they could determine how many names are on a page in the phone book. Encourage the children to think of a more efficient way than counting all the names. Children could count the names in a single column and then use their calculator to multiply the number of names in a column by the number of columns.

Variation: Count the number of seats in one row of the school hall and work out how many people the hall will hold.

Adding ages

Aim: Solving problems with number

Materials: Calculators

Activity: The combined age of two brothers is 16. What ages might they be? The children use their calculators to explore all the combinations of numbers that add to 16.

Figure 5.33: *Adding ages*

Adding numbers

Aim: Solving problems with number

Materials: Calculators

Activity: Use the numbers 2, 5, 7 and 8, and the + sign. Create pairs of numbers (e.g. 25, 78) and add them together. Change the order of the digits to make different combinations and see how many answers you can get. Think about which order of digits will give you the largest and smallest totals.

Further resources

Books

Burmingham, J., *The Shopping Basket*, Red Fox (subtraction, triangular numbers)

Burns, M., *Spaghetti and Meatballs for All*, Scholastic (division, multiplication, equal share)

Carle, E., *The Grouchy Ladybug*, HarperCollins (subitising)

Cave, K., *Out for the Count*, Frances Lincoln (counting, large numbers)

Dodds, D. A., *Full House*, Candlewick (fractions)

Dodds, D. A., *The Great Divide: A Mathematical Marathon*, Candlewick (halving)

Friedman, A., *The King's Commissioners*, Heinemann (counting on, tallies, skip counting, place value)

Frith, M., *I'll Teach My Dog 100 Words*, Random House (numbers to 100)

Fromental, J. and Jolivet, J., *365 Penguins*, Abrams (factors, grouping)

Gerth, M., *Ten Little Ladybirds*, Piggy Toes Press (counting backwards)

Harris, T., *100 Days of School*, Milbrook Press (counting to 100 by 10's)

Leibrich, J., *Nesta and the Missing Zero*, Scholastic (place value)

Losi, C., *The 512 Ants on Sullivan Street*, Cartwheel Books (sequences, doubling)

Mahy, M., *Seventeen Kings and Forty Two Elephants*, Dial (division)

Mathews, L., *Bunches and Bunches of Bunnies*, Scholastic (multiplication and square numbers)

Mewburn, K., *The Eleventh Sheep*, Scholastic (ordinal)

Neuschwander, C., *Amanda Bean's Amazing Dream*, Scholastic (multiplication)

Pavey, P., *One Dragon's Dream*, HarperCollins (counting to 10)

Rocklin, J., *One Hungry Cat*, Cartwheel (division)

Trinca, R., *One Woolly Wombat*, Kane/Miller (numbers to 10)

Wild, M., *Something Absolutely Enormous*, Scholastic (large numbers)

Apps

10 Frame Fill (Classroom Focused Software)

123 Animals Counting (Hien Ton)

Line 'Em Up (Classroom Focused Software)

Marble Math Junior (Artgig Studio)

Math Cakes (Funflip Studios)

Math Kid (Alex Drel)

Penguin Jump Maths (Pilot Fish Media)

Splosh (Yash Adukia)

Stickboy Numbers (Eike Interactive)

Tap Shapes (Infinite Loop)

Summary

The activities in this chapter have been designed to help children build and consolidate the foundational understandings of number. Because number has many aspects (e.g. counting, recognising numerals), children should engage in activities related to each of these aspects. Children will differ in how easily they learn about number. Some children will need to undertake a variety of activities before they understand a particular concept. The variations in activities are included to provide additional practice with a concept or a new context in which to apply this concept. Other children will master the basic ideas in number quickly and easily. These children can be challenged with activities involving large numbers or fractions.

Chapter 6

Patterns and algebra

Overview

In this chapter you will become familiar with:

- describing, copying, extending and creating repeating patterns
- identifying the 'rule' in growing patterns, and continuing and creating these patterns
- the notion that the rule to extend a growth pattern in number is the same as a function to change the value of a set of numbers
- finding key mathematical relationships among numbers or sets of numbers.

Recognising and working with patterns is fundamental to mathematics. Some patterns have units that repeat. Continuing a *repeating pattern* involves simply copying the repeating unit and adding it onto the existing pattern. There are also *growth patterns*. In a growth pattern, each new term includes the one before and grows according to an inbuilt 'rule'. The rule in the growth pattern below is to copy the letters and include the next letter of the alphabet.

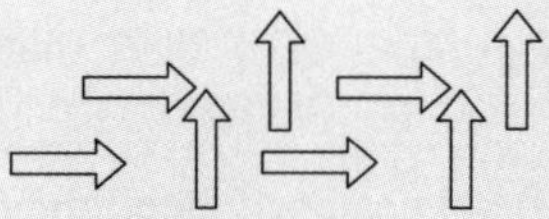	a, ab, abc, abcd, abcde
Repeating pattern	Growth pattern

Number can be used to create repeating patterns and growth patterns. The rule in the growth pattern below is to 'add 2'. The mathematical rule (+2) that changes one value (1) into another value (3) is referred to as a 'function'.

1, 2, 3; 1, 2, 3; 1, 2, 3; 1, 2, 3	**1, 3** (1 + 2), **5** (3 + 2), **7** (5 + 2), **9** (7 + 2)
Repeating pattern	Growth pattern

Understanding number patterns involves knowing about *equivalence* – for example, that 3 is equivalent to 1 + 2. This knowledge can be expressed as an *equation*: $1 + 2 = 3$. Arithmetical thinking about growth patterns in number, functions, equivalence and equations forms the foundation for algebraic thinking, which incorporates generalisations and dealing with unknown values. The difference between arithmetical thinking and algebraic thinking is that the former focuses on numerical answers while the latter focuses on relationships between numbers (MacGregor & Stacey 1999).

Pattern and algebra experiences

Patterns. Patterns can be made using colours, shapes, objects, body actions (clapping) or numbers. Young children should be encouraged to describe, copy, extend and create patterns. They should have many opportunities to engage with repeating patterns, which can be presented in different formats – horizontal, vertical, diagonal and circular patterns. They should also be introduced to growth patterns using various materials. When children skip count by twos, fives or 10's, they are verbalising number growth patterns.

Algebra. Young children's introduction to algebra should be supported by concrete materials as they explore some fundamental relationships in mathematics, such as:

- the equivalence of numbers ($2 + 3 = 5$; $2 + 3 = 4 + 1$)
- the inverse operations of addition and subtraction, and multiplication and division
- the effect of adding and subtracting zero, or multiplying and dividing by 1
- the commutative principle where you can add (or multiply) numbers in any order but still get the same result ($3 + 4 = 4 + 3$), sometimes referred to as 'turnarounds'
- the associative principle where you can add (or multiply) either group of numbers to achieve the same result: $(2 + 3) + 4 = 2 + (3 + 4)$.

A balance scale can show some of these relationships. For example, children could balance different masses on either side of the balance scale (equivalence). These amounts could be recorded in an equation, such as $3 + 2 = 4 + 1$. A balance scale is also useful for showing what happens when something is changed on one side, such as one block being removed. The action results in the scale being out of balance. To rebalance the scale, there is a need to do the same action on the other side – that is, remove one block. This function that acts on the original value or amount and changes it can be expressed numerically (e.g. as –1). The concept of change and generalisation comes in when the children verbalise that 'one block was removed from both sides' and that 'if you change something on one side, you need to do the same on the other side'. Thus, the balance scale is providing children with a visual experience of 'balancing an equation', an important concept in algebra.

Pattern

Body and movement patterns

Aim: Recognising and working with repeating patterns

Activity: Use spatial orientation to develop an understanding that pattern involves the repetition of a sequence. Encourage the children to chant the pattern as they perform each action. For example:

foot out, foot in, foot out, foot in

head, shoulder, knees, head, shoulder, knees

Create movement patterns for the children to copy, such as:

stomp/stomp/jump

clap/roll/clap

Provide a variety of musical instruments so the children can copy, create and perform patterns:

drum/shaker/bell

Variations: Use the children to create a pattern. They can gather in a circle, a straight line or a wiggly line across the room. Examples include:

happy/sad faces

tall/short

boy/boy/girl

Ask a group of children to make a pattern. Have the class guess the pattern. To end a morning of pattern work, provide skewers and pieces of fruit so that the children can make a healthy fruit pattern for lunch.

Pattern centre

Aim: Investigating patterns

Materials: A variety of materials that can be used to make patterns: toothpicks, seeds, pegs, bottle tops, stickers, Lego, blocks, stamps, buttons and shapes. Materials that can be used for threading: coloured beads or pasta, and straws cut into four-centimetre lengths.

Create situations where children have the opportunity to do the following:

- copy a pattern
- describe a pattern
- extend a repeating pattern in both directions
- identify missing parts in a repeating pattern
- write about a pattern.

Gridded pattern cards can help with spacing and keep objects in a row. As children are exploring patterns, ask the following questions:

Why is this a pattern? What part is repeating? What's next in the pattern? What is missing in the pattern?

Provide opportunities for children to make an arrangement that is not a pattern. Discuss why it is not a pattern. Encourage each child to point to the pattern and read it aloud. This allows him to assimilate information through his senses.

Variation: Make a pattern on a strip of cardboard. Strips can be used as a decorative frieze or to frame a picture.

Extension: Make a repeating pattern. Ask the children to close their eyes while one piece is removed. Guess what's missing. Remove two or three pieces and see whether they can guess what is missing. The children could work in pairs with one child removing items and another guessing.

Figure 6.1: *Pattern centre*

Patterns in songs and stories

Aim: Recognising and describing patterns

Activity: Use a variety of songs, finger plays and books that incorporate pattern. The books could include *We're Going on a Bear Hunt* by Michael Rosen, *Possum in the House* by Kiersten Jensen or *Wheels on the Bus* by Maryann Kovalski.

Variation: Go on a hunt for real-world patterns in carpet, artwork, nature, buildings and fences. Record objects that are patterns and not patterns. Challenge the children to design quilt covers for their bedrooms that incorporate a pattern.

Concertina pattern

Aim: Creating patterns

Materials: A template, paper, felt pens and craft material for decorating

Activity: Fold the paper into a concertina (backwards and forwards). Trace around a template on the top of the paper. Hold the paper firmly and cut carefully, ensuring the pieces on the fold remain uncut. Open out and decorate in a pattern using felt pens and craft material. Ask the children to describe their patterns to their classmates. Display the concertina patterns across the room.

Figure 6.2: *Concertina patterns*

Print patterns

Aim: Matching prints and shapes

Materials: Shapes and playdough

Activity: A child creates a pattern by making impressions of various shapes (e.g. cookie cutters) in playdough. When the pattern is finished, another child identifies the shapes that were used and checks the shapes by matching the shape to the imprint.

Box patterns

Aim: Representing the two-dimensional shapes that make up a three-dimensional shape

Materials: Small cardboard box, paint and butcher's paper

Activity: Children number the four adjoining sides of the box from 1 to 4. (Note: Leave a pair of opposite ends unnumbered.) Cover side 1 with paint and stamp it onto the paper. Then do the same for sides 2, 3 and 4 in turn. After each side has been stamped in order the process is repeated to form a pattern.

Hexagon pattern

Aim: Making patterns from composite shapes (i.e. shapes made from other shapes)

Materials: Pattern blocks

Activity: Ask the children to identify a hexagonal pattern block. Challenge them to make a hexagon using other shapes. Children use the different-coloured hexagons to make a hexagon pattern. Make patterns using other composite shapes.

Pattern block patterns

Aim: Creating patterns

Materials: Pattern blocks

Activity: Pattern blocks can be used to create horizontal, vertical, circular, symmetrical or growing patterns. Spatial patterns can be created with tessellations.

Figure 6.3: *Pattern block patterns*

Symmetrical pattern

Aim: Creating a pattern

Materials: A mirror and shapes, or grid paper

Activity: Use a mirror or grid paper to create a symmetrical pattern.

Variation: Children work in pairs with a barrier between them. One child makes or draws a pattern and describes it to his partner. The partner has to listen to the description and make the pattern. Remove the barrier and see if the patterns match.

Growing patterns

Aim: Making a growing pattern

Materials: Coloured toothpicks and long strips of cardboard

Activity: Use coloured toothpicks to make a triangle. Label how many toothpicks were used. Next, make two triangles and label how many toothpicks were used. Challenge the class to decide how many toothpicks are needed to make the next part of the pattern.

Continue the pattern by adding toothpicks. Label the number of toothpicks used each time. Ask:

How many are being added each time? Is there a pattern in the number? Is it odd or even? Will there be a 12 in this pattern?

Repeat this activity by making a growing pattern of squares. Encourage the children to make their own patterns and to explain the pattern to the person next to them.

Variation: Provide a variety of opportunities for children to use addition and subtraction to make a growing pattern. For example, they could use towers of cubes or pattern block shapes. Draw and write about the growing pattern. Discuss how a growing pattern is different to a repeating pattern.

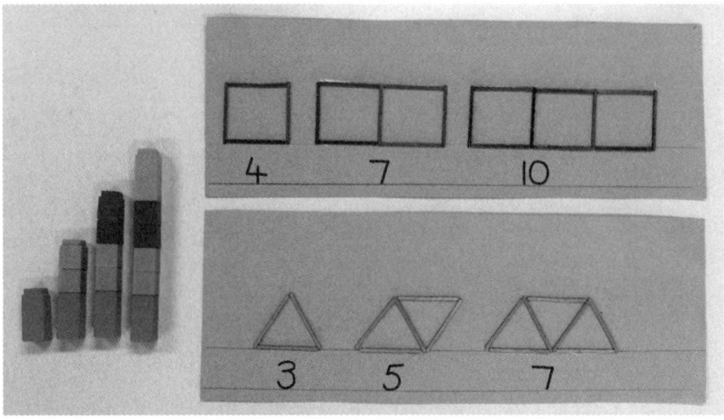

Figure 6.4: *Growing patterns*

100's board patterns

Aim: Finding patterns in numbers

Materials: 100's board, coloured pencils

Activity: Give each child an individual 100's board and explore the number patterns on the board. You could cover:

numbers that end in 6

numbers that start with 4

counting in 2's, 5's and 10's

multiples of 4

odd/even

Variation: Use a monthly calendar to highlight patterns. For example:

Days in a week are shown on a horizontal pattern.

Sundays in June form a vertical pattern.

The date on each Saturday increases by 7.

Look and count

Aim: Creating number patterns

Materials: Calculators

Activity: Show children how to use the constant function on a calculator to count (e.g. press 0 + 1 = = = to count by ones). Have the children practise counting aloud and simultaneously pressing the = button. Establish a slow rhythm for the counting and periodically call 'Stop' so children can check the correctness of their neighbour's calculator display.

Variation: Children can use the constant function to count by different numbers.

Figure 6.5: *Look and count*

Multiples of three

Aim: Exploring patterns of three

Activity: Write the multiples of three on the board and question as follows:

How can you quickly decide whether a number is in the pattern of threes? (Check whether the sum of its digits is 3, 6 or 9.)

Will 51 be in the pattern of threes?

Make a large number that you know will be in the pattern of threes.

Growing patterns in number

Aim: Exploring the growing pattern in a sequence of numbers and writing the pattern rule

Activity: Write a number pattern on the board, such as 4, 8, 12,16, 20. Ask the following questions:

Is this an addition number pattern or a subtraction number pattern?

What is the rule?

How do we figure out the increase in an addition number pattern?

How do we figure out the decrease in a subtraction number pattern?

What do we do to the first number to get the second number?

Variation: Explore a growing and repeating pattern, such as 5, 10,15, 20, 25, 30.

Equivalence

Balancing hunt

Aim: Exploring equivalence with a balance scale

Materials: Balance scale, classroom items and units of measure, such as blocks or iceblock sticks

Activity: Children select an object such as a shoe. Using a balance scale, have them find and record different units that match the weight of their object. For example:

My shoe is the same weight as 6 blocks.

Draw the slope of the balance beam before and after placing the unit of measure on the scale. Encourage the use of language such as *more than, less than, same, different, balanced, unbalanced, equal* and *not equal.*

Variation: Provide opportunities for children to create collections that have an equal quantity, length or height. They could use strings of beads, towers of cubes, gardens of flowers or plates of cookies.

Does it balance?

Aim: Using a concrete model to explore addition and turnarounds

Materials: Counters, balance scale and an equals symbol printed on a piece of paper

Activity: Place four red counters on one side of the balance scale and ask:

How can we balance the scale?

Then place two yellow and two blue counters on the other side. Ask whether the balance scale is balanced. Stick the equals symbol in the middle of the scale as a way of showing that the scale is balanced. Write the number sentence 2 + 2 = 4. Turn the scale around. Ask whether it is still balanced. Write the new number story: 4 = 2 + 2.

Variation: Demonstrate that when we add or subtract zero there is no change in the answer. So, 4 + 0 = 4.

Watch the scales

Aim: Adding the same amount to both sides so the equation remains balanced

Materials: A balance scale and cubes of various colours

Activity: Place two red cubes and three green cubes on the left side of the scale and four red cubes and one green cube on the right side of the scale. Ask whether the scale is balanced. Model how you would write this example: 2 + 3 = 4 + 1. Then add two green cubes to one side and ask:

Is the scale still balanced? Which side has more? How would we write this?

Introduce the 'not equals' sign. Then ask the children how they would balance the scale. Have the children experiment and write their own balancing equations. Encourage a discussion about the meaning of *equal* and *not equal*, and the fact that if we add to one side we must add to the other side to keep the scale balanced.

Variation: Explore equivalent stories that include subtraction. For example: 2 + 3 = 7 – 2 and 6 – 3 = 8 – 5.

Figure 6.6: *Watch the scales*

Count the eggs

Aim: Using real-world situations to model equivalence

Materials: Whiteboard, markers, counters and balance scale

Activity: Draw a picture of two nests. Place four yellow eggs and two brown eggs in one nest, and five yellow eggs and one brown egg in the other nest. Instruct the children to:

- tell a story that describes the picture
- use a balance scale and counters to represent the story
- draw a picture that illustrates the story.

Ask:

Is there the same number of eggs in each nest? How do we write this?

Write the number sentence 4 + 2 = 5 + 1. Ask the children what they think the equals sign means. Encourage a discussion about the fact that each side is the same or must balance.

Variation: Explore the terms *more than, less than* and *not equal*, and the written symbols for these terms.

Equal share for ted

Aim: Exploring *equal* and *not equal*

Materials: Two teddies and two paper plates

Activity: Discuss how six cookies can be shared equally between two teddies.

How do we know the shares are equal?

Place the equals symbol between the two plates. Then ask:

How would we share 5 cookies between 2 teddies?

Introduce the 'not equal' sign (≠). Discuss what the children would have to do to make the shares the same or equal.

Which part?

Aim: Exploring the *part-part-whole* concept in addition

Materials: Interlocking cubes

Activity: Hold up five interlocking cubes and model the story:

I had 3 cookies [*hold up three cubes*] and my friend gave me 2 more cookies [*hold up the two remaining cubes*]. How many cookies do I have altogether?

3 cookies add 2 cookies make 5 cookies.

Write the number story 3 + 2 = 5. Repeat this for 2 + 3 = 5. Reinforce which numbers represent the *parts* and which number represents the *whole*. Give each child six interlocking cubes and ask him to make up his own *part-part-whole* number stories for 6.

Variation: Encourage the children to use a ten frame and coloured counters to explore part-part-whole stories for 10. For example:

5 red counters and 5 yellow counters make 10 counters.

Relationships between numbers

Alien encounter

Aim: Making an ordered list and recording it on a table

Materials: Magnetic counters, magnetic board and a table for recording

Activity: Draw a spaceship on the magnetic board. Use six counters to model the story:

There are 4 aliens in the spaceship. How many aliens are out of the spaceship?

Record the answer in a table under the headings 'in the spaceship' and 'out of the spaceship'. Ask the children to work in pairs with six counters and find out how many different ways six aliens can be *in* and *out* of the spaceship. Discuss and demonstrate how this information could be systematically represented on a table. Encourage the children to list their findings in order and explain their list.

For example:

In the spaceship	Out of the spaceship
0	6
1	5
2	4
3	3

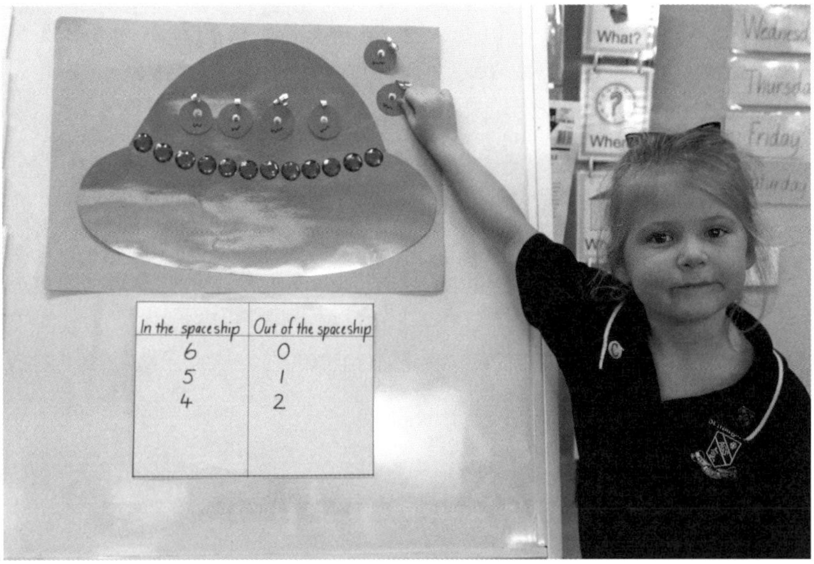

Figure 6.7: *Alien encounter*

How far can it travel?

Aim: Developing the understanding that change can be predictable

Materials: Toy car and a wooden ramp

Activity: Explore the fact that a toy car will travel further as the height of a ramp is increased. Set up the ramp with a small incline. Measure and record the height of the ramp and the distance the toy car travels along the ramp. Gradually increase the height of the ramp and continue to measure the distance the car travels. Discuss the relationship between the height of the ramp and the distance travelled by the car. Enter data in a table to describe the change. Ask whether there is a relationship between the measurements. Present the findings in graph form or plot the findings on a grid.

Variations: Provide a variety of opportunities to explore change in relation to quantity or time. For example, a bean plant will grow taller over time, a bag of marbles gets heavier as marbles are added and a jug will get fuller as water is added. Display these results in a graph or table format and discuss trends and relationships. Encourage the use of comparative terms such as *smaller, taller, fuller* and *heavier.*

How many ears?

Aim: Using a model to represent and teach quantitative relationships

Materials: Counters, lids, and paper for recording

Activity: Pose the question:

How many ears in a group of 3 people?

Generate a discussion about what you could do to find the answer to this question. Encourage the following responses:

Gather 3 people and count the ears.

Draw pictures of people with ears.

Use 3 lids with 2 counters on each lid.

Write the number sentence 2 + 2 + 2 = 6.

Ask:

What kind of pattern do you see? What if there were only 2 people?

Plot the results on a coordinate grid and discuss the relationship between the numbers.

Count and record

Aim: Exploring quantitative relationships

Materials: Marbles, and 100-, 200- and 500-gram containers

Activity: Work in small groups to determine how many marbles it will take to fill a 100-gram container. Record the results. Estimate how many marbles it would take to fill a 200-gram and a 500-gram container. Test the estimates and display the results on a table. Ask:

Is there a pattern in the results? What is the relationship between the size of the container and the number of marbles it holds?

Pizza tonight

Aim: Making an ordered list and recording it on a tree diagram

Activity: Draw two pizza bases, one with a thin crust and the other with a thick crust. Discuss three choices of topping: cheese, salami and ham. Explore the number of pizza creations. Encourage the children to work systematically to show all the variations. For example, use the same base and vary the topping or use the same topping and vary the base. Record the variations in table format and display them in a tree diagram.

Tree diagram

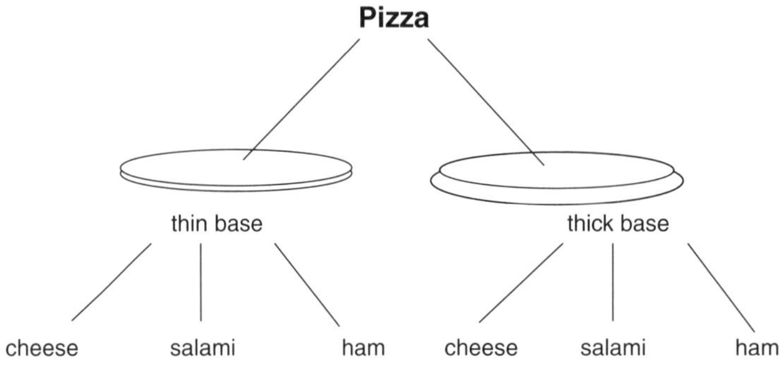

Ordered list

Pizza	Topping
thin base	cheese
thin base	salami
thin base	ham
thick base	cheese
thick base	salami
thick base	ham

Figure 6.8: *Pizza tonight*

Magic change machine

Aim: Applying rules to determine outcomes

Materials: A 'magic change machine' made out of a shoe box, strips of card, and a set of rule cards (e.g. +5, –3)

Activity: Provide a variety of opportunities to:

- calculate the 'out number' when you know the 'in number' and the rule
- develop an understanding that you need to use the rule to find the 'out number'
- calculate the 'in number' when you know the 'out number' and the rule
- develop an understanding that you need to reverse the rule to find the 'in number'
- find the rule when given the 'out' and 'in' numbers.

Questions you could ask include:

How much do we add to the 'in number' to get the 'out number'?

How much do we subtract from the 'out number' to get the 'in number'? What is the rule?

Stick the rule on the front of the machine (e.g. +5 or –3). Play in pairs and have a friend guess your rule.

Variation: Represent the information using drawings, number sentences and tables. Use a 'magic change machine' to demonstrate multiplication. Explore the fact that the inverse of multiplication is division.

Figure 6.9: *Magic change machine*

Number line travel

Aim: Exploring the commutative principle with addition

Materials: Number line on the floor or desk

Activity: Use a number line to demonstrate that order is irrelevant when adding.

Add the same three numbers in different orders; the answer will always be the same. For example:

2 + 4 + 3 = 9

4 + 3 + 2 = 9

3 + 2 + 4 = 9

A number line can also be used to show how you can multiply numbers in any order and still get the same answer. For example:

3 x 2 = 2 x 3

Variation: Use a number line to demonstrate that when we subtract two numbers, the order of the numbers does matter. So 6 – 2 is not the same as 2 – 6. 'Turnarounds' are not possible in subtraction.

Comparing towers

Aim: Showing how addition and subtraction are related

Activity: Present the following problem:

Fin has 5 lollies and Josh has 8 lollies. How many more lollies does Josh have than Fin?

Model this problem with two towers of cubes – one tower of five and one tower of eight. Ask:

How can we find the difference between the two towers?

Show that it is possible to solve this problem in two ways. We can count up from 5 (5 + 3 = 8) or count down from 8 (8 – 3 = 5). Draw diagrams to represent the towers.

Who has more?

Aim: Exploring the commutative principle with multiplication

Materials: 12 counters and five paper plates

Activity: Present six counters and share them between two plates. Question the children:

How many groups are there? How many counters are there in each group? How many counters are there in total?

2 groups of 3 equals 6, or 2 x 3 = 6.

Present another six counters and share them between three plates. Ask the same question as above. This time the answer will be:

3 groups of 2 equals 6, or 3 x 2 = 6

Then ask:

Is 2 groups of 3 the same as 3 groups of 2? How do you know? Is this correct: 2 x 3 = 3 x 2?

Does it matter if we change the order in which we multiply two numbers?

Find the missing part

Aim: Using a number line to find the unknown quantity

Materials: A number line on the desk or floor

Activity: Write '4 + □ = 6' on the board. Develop the part-part-whole concept by asking:

Do the numbers represent the parts or the whole?

What number is unknown? Is it one of the parts or the whole?

Demonstrate how you can use a number line to solve this problem.

Repeat this activity where the unknown is the first number. For example, □ + 2 = 6, and where subtraction is involved, 6 – □ = 2. Work towards developing an understanding that if the addend is unknown it can be solved by subtracting or vice versa. If the whole quantity is unknown, addition is required.

Further resources

Books

Base, G., *Uno's Garden*, Penguin Viking (pattern)

Berenstain, S. and J., *Bears on Wheels*, Random House (combinations of numbers to 10)

Brown, B., *Fifty-Five Feathers*, Reed (number sequences)

Gravett, E., *The Rabbit Problem*, Macmillan (number patterns)

Hunter, J., *Wild Fibonacci – Nature's Secret Revealed*, Tricycle Press (number patterns)

Irons, C., *The Doubling Duo*, McGraw-Hill (number patterns)

Knowles, S., *Edwina the Emu*, HarperCollins (partitioning)

Kroll, V., *Equal Shmequal*, Charlesbridge (equivalence)

Leedy, L., *The Great Graph Contest*, Holiday House (graphs)

Neuschwander, C. and Langdo, B., *Patterns in Peru: An Adventure in Patterning*, Henry Holt and Co (patterning)

Pulley Sayre, A. and Sayre, J., *One is a Snail, Ten is a Crab: A Counting Feet Book*, Walker (part/whole)

Slobodinka, E., *Caps for Sale*, HarperCollins (pattern)

Apps

10 Frame Fill (Classroom Focused Software)

A 2nd Grade Pattern Recognition Game (Nth Fusion LLC)

Line 'Em Up (Classroom Focused Software)

Summary

The activities in this chapter have been designed to capitalise and expand on children's interest in patterns. They can be supplemented by similar activities to ensure children experience patterns in a breadth of situations and formats. Children need to observe patterns closely to identify what is repeating or what the rule is in a growing pattern. Hence, encourage children to talk about or record the patterns. This chapter included early algebraic activities related to functions, equivalence, change and unknowns, which draw on children's pattern knowledge (combined with their number understanding). Children who are competent in mathematics may particularly enjoy algebra because it is a powerful tool in mathematics. These children's interests can be fostered with more challenging activities.

References

MacGregor, M. and Stacey, K., 1999, 'A Flying Start to Algebra', *Teaching Children Mathematics*, 6(2), 1978–85

Chapter 7

Measurement

Overview

In this chapter you will become familiar with:

- the ways in which measurement can be an important part of children's everyday lives and how measuring experiences can be personally relevant to them
- the understanding that measuring is about the quantity of a particular unit of measurement[1]
- using different measures in order to teach children which measures are appropriate for a particular measuring context.[2]

[1] For example, the length of a table can be measured by counting the number of pencils that can fit along its length. Here, the pencil – a familiar item – is the unit of measure. Other non-standard units such as blocks or handspans can be used to build an understanding of length measurement.

[2] For example, a cupful is appropriate for measuring the volume of a jug but not for measuring the volume of a bathtub.

Measurement is part of a young child's everyday life. Initially, children are exposed to measuring through interactions with adults. We measure children's *height* and *mass*. We give children *money* to buy a drink. We tell children when it is *time* to go to play. But as children get older, they need first-hand experiences to develop their ability to measure many different attributes – length, area, volume, capacity, mass, time and money. Measuring is finding out 'how much' there is of a particular attribute. It involves an understanding of the attribute to be measured, and knowledge of an appropriate unit of measure and how to measure with this unit. It also requires good number understanding.

Measurement experiences

Length. Length is the measure of something from end to end, such as the height of a person. Children enjoy finding out how tall they are and checking to see how much they have grown. When measuring length, a child's understanding of numbers needs to be considered. A height of 100 centimetres will have little meaning for a child who is working on the numbers up to 10. It is useful to refer to a child's height in comparison to other objects, so she can have a point of comparison to connect with her existing knowledge. We can do this in simple statements, such as:

Paula, you are taller than the blackboard ruler.

Initially, we can use arbitrary measures, such as tiles on the floor, and state:

You are the same length as 8 floor tiles.

As children become familiar with the concept of the standard units for length, the metre (m), the centimetre (cm) and the kilometre (km) are introduced.

Area. The 'Big Idea' associated with area is 'coverage'. Look for areas that are covered by objects that can be counted. Tell the children:

The area of the path is 20 pavers. The block construction covers 16 floor tiles.

Volume. Volume refers to the three-dimensional space that can be occupied by a substance, such as water or sand. To develop an understanding of volume, children need to focus on how much a container holds rather than the height or shape of the container. As with other units of measurement, we can begin with arbitrary units of measure, such as cupfuls, to determine how much a container holds. The standard units for volume are the litre (L) and the millilitre (ml).

Capacity. Capacity refers to how much a container can actually hold and often relates to volume. For example, the capacity of a hot water tank is the volume of water that can fit inside the tank. The capacity of a petrol tank is the volume of petrol that can fit inside the tank. An empty one-litre jug has a capacity of one litre, but because it is empty it has nil volume.

Mass. The focus with mass should be on the heaviness of the object and not its size. Children can be misled with mass due to the 'look' of an object. The standard units for mass are the kilogram (kg) and the gram (g).

Time. Time is an abstract and complex concept. Children need to understand the sequence of events (e.g. play time is after lunch), the length of the various units of time (e.g. a minute) and the duration of events (e.g. lunchtime is 20 minutes long). Children also need to be able to tell the time. Reading a digital clock requires an understanding of two-digit numbers and the positions of hours and minutes on the clock. Reading an analogue clock requires an understanding of the role of each hand and the relationship between each hand and the number it is pointing to. For example, if the hour hand is pointing to 4, we say '4'. However, if the minute hand is pointing to 4 we say '20 past'. Telling the time also requires knowledge of position (past and to) and simple fractions (half and quarter). The calendar is also a measure of time. Children need to be able to order months and seasons and describe duration of time using days, weeks and months. They should be encouraged to use the calendar to identify the date and determine the number of days in each month.

Money. Children need to develop a functional understanding of money so that they know how much money is necessary for the bus and whether they have enough money to buy something at the shop. Some children have difficulty with money because it is non-proportional. The $2 coin is smaller than the $1 coin but is worth twice as much.

In this chapter we cover each of these topics through activities that will help children to develop their understanding of measurement.

Length

Train tracks

Aim: Estimating and comparing length in non-standard units

Materials: Plasticine and paper clips

Activity: Roll a piece of plasticine into a long train. Estimate the length of the train in paper clips. Discuss how this could be measured using only one paper clip. Reinforce the idea that the first imprint of the paper clip needs to be made at the end of the train and that each imprint must touch the one before it.

Variation: Challenge the children to roll a train that is a specific length – for example, six paper clips long. Have them make paper clip imprints to check their guess. Make a train and give it to a partner to guess and check the length.

Figure 7.1: *Train tracks*

How tall are you?

Aim: Estimating and measuring in non-standard units

Materials: Streamers or tape and scissors

Activity: In pairs, one child lies down on the floor while the other child measures her partner's length using the tape. The strip is then cut and the process is repeated for the second child. In small groups the children order themselves by height and then pin their tapes to the wall in that order. Initiate a discussion as to who is the *tallest, shortest* and *the same height*. The following poem can be used when making comparisons:

> Short, Taller, Tallest.
> [*First child's name*] is short,
> [*Second child's name*] is tall,
> [*Third child's name*] is in the middle of them all.
> Line them up,
> You will see,
> Children in order,
> One, two, three.

Variation: Repeat the activity in a few months time and compare the children's height. Provide a variety of materials such as straws, pegs and iceblock sticks. Encourage the children to find out how tall they are using these materials. For example:

I am 21 pegs tall. I am 6 straws tall.

My first measuring tape

Aim: Measuring in non-standard units

Materials: Strips of cardboard, coloured paper, and objects for printing

Activity: Make a measuring tape on a strip of cardboard using one of the following:

- handspans
- footprints
- object printing.

Discuss the need for each unit to touch the unit on either side of it and for the units to be placed in a straight line. Number the units to make measuring easier. Go on a measuring hunt and use the tape to measure various objects in the room or around the playground.

Extension: Hide a treasure and write a list of measurement instructions to find the treasure using one of the measuring tapes above. Include what direction to go (forward, backward), how far to walk (in handspans or footprints) and which way to turn (left, right).

Figure 7.2: *Making a measuring tape*

My piece of string

Aim: Measuring length using non-standard units

Materials: String or tape and scissors

Activity: Introduce this activity by reading the following story.

'My String'

I use my string to measure things. It was 6 and a bit strings from the wall to the door. My desk is 2 strings wide. I wanted to measure the cat but she ran away. I'd like to measure a giraffe or a bear in the zoo. My friend Tara is 5 strings tall. (By Brianna, Grade 2)

Cut and distribute different lengths of string. Encourage each child to use her string to measure the length of different items.

Variation: Send the children on a hunt to find something that has the same length as their string. When they have completed their search, have them report their findings to the group. Alternatively, have them find something that is longer or shorter than their string, or find a person who has the same length of string as theirs. Allow the children to experiment by measuring with a variety of objects (e.g. sticks, straws, counters).

Extension: Place cans of varying sizes, string and scissors at a centre. Investigate the height and circumference of each can by measuring the distance with string and cutting the string to the appropriate length. The strings are glued onto a sheet of paper and compared.

Figure 7.3: *My piece of string*

Fairy trail

Aim: Measuring straight and curved lengths with non-standard units

Materials: Glitter glue, paper, and objects for measuring such as paper clips, string and buttons

Activity: Use glitter glue to make a curved fairy trail. Ask the child to select from a variety of objects to measure the trail. Discuss how you would measure the curved part of the trail. Create a fairy trail for a friend to measure or design a fairy trail that is a specified length.

Metre man

Aim: Measuring using a standard unit of measure – a metre

Materials: A metre ruler, paper bags, glue and collage material.

Activity: Make a metre man by joining paper bags together until you have a one-metre length. Decorate the bags to make a metre man. Use the metre man for measuring things. Make a list of things that are longer or shorter than a metre.

Measure a friend to see if she is more or less than a metre.

Figure 7.4: *Metre man*

Body parts in centimetres

Aim: Measuring using a standard unit of measure – a centimetre

Materials: Drawing paper, centimetre tape, and paint or felt pens

Activity: The children draw a picture of themselves. In pairs, they then help each other measure their body parts in centimetres. Children record their measurements on their pictures. Initiate a discussion:

Is the distance around your neck longer than the distance around your thigh?
What is the shortest body part you measured?

Repeat this activity later in the year so that the children can make comparisons.

Variation: Invite each child to take a close look at her partner's face and ask her to make statements about the location of facial features – for example, 'The nose is in the middle of the face. The ears line up with the eyes'. Have each child draw her partner's face. Encourage her to estimate before measuring the overall dimensions in centimetres.

Figure 7.5: *Body parts in centimetres*

Mini Olympics

Aim: Measuring in standard units – a metre and a centimetre

Materials: Measuring tape, paper and pencil for recording

Activity: Hold a Mini Olympics in the gym or playground. Have the children measure in centimetres or metres how far they can throw a beanbag or jump from a standing position. The information could be presented on a graph or as a slideshow presentation.

Area

Fill the space

Aim: Arranging shapes to cover an area

Materials: One packet of Freddo Frogs™ (or Hershey's®) per group, scissors, tracing paper and glue

Activity: Each group traces around the empty packet of Freddo Frogs. Encourage the children to predict and experiment with ways of covering the area of the packet with Freddo Frogs. They could stick each arrangement of Freddo Frogs onto the paper outline with Blu Tack. Compare and discuss the different arrangements.

Variation: Try covering different shapes with Freddo Frogs.

Figure 7.6: *Fill the space*

Coloured tiles

Aim: Covering surface area

Materials: A large collection of coloured paper squares or rectangles

Activity: As an introduction, have the children look at floor tiles or pictures of floor tiles and ask the following questions:

Do all the tiles touch? Are there any spaces? Do any of the tiles overlap? What shape are the tiles? Can you see a pattern?

In pairs, the children select a surface they want to cover, such as a desk top or the seat of a chair. Provide a large number of squares or rectangles and instruct them to estimate how many shapes they think they will need to cover the surface. Ask them to cover the surface and count the number of shapes used. The children can record their predictions and measurements to share with others.

Variation: Choose a second surface to cover. Encourage the children to create a pattern as they tile. Include some different shapes, such as triangles and diamonds.

Figure 7.7: *Coloured tiles*

Design a room

Aim: Estimating and measuring surface area

Materials: One small box (e.g. a shoe box) per child, old wallpaper books cut into strips, and a variety of uniform geometric figures (e.g. squares, hexagons, triangles)

Activity: Design a room of choice. Each child is given a box and asked to tile the floor and paper the walls. The geometric shapes can be used as floor tiles. The strips of wallpaper can be used to cover the walls. To finish the room, draw a design or pattern on the tiles and wallpaper. Curtains and furniture can also be added.

How many squares?

Aim: Measuring and comparing area

Materials: Geoboards and elastic bands

Activity: Using elastic bands and a geoboard, the child explores the different shapes that can be made using six whole squares. Change the number of squares that can be used.

Variation: In pairs, one child makes a shape without showing it to her partner. This is then described to the partner, giving enough information for the partner to copy. For example:

Start 1 square in and 3 squares down. It is 3 squares across and 4 squares down.

Figure 7.8: *How many squares?*

Design a quilt

Aim: Covering surface area

Materials: Sheets of cardboard and coloured paper shapes

Activity: Give each child a uniform-sized sheet of cardboard and a number of smaller paper shapes. Encourage them to design a quilt by covering the cardboard with the different shapes. Experiment with shape, colour and pattern before gluing the final attempt.

Variation: Present the outline of a shape and ask the children to use pattern blocks to solve the following problems:

Fill the space using 4 blocks. Fill the space using blocks of the same colour. Fill the space using blocks that are the same shape.

Figure 7.9: *Design a quilt*

What's the area?

Aim: Comparing surface area

Materials: Centimetre grid paper and felt pens

Activity: Ask the children to draw their initials on centimetre grid paper with their pens. Count the number of squares the letters cover. Discuss whose initials covered the largest and smallest areas. Repeat this activity by tracing around their hand or foot.

Volume

How many jugfuls?

Aim: Estimating volume

Materials: Transparent containers, a jug, coloured water, rubber bands (to mark water levels) and felt pens

Activity: Use a container and a jugful of coloured water, and ask the following questions:

What will happen if we pour this jugful of water into this container? Will the container be full?

Encourage the children to estimate the water level after one jugful has been poured into the empty container. Place a rubber band around the container to show each estimate. Pour the coloured water into the container and mark the actual water level with the felt pen. Allow time for the children to discuss the accuracy of their estimates. Predict how many jugs of water will be needed to fill the container. Repeat this activity with a variety of containers.

Which jug holds enough?

Aim: Estimating volume

Materials: Three different-sized jugs and six party cups

Activity: Provide the group with three different-sized jugs and six party cups. Pose the following problem:

Six people will be at your party. Which jug will hold enough cordial for everyone to have a full glass?

Figure 7.10: *Which jug holds enough?*

Looking for litres

Aim: Estimating and measuring volume using a litre container

Materials: Each group needs three hoops, a litre container and a variety of different-sized containers

Activity: At work areas, place three hoops and three cards to label the hoops as *more, less* and the *same as* a litre container. Direct the children to estimate, then measure, the size of each container in comparison to the litre container. Sort the containers into the appropriate hoops: those holding more, less or the same as the litre container. Discuss the findings.

Variation: Encourage the children to go on a shopping hunt to find items that are sold in millilitres and litres. Make a digital presentation of the findings.

Figure 7.11: *Looking for litres*

Capacity

Which holds more?

Aim: Estimating and comparing capacity

Materials: Three different-sized containers, water, rice or sand

Activity: Work in pairs with three different-sized containers. Estimate which container holds the most and which container holds the least. Encourage the children to use the materials to measure and compare the capacity of the containers. Ask questions to initiate discussion, such as:

How did you find out which container holds the most? Does the tallest container always hold the most? Does the shortest container always hold the least?

Order the containers on a strip of paper according to their capacity. Trace around the containers and label the drawings.

Figure 7.12: *Which holds more?*

Make a cylinder

Aim: Exploring capacity

Materials: Different-sized sheets of cardboard, stapler and marbles

Activity: Provide different-sized sheets of cardboard. Ask the children to make a cylindrical-shaped container using the cardboard. Use marbles to test the capacity of the container. Compare and discuss dimensions and capacities of different-shaped cylinders. For example:

My cylinder is shorter but has a greater capacity. Does a small circumference always mean less capacity?

Figure 7.13: *Make a cylinder*

Which lunch box holds more?

Aim: Comparing capacity

Materials: Cubes and a lunch box

Activity: Use cubes to work out the capacity of a lunch box. Explore how rows and layers of cubes help to determine how many cubes fit.

How could a calculator help? How can you work out the capacity if you don't have enough cubes to fill the lunch box?

Mass

My pet rock

Aim: Making comparisons of weight with a non-standard unit

Materials: Rocks of various sizes, collage materials and a balance scale

Activity: Choose a rock and decorate it with hair, facial features and so on. Find items that are *heavier/lighter* or the *same* weight as the rock. Check on the balance scale. Write a story about your findings. For example:

'Mr Wiggles'

My pet rock is called Mr Wiggles. He is heavier than a rubber. He is lighter than 2 glue bottles. He is the same weight as 5 blocks. I know this because the scales balance. Mr Wiggles is heavier than my friend's pet rock. He has crazy hair. (By William, age seven)

Figure 7.14: *My pet rock*

Mass graph

Aim: Estimating and measuring mass in non-standard units

Materials: A balance scale, iceblock sticks, large sheets of paper and objects for weighing (e.g. small glue bottle, a pencil, a pair of scissors, eraser)

Activity: Invite a small group of children to sit in a circle. Ask one child to place an object on one side of the balance scale. Ask a second child to balance the scales by placing iceblock sticks in the other pan. When the scale is balanced, have the children count the number of iceblock sticks. Display the findings by pasting or drawing iceblock sticks onto the paper to make a graph. Discuss the results. Repeat this procedure with other items. Encourage the children to estimate before measuring.

Figure 7.15: *Mass graph*

Guess and measure

Aim: Estimating and measuring mass in non-standard units

Materials: A balance scale and identical containers filled with foam, shells, cotton wool, sand, blocks, flour, rice, counters or nails

Activity: Prepare four containers and label them so that the children know the contents. Invite the children to estimate which container they think will be the lightest or heaviest and to explain why. Ask the children for ways to check their estimates and encourage them to try out their suggestions.

Are there two containers that have the same mass?

Order the containers from *lightest* to *heaviest*. Discuss results.

Variation: Children choose their own materials to put in the containers and challenge a friend to find the lightest and heaviest containers.

Figure 7.16: *Guess and measure*

Playdough measuring

Aim: Making comparisons of length, area and mass

Materials: Playdough and kitchen scales

Activity: Use playdough to make snakes ranging from short and fat to long and thin. Order by length. Discuss the need for the snakes to be lined up against a baseline so that lengths can be compared. Coil the snakes and reorder them by the table space they will take up. Re-form the playdough into balls and order by mass using a scale.

Figure 7.17: *Playdough measuring*

How much is one kilogram?

Aim: Estimating and measuring in kilograms

Materials: A balance scale, a kilogram weight, a kitchen scale and a variety of food items such as pasta, cornflakes, rice and sugar

Activity: Provide a balance scale and a kilogram weight and ask the children to find items that are *greater than, less than* or *equal to* a kilogram. Then, using the kitchen scale, have the children explore quantities of food that measure one kilogram. Encourage the children to find items at home that are packaged in one-kilogram amounts.

Variation: Provide a variety of boxed food items and ask the children to classify them according to different attributes, such as height, capacity, mass, brand, type of food, and colour. Encourage the children to label different collections: for example, *short, tall, tallest, light, heavy, heaviest.*

M&M grams

Aim: Estimating and measuring in grams

Materials: A kitchen scale and a 25-gram packet of M&M's® for each group

Activity: Give each group a packet of M&M's and ask them to investigate the following:

How many grams of M&M's does the packet hold?

How heavy is each M&M?

What is the mass of the red M&M's?

What is the mass of the blue M&M's?

Which colour has the smallest mass?

Which colour has the heaviest mass?

Which colours have a mass of less than 10 grams?

Which three colours have a total mass of 15 grams?

Encourage each group to make up stories or problems about the packet of M&M's. Children report their findings to the other groups or make a class book.

Variation: Estimate, then measure, the width and length of the packet with the M&M's. Make a graph of the number of different-coloured M&M's found in the box. Make a pattern with the M&M's.

Shopping for grams

Aim: Estimating and measuring in grams

Materials: A kitchen scale, full packets of food items (e.g. a box of cereal, pasta)

Activity: Encourage the children to read the labels to find the mass of each food item. Weigh the contents of the package to determine the accuracy of the measurement on the label. Discuss some examples of different-sized packages that have the same mass. Children could also investigate the mass of the packaging.

Variation: Make a 50-gram ball of plasticine. Ask a volunteer to roll the ball of plasticine into a sausage. Measure the mass of the plasticine again. Ask:

Is it still the same mass? Why do you say that?

Repeat this activity several times, making different shapes with the plasticine. Break the plasticine into several smaller pieces. Ask:

Has the total mass of the plasticine changed?

Time

How fast?

Aim: Measuring passage of time in non-standard units

Materials: Lid with a hole in it, a container of water, and beads for threading

Activity: Children work in pairs. Each pair needs a lid with a hole in it and a container of water. One child is the timer while the other is the worker. The worker selects a task to complete, such as threading beads or building a tower. The timer places the lid in the container of water, and when the lid sinks, the worker stops the activity. The pair reverse roles and the activity is repeated several times. (A few drops of detergent in the water will ease the surface tension and allow the lid to sink faster.) Compare results:

Did you get faster or slower at the activity? Which activity was the easiest to perform in the timeframe? Why?

Figure 7.18: *How fast?*

Alarm! Alarm!

Aim: Telling the time to the hour

Materials: An alarm clock, clock cut-outs and cards for recording

Activity: Set an alarm clock to ring on the *hour*. When the alarm rings – for example, at 9:00 a.m. – direct the children to stop what they are doing and look at the clock. A volunteer records the time on a clock cut-out. Paste the clock onto a piece of card and draw and label the activity being performed at the time when the alarm went off. Display the completed cards in order across the room to create a timeline.

When several times and activities have been recorded and displayed, question as follows:

What did we do at 2 o'clock?

Did we go to music at 10 o'clock?

What did we do one hour before 12 o'clock?

At a later date, set the alarm clock to ring every *half hour* and record the time and events in the same way.

Variation: The children can create their own charts showing what they did each hour after school.

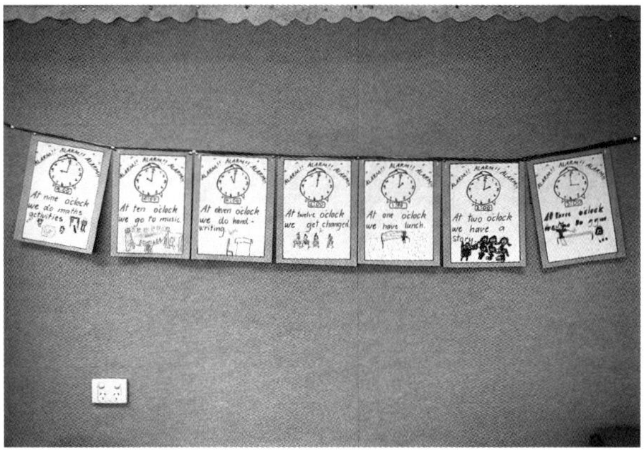

Figure 7.19: *Alarm! Alarm!*

Can you tell the time?

Aim: Telling the time to the hour

Materials: Paper plates, split pins, cardboard, markers and scissors

Activity: Guide each child in the making of a clock with movable hands. Sit in a circle and invite a leader to call out a time for the others to show on their clocks. The following rhyme can be used to add interest to this activity:

> When the long hand stands up tall,
> The short hand tells the time.
> It's [7] o'clock, it's [7] o'clock,
> Can you tell the time?

Figure 7.20: *Can you tell the time?*

Where is half past?

Aim: Telling the time to the half hour

Materials: A large clock drawn on the ground

Activity: Draw a large clock on the ground showing the big hand pointing to '6' for half past. Select a volunteer to be the small hand and stand on the clock in the position where the small hand should be. For half past three, the volunteer should stand halfway between the three and the four. Continue to do this, while interest is maintained, to reinforce the position of the small hand on the clock face.

Extension: (quarter to, quarter past) Use a paper plate and split pin to make a clock with movable hands. Cut a second paper plate into quarters and glue it on the first plate. Discuss first, second, third and fourth quarters as children are gluing. Connect the minute and hour hands in the middle.

Figure 7.21: *Where is half past?*

In a minute!

Aim: Estimating and measuring a passage of time – one minute

Materials: Stopwatch

Activity: Work in pairs. Estimate and then time how much of an activity can be performed in one minute. Activities could include:

- skipping
- catching a ball
- completing an obstacle course
- bouncing on the trampoline
- writing a name.

Repeat this activity later in the year and compare results.

Variation: Use a paper plate and split pin to make a clock with movable hands. Develop an understanding that the numbers around the clock face also have a minute value when you count by fives. This can be done by placing a minute value under the flap of each number on the paper plate clock. Discuss and compare digital time.

Daily schedule

Aim: Writing a daily schedule

Activity: Encourage the children to write a daily schedule and compare their schedule with a friend's. For example:

I get up at 7:30 a.m., I eat lunch at 12:00 p.m. and I have a piano lesson at 5:15 p.m.

Create a digital presentation about your day to share with the group.

Variation: Measure and compare how much time is spent on daily routines in a 24-hour period – for example, sleeping, going to school, eating, playing sport. Make a graph to display the results.

Extension: Choose four countries that are at approximately equal distances around the globe. Research the time in each country and display on labelled clocks in the classroom. Generate questions such as:

What time is it in New York today?

What would the children be doing in London now?

Time the event

Aim: Measuring and comparing time in minutes

Materials: Stopwatch

Activity: Provide a variety of opportunities for children to time events. This could involve selecting a favourite TV show and measuring how much time is taken up for commercials and how much time for the actual show. Or you could ask the children to time and record how long it takes them to get to school. Explore questions such as:

Who takes the longest to get to school? How does that person get to school? Who lives the closest to school? Does this person take the shortest time to get to school?

What day is it?

Aim: Recognising and ordering the days of the week and the months of the year

Materials: Strips of coloured paper and a stapler

Activity: Make a paper chain that displays the days of the week in the correct order. String it across the classroom to create a colourful visual aid. Extend to seasons and months of the year. Make each season a different colour.

Calendars

Aim: Reading weekly and monthly calendars

Materials: Class calendar

Activity: Make a class calendar. Refer to it every day, using terms such as *yesterday* and *tomorrow*. Schedule holidays, classroom activities and special events on the calendar. Start with a weekly calendar and label activities for each day. Move to a monthly calendar and discuss days in a month and months in the year. Describe the weather and various events – for example, for April, talk about autumn and Anzac Day. Discuss writing the date and the use of ordinal numbers. Encourage the children to make individual calendars.

Money

Set up a shop

Aim: Working with money

Materials: Money and items for a shop

Activity: Create interest by visiting a shopping centre or reading books about shops. Have the children choose the type of shop they want and the materials they are going to sell. Encourage them to collect and price items for their shop. Make signs and posters advertising what is for sale. When the shop is complete, children can take it in turns to dramatise shopping situations. During free play, encourage the children to act out the shopping process. 'What might you say when you go into the shop? What might the shopkeeper say?' As you discuss the shopping process, emphasise the trading aspects so that the children are used to giving money and receiving change. Encourage the children to make a shopping list and then let them purchase their list of items or give their list to a friend.

Variation: Go on a shopping hunt to find selected items, such as items under $1.50, items over $5, or two items that have a combined value of $6.

Figure 7.22: *Set up a shop*

Money riddles

Aim: Recognising coins

Materials: Coins

Activity: Provide each child with a set of coins and initiate activities that will help the children to become familiar with the different coins.

(1) Ask riddles:

I am the coin with [the picture on the coin]. I am the smallest coin. What am I?

I am silver in colour. I have [a person] on me. What am I?

I am not round. What am I?

(2) Have the children line their coins up in order of size, from largest to smallest, and then discuss:

Which coin is the smallest?

Which coins are larger than the 10-cent coin?

Which coins are the closest to being the same size?

Place your largest coin on the bottom and build a coin tower in order of size. Now start with the smallest coin. Is the largest coin worth the most? Which coin is worth the most/least?

Encourage the children to do some rubbings of the coins and discuss the similarities and differences.

Make a list

Aim: Calculating total cost

Materials: A price list of items ranging from $1 to $10, and $1 and $2 coins

Activity: Prepare a price list that displays a variety of items with prices ranging from $1 to $10. Display the price list and ask the following questions:

What costs the most?

What costs the least?

Which items cost more than $5?

What could you buy with $4?

What could you buy with $10 and get $2 change?

How much would two items cost?

Variation: Set an allowance of, say, $6. Ask the children to select from the list of items and suggest ways they would spend their allowance. Compare and discuss the different ways of spending $6. Make up an order form for each group. Explain to the group that they are to fill out their order form using items from the list. Then, pass the form on to the next group who price each item and find the total cost. As the children's understanding of number improves, add more complicated purchases with the use of paper money and all the different coins.

Bus, anyone?

Aim: Identifying money and giving change

Materials: Play money, play tickets and classroom chairs

Activity: Arrange chairs in rows so as to set up a bus or train in the classroom. Take it in turns buying and selling tickets and giving change.

Figure 7.23: *Bus, anyone?*

Money spinner

Aim: Identifying coins, finding total amounts and giving change

Materials: A money spinner and a large collection of coins

Activities:

(1) Children work in groups of four. A selection of coins is placed in the middle of the group. The children take it in turns to spin the spinner and select the appropriate coin from the pile to match where the spinner lands. After several turns each child adds up her money to see who has the most.

(2) Give each child a certain number of coins. The children take it in turns to spin the spinner and pay the amount to a chosen banker, who gives change if necessary. The group then checks to see that the correct change has been given. Play continues in this way until one player has spent all her money. She then becomes the banker. Encourage the children in the

group to work out their own strategies for giving change. Methods might include counting on to find the change, counting back to find what is left, or changing a $1 coin into ten 10-cent coins and taking only the correct amount.

Variation: Repeat the activities using two spinners.

Figure 7.24: *Money spinner*

Shopping games

Aim: Working with money up to $20

Materials: Magazine cut-outs, blank cards and play money

Activity: Make some shopping cards from magazine cut-outs pasted on card. Label the pictures with a price up to $10. Give each child $20 in coins. Shuffle the cards and place them in the middle. The children take it in turns to select a card and purchase the item. The first child to spend all her money is the winner. Repeat this game but have the children take two cards from the centre. This way, they have to work out the combined value of the cards and whether or not they can purchase the items.

Variation: Ask the children to cut out pictures from magazines, paste them in a book and price them. Pass the book to a friend who has to match the price with play money or money stamps.

Problem solving using measurement

Build a tower

Aim: Solving a problem related to height

Materials: Straws and plasticine

Activity: Using eight straws and pieces of plasticine, challenge the children with the following problem:

How high can you build a tower?

Figure 7.25: *Build a tower*

How do you weigh a sack of toys?

Aim: Solving a problem related to mass

Materials: A bathroom scale and a sack of toys (light enough to be carried by a child but that does not fit easily onto the scale)

Activity: Pose the following problem:

How could you find out how heavy the sack is when it does not fit on the scales?

Allow the children to suggest ways of solving this problem and give them the opportunity to try their suggestions. Discuss the efficiency and practicality of their methods. During the discussion someone may suggest holding the sack while standing on the scales, then subtracting that person's weight from the combined weight to work out the mass. Using this strategy, the children can estimate and then measure the weight of other large objects in the room.

A perfect day

Aim: Exploring time

Materials: Paper, paper clocks, glue and scissors

Activity: The children are to plan and record to the hour their perfect day. For example, for each hour of the day the children could draw pictures and write descriptions of what they would like to be doing. A clock face showing the time of day could be added to each picture. These pages can then be glued in order onto a long sheet of paper to create individual timelines. Discuss with the class their ideas of a perfect day.

How does incline affect distance?

Aim: Exploring the relationship between measurements

Materials: Toy cars and a ramp

Activity: Using toy cars and a ramp, the children investigate the effect the incline of the ramp has on the distance the cars will travel. Encourage children to change the slope of the ramp to make the cars go further.

Further resources

Books

Alborough, J., *Tall*, Walker Books (length, volume, mass)

Cronin, D., *Diary of a Worm*, HarperCollins (time, date, months)

Godwin, J. and Walker, A., *All Through the Year*, Penguin (months and seasons)

Hutchins, P., *Titch*, Aladdin (height)

Hillman, B., *How Big Is It? A Book All about Bigness*, Scholastic (length, volume and area)

Hillman, B., *How Strong Is It? A Mighty Book All about Strength*, Scholastic (rate and mass)

McNicholas, S., *In a Minute*, Little Bee (time)

Milbourne, A., *How Deep Is the Sea?* Usborne (length)

Pilegard, V., *The Emperor's Army*, Pelican (volume and space)

Slawson, M., *Apple-Picking Time*, Crown (money)

Stevens, G., *Counting on Frank*, Angus and Robertson (counting, measuring and calculating)

Wells, R., *Bunny Money*, Puffin Books (money)

Wells, R., *Is a Blue Whale the Biggest Thing There Is?* Whitman & Co (size and comparison)

Apps

Amazing Scales Challenge (JKQ)

Bucketz (Picnichippo)

Dr Panda's Supermarket (Tribe Play)

Geoboards (Maths Learning Centre)

Geo-Measure (Object Graph LLC)

Interactive Telling the Time (GiggleUp)

Measure (Tap to Learn)

Tell Time (Matchups)

Toca Store (Toca Boca)

Where's My Water? (Disney)

Figure 7.26: *Computers can enhance learning*

Summary

The activities in this chapter have been designed to interest and cater for diverse learners. Using non-standard units to measure is highly recommended as a first step in measuring any attribute. It enables children to become familiar with the unit to be used (e.g. a paper clip) and, in the case of handspans or other personal units of measurement, to realise that we need a *standard* unit of measure for accurate and consistent results. Since each of our two handspans is different, we might get different results. When commencing standard units of measure, select activities relevant to children's interests and everyday lives (e.g. calendar). Due to the number of characteristics of objects and people that can be measured (e.g. foot length, body temperature, lung capacity), it will take children some time to acquire deep understandings about the various types of measurement. Teachers are encouraged to revisit these activities over time, and to adapt activities to provide students with new opportunities to build their measurement knowledge.

Chapter 8

Space

Overview

In this chapter you will become familiar with:

- the importance of knowledge of space in the early years – it enables children to explore the world around them and develop the vocabulary to label and talk about it
- the role of shape in children's understanding of space, and the related concepts of location and transformation
- the seven spatial perception skills.

In addition to the ability to work with numbers and reason logically, children need opportunities to develop their spatial skills and understanding of *shape*, *location* and *transformation*, and to engage in geometric or spatial reasoning. This form of knowledge is referred to broadly as spatial sense – an important objective of mathematics education in the 21st century. Some aspects of spatial sense are evident in the drawings from seven-year-old Laura's journal (see below). Compared to her age peers, Laura has a well-developed spatial sense. However, her drawings suggest that she needs to develop an understanding of the *relative size* of adults and children. Hence, encouraging children to express themselves through drawing provides an insight into their spatial sense. Comparing a child's drawings over time is one method of monitoring the progression of his spatial sense.

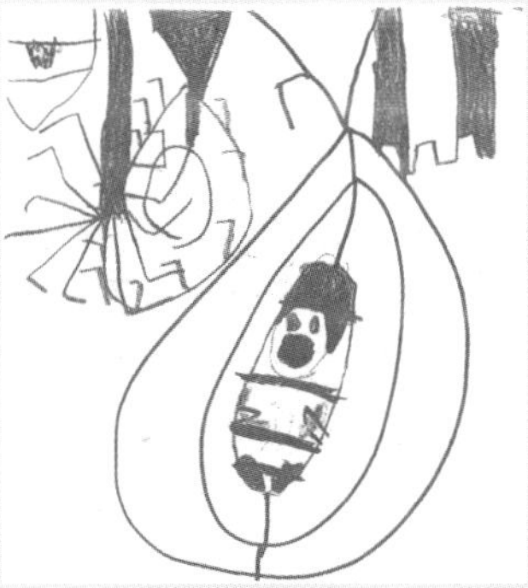

Laura's drawing of rides at a school fair shows her understanding of *orientation* (upside down) and *direction* (anticlockwise).

The drawing of a gymnast in action shows an awareness of *direction* (downward). Laura's attempt at drawing a three-dimensional beam shows some understanding of *perspective*.

An understanding of *perspective* is evident in the illustrations of the side and back views of the children. As the teacher is very large in proportion to the children, the understanding of *relative size* needs to be developed further.

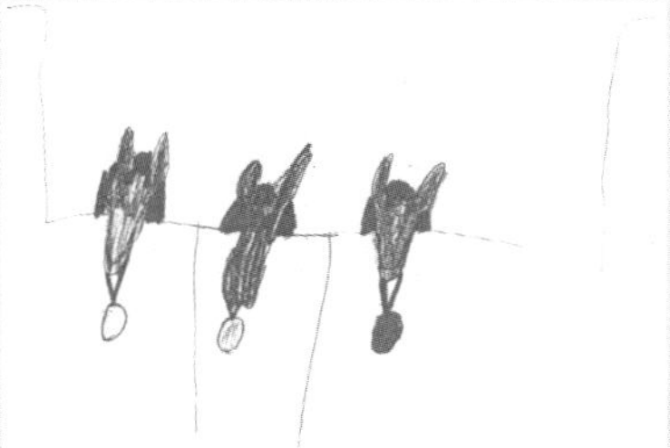

Laura's drawing of three horses in a stall after a medal ceremony shows attention to the viewer's *perspective*. In this drawing she demonstrates her awareness of the *shape* of objects in her depiction of the horses' heads, the medals and the stall doors.

Space experiences

Developing an understanding of shape involves being able to identify, represent, visualise and analyse two-dimensional (2D) (e.g. square) and three-dimensional (3D) shapes (e.g. cube). Shapes can be represented through drawing, constructing and modelling. Visualising is particularly important when children interpret drawings of three-dimensional shapes – for example, in building from a Lego plan. Analysing shapes involves knowing the properties of particular shapes and the relationships between shapes.

Drawing and making objects helps children to develop an understanding of how parts go together and the relative location of objects. Using plans for construction activities and drawing plans after construction provides children with experience in creating and interpreting two- and three-dimensional representations of the same object. Simple tools and techniques can be used in this process. For example, rulers can be used to produce straight lines and an upturned cup can be used to produce curved lines. The shapes produced can also be changed.

Two- and three-dimensional shapes can be transformed in many ways. They can be flipped, slid, turned or rotated. Two-dimensional shapes can also be mirror-reversed, enlarged or reduced. However, irrespective of the transformation, the properties of the final shape should correspond to the initial shape.

How shapes are arranged highlights the importance of location in space. Everyday positional language, such as *above* and *below*, is important in understanding location. More advanced positional language, such as *horizontal* and *vertical*, should also be developed. Children should also engage in simple mapping of familiar and imaginary locations.

A range of activities to develop spatial sense are presented in the following pages. These activities provide children with an opportunity to learn key vocabulary related to space. Because of the visual nature of space, many of these activities give children the opportunity to engage in the visual-spatial aspects of tasks. Such activities can include the virtual world.

Spatial perception skills

Underpinning spatial sense are seven unique spatial perception skills. The following table shows these skills and gives examples of activities that would facilitate the development of that skill. Many of the experiences that children engage with in the years before school, such as construction, drawing and puzzles, continue to be of value. However, many children need ongoing attention to spatial perception skills in the early years. These skills are important not only in mathematics but across the curriculum. For example, visual discrimination is important in reading.

DESCRIPTION	TYPES OF ACTIVITIES
Hand–eye coordination: Coordinating hand and eye movements.	• Drawing, tracing, painting, colouring, dot-to-dots, completing mazes, modelling, building and pulling objects apart.
Figure–ground perception: Distinguishing between the foreground and the background.	• Asking children to locate and colour items in the foreground and background in pictures.
Perceptual constancy: Recognising that the shape of an object is unaffected by its size.	• Using plans to build objects and making plans from constructions.
Position-in-space: Locating objects in different positions in space after flips, slides or turns.	• Making patterns with a set of objects by changing the position of the shape: e.g. a rectangle placed lengthways, then widthways, then lengthways, then widthways …
Perception of spatial relationships: Establishing the relationship between the positions of two objects.	• Copying, enlarging or reducing a drawing that has been done on dot paper.
Visual discrimination: Identifying similarities and differences between objects.	• Finding which objects match and which object doesn't belong in a group.
Visual memory: Recalling objects and their positions.	• Remembering a group of objects that is no longer in view.

Shape

Spot the shape

Aim: Identifying plane shapes in everyday objects

Materials: Magazines

Activity: Children search for particular two-dimensional shapes (e.g. circle) in a magazine and mark all shapes with a coloured spot.

Variation: All items 'spotted' for a particular shape could be cut out, put into a shape book and given a simple caption.

Figure 8.1: *Spot the shape*

Fabulous flags

Aim: Identifying matching shapes

Materials: A reference book of flags, cardboard, iceblock sticks and a sand tray

Activity: Children select two flags that have the same shapes and the same number of those shapes (e.g. three rectangles). They make and colour these flags, and any other flags that have the same attribute. When several flags are made, the children can add iceblock sticks and stand the flags up vertically in a sand tray. The flags can then be sorted by focusing on one colour, such as red. The flags with a red section can be sorted again by the position of the red section.

Rectangle ladder

Aim: Exploring squares and rectangles

Materials: A strip of paper one square centimetre in size, scissors

Activity: In small groups, have the children cut out as many different-sized rectangles as they can from the squared paper. Each rectangle should be labelled with its size (e.g. 1 x 1; 1 x 2; 1 x 3; 1 x 4) and then arranged in order. Look for a square in each group's shapes. Question the children about whether or not a square can also be a rectangle. (To help a child understand that a square is also a rectangle, refer to how he can be both a son and a brother.) Explain that a square is a special kind of rectangle. If any group has not cut out a square, ask the children to look carefully at the pattern to see whether anything is missing and have them cut out a square. Colour the square red and the other rectangles another colour.

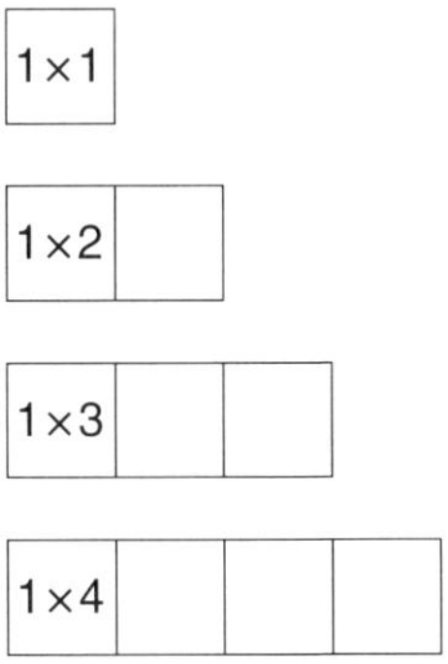

Figure 8.2: *Rectangle ladder*

Making circle pictures

Aim: Create triangles on the geoboard

Materials: Objects with a circular face (e.g. cups, glasses, plates, cans, vases, cones, coins, empty pill bottles), drawing paper, coloured pencils

Activity: Encourage the children to explore how to use everyday objects, such as cups and plates, to produce circles of different sizes. The children turn these circles into an object, animal or person.

Variation 1: Encourage the children to draw part of the way around a circle to produce a semicircle that can be used for a smile or eyebrows on a person, or waves on a beach.

Variation 2: Encourage the children to overlap the drawings of their circles and make pictures from their overlapping circles (e.g. a caterpillar).

Extension: Interested children can be introduced to the use of the compass to make circles of different sizes.

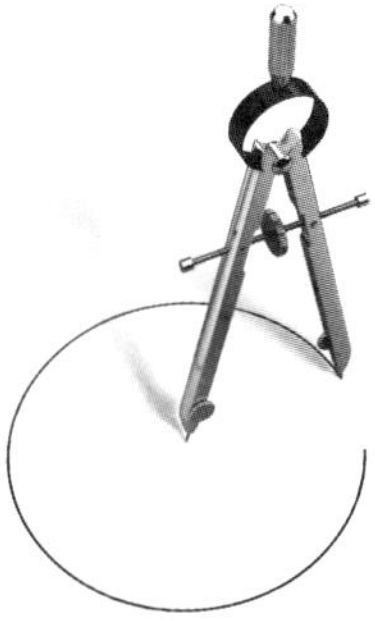

Figure 8.3: *Compass and pencil*

Geoboard challenge

Aim: Creating triangles on the geoboard

Materials: Geoboards and rubber bands

Activity: Challenge the children to make as many different triangles as they can using rubber bands on geoboards. Triangles can vary in their size, the relative lengths of their sides, the relative size of their angles and their position.

Variation: Other shapes can be made.

Figure 8.4: *Geoboard challenge*

Odd one out

Aim: Identifying which shape does not belong

Materials: Sets of four similar shapes (e.g. rectangles of different sizes) and one different shape (e.g. triangle)

Activity: Ask the children to identify which shape does not belong in a set of shapes of the same type and explain why it does not belong.

Variation 1: Add another shape that does not belong so the children need to identify the two shapes that do not belong.

Variation 2: Children can make shape sets with an odd shape for their peers.

Shadow shapes

Aim: Making shapes with shadows

Materials: Pattern blocks or attribute blocks, white cardboard, black paper, scissors and an overhead projector

Activity: Tape the white cardboard to the wall. Have the children make a shadow shape (e.g. a person, a house) by placing the blocks on the overhead projector. Trace around the shape that is projected onto the cardboard. Use this shape as a template and trace around it onto black paper to create a 'permanent' shadow. (Note: adult supervision of the overhead projector is advised, as the projector may become hot.) Children can write about their shadow shapes or other children can guess which shapes were used to make the shadow.

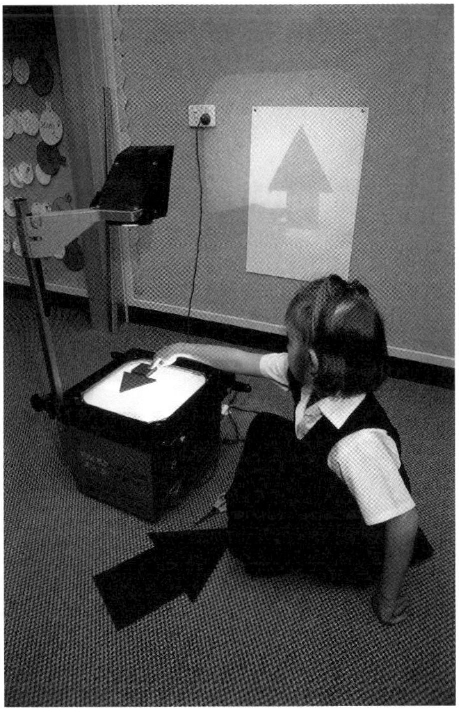

Figure 8.5: *Shadow shapes*

Variation: Use the blocks to create large shadow letters and numbers. Which letters or numbers cannot be made?

Matching 3D shapes

Aim: Matching 3D shapes in the everyday world with wooden blocks

Materials: A wooden or plastic set of 3D shapes, a collection of everyday 3D objects (e.g. grocery cartons) and labels for each of the 3D objects

Activity: Children make a collection of everyday objects that resemble each of the 3D shapes (e.g. an ice-cream cone). The everyday objects can be displayed together with the wooden shape and labelled with the shape name.

Variation: The children can use pictures to identify objects with more than one 3D shape (e.g. an ice-cream cone has a sphere and a cone).

Fruit and vegetable jigsaws

Aim: Analysing 3D shapes

Materials: Fresh fruit or vegetables, coloured playdough, plastic knives, and plates

Activity: A child models a piece of fruit or a vegetable from the appropriately coloured playdough. The child cuts the item into a couple of pieces and puts them on a plate. Another child identifies common 3D shapes on the plate and tries to recreate the piece of fruit or the vegetable. For example, a carrot would be made from orange playdough and when cut could form a cone and a cylinder.

Figure 8.6: *Fruit and vegetable jigsaws*

Making robots

Aim: Creating a 3D object from smaller 3D shapes

Materials: Junk material suitable to construct a robot, scissors and sticky tape

Activity: Read a story about a robot or sing the song 'I'm a Little Robot'. Have the children make a life-size robot using junk material (e.g. juice bottle lids).

'I'm a Little Robot' (sung to the tune of 'I'm a Little Teapot')

> I'm a little robot,
> Short and square,
> I have no toenails,
> I have no hair.
> If you want the answer to a sum,
> Just press my button [*belly button*]
> And out it comes.

What makes a cube a cube?

Aim: Identifying the critical characteristics of cubes.

Materials: A selection of different-sized cubes that vary in colour and composition

Activity: Give a small group of children a selection of cubes (at least one each) and ask them to find the common attributes of the cubes. Help them focus on the attributes of the cubes by using the language 'all' and 'some'.

Some of the cubes are wooden. Are *all* of the cubes wooden? Can you find a cube that *is not* wooden?

The children should be able to make a general statement about cubes. For example:

Cubes have six square faces but they do not have to be made of wood.

Variation: The same activity can be done with other 3D shapes (e.g. cone).

Which shape am I?

Aim: Identifying shapes from verbal descriptions

Materials: Set of 12 cards with the names and pictures of 2D and 3D shapes

Activity: The children work in a group of four. The cards are placed face down on a pile. The first child draws a card, looks at it and passes it on to the second and third children. The third child puts the card face down in front of him. If the card was a triangle, the first child would make a statement about the shape without identifying it.

I have (*3 sides*).

The other two children make different statements.

I have no (*curves*).

I am one of the faces on a (*pyramid*).

After the third child has given his statement, he asks the fourth child to identify the shape.

Which shape am I? (*triangle*)

The fourth child guesses the shape and checks the card. If he is correct, he keeps the card. If he is incorrect, the card is returned to the bottom of the pile. The game continues until no cards remain. The child with the most cards wins.

Variation: More cards can be added with less common 2D and 3D shapes.

Making plans

Aim: Linking 2D and 3D representations

Materials: Blocks or Lego or multilink cubes, paper and pencils

Activity: Children draw and talk about a plan before building with blocks. When the construction is completed the plan is compared to the final product.

Variation: Children draw a block construction before it is dismantled as a record of the construction.

Building blocks

Aim: Using a net to create a 3D shape

Materials: Cardboard packets (e.g. cereal or biscuit), paint and sticky tape

Activity: Open the boxes out flat in preparation. The children paint the non-printed side of the opened-out box. Once the box is dry, they can remake and tape the box with the painted side to the outside. These new boxes can be used for construction activities.

Location and transformation

Places to be

Aim: Developing positional language (e.g. around, behind)

Materials: A page for each child with a positional word written on it (e.g. in, on, under)

Activity: Each child writes a simple sentence containing the word and illustrates the sentence. For example:

Sam is *near* the tree.

Collate the pages and a cover to make a book of *Places to Be*.

Treasure tracks

Aim: Using directions to locate a position

Materials: Hundreds board, stickers

Activity: The teacher attaches a sticker to the back of a number on the hundreds board. The teacher nominates a starting number and gives a series of directions that lead to the stickered number. A child follows the directions and 'guesses' the number. For example, if a sticker is hidden under 59 and the teacher starts at 17, a possible track to the treasure is:

Down 7 rows, right 2 numbers, up 3 rows.

Figure 8.7: *Treasure tracks*

Variation: This activity can be played in the same way by adding and subtracting numbers instead of using the hundreds board. If the sticker was hidden behind 59, the teacher could say:

Start at 17, add 70, add 2, subtract 30.

Follow my lead

Aim: Using geometric terms

Activity: In the playground, describe a path for children to follow.

Start at the swing, climb *over* the cargo net, walk *along* the bridge, slide *down* the fireman's pole.

Figure 8.8: *Follow my lead*

Variation: Children can work in pairs with one child describing the route to take and the other child following the instructions.

Tumbling teddies

Aim: Investigating the rotation of shapes

Materials: Long strips of paper and five copies of an identical teddy-bear shape for each child

Activity: Have each child colour five teddies alike. Children glue the teddies onto the paper to show them tumbling in a clockwise direction.

Figure 8.9: *Tumbling teddies*

Swinging shapes

Aim: Viewing shapes in different orientations

Materials: Four sets of common 2D shapes (e.g. square, triangle, circle, rectangle) cut from stiff cardboard, string, and one coathanger per set of shapes

Activity: The teacher cuts out the shapes and punches a hole in each of the shapes to allow them to be suspended with string. In each set of shapes, the hole needs to be punched in a different place. For example, in a set of rectangles, a hole could be punched on the long side of one rectangle, a hole on the short side of another rectangle and a hole in the corner of further rectangle. The children work in groups to paint one set of shapes (e.g. rectangles). Each shape in the set should be painted a different colour. Each set of shapes is attached by string to a different coathanger and placed overhead in the room. Draw the children's attention to how different the same shapes can look.

Variation: Use 3D shapes made from cardboard.

Forever friends

Aim: Exploring symmetry

Materials: Paper, scissors and coloured wool

Activity: Children make a chain of paper dolls to represent themselves and their friends. They add facial features to each of the dolls to show the individual characteristics of each person and add clothing. Wool can be added for hair.

Figure 8.10: *Forever friends*

Variation 1: At the beginning of the year, a class chain could be made. After each child has added his own features, the chain is displayed on the wall and the class plays 'Guess Who?'

Guess who has brown eyes and black hair? Guess who is wearing a striped shirt? Guess who is in between Sally and David?

Variation 2: Children could make identical twins, triplets or quadruplets by making paper dolls and cutting on the fold line to make two, three or four dolls joined together.

Butterfly pictures

Aim: Creating shapes with line symmetry

Materials: Paper and paint

Activity: Children fold a piece of paper in half and paint a brightly coloured 'butterfly wing' on one side. The paper is then folded so the butterfly wing is printed on the other side.

Variation: Challenge the children to make other symmetrical pictures (e.g. house, person, tablecloth).

Mirror pictures

Aim: Exploring mirror images

Materials: Pattern blocks and rectangular mirrors at least 20 centimetres in length

Activity: Children work in pairs to create mirror pictures using pattern blocks. One child makes a simple picture and then places a mirror vertically near the picture. If the mirror is at the top or bottom of the picture, the second picture should be horizontally inverted. If the mirror is positioned to the left or right of the picture, the second picture should be vertically inverted. The other child makes the picture after the mirror has been removed. The 'mirror picture' can be checked by placing the mirror next to the original picture.

Partner pictures

Aim: Creating a picture from a verbal description

Materials: Pattern blocks

Activity: Children work with a partner and take turns to make and describe a picture using pattern blocks. One child makes a simple picture, covers it and describes it to the other child, who tries to make a matching picture (e.g. 'Put the square to the left of the triangle. Children are best seated side by side, rather than opposite their partners to avoid confusion regarding the instructions.

Figure 8.11: *Partner pictures*

Variation: Increase the complexity of the task by increasing the number of blocks in the initial picture or restricting the colour choices so the blocks are more similar.

Problem solving in space

Making shapes

Aim: Investigating lines and squares

Materials: Paper and pens

Activity: Think of different ways to divide a square into quarters using two lines. How many different ways can you think of dividing a square using only three lines?

Variation: Divide a rectangle into quarters using two straight lines. Can you do it with three straight lines?

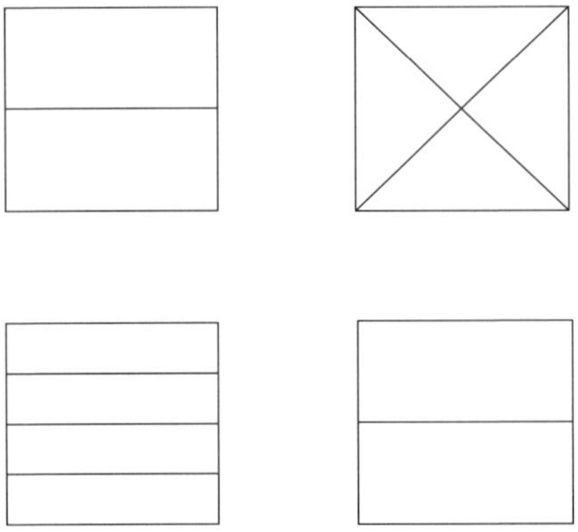

Figure 8.12: *Making shapes*

One, two, three, four

Aim: Making shapes through paper folding

Materials: Newspaper sheets

Activity: Challenge the children to make as many different shapes as they can from one, two, three or four folds of paper. Have them draw or photograph the final shape of the paper and record how many folds it took.

Cat and mouse

Aim: Problem solving in games

Materials: Counters and diagram

Activity: The cat and mouse move in turn from one corner of the house to the other. The mouse moves first. Find the fewest number of moves for the cat to catch the mouse.

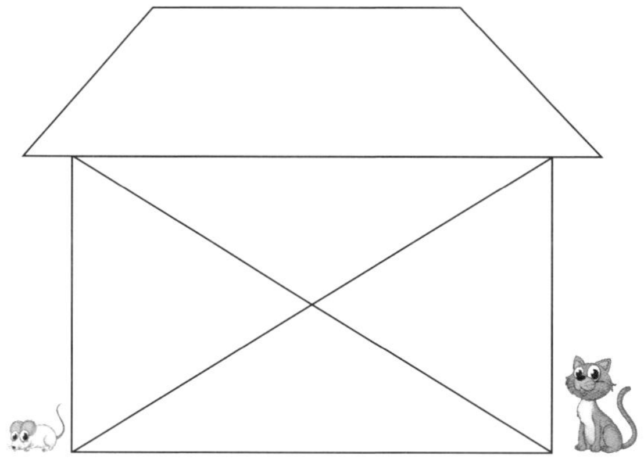

Figure 8.13: *Cat and mouse*

What should we build?

Aim: Creating a mini town

Materials: Junk material, tracing paper, and a plastic play mat showing land and roadways (available at toy stores)

Activity: Discuss what buildings are required in a community. Have groups of children select a section of the mat and decide on a building project. Children trace the land portion, so that their buildings will be the correct size, and create their building. When all the buildings are complete, they are placed on the mat in the appropriate position and an instant 'town' is created. Children can photograph and draw the town.

Famous shapes

Aim: Making replicas of landmarks

Materials: Photos or reference books showing famous landmarks, and construction materials (e.g. paper, straws, blocks, clay, glue, tape)

Activity: Children select a famous landmark (e.g. the Eiffel Tower, the Sydney Opera House). They make their favourite landmarks with materials, such as straws or modelling clay.

Figure 8.14: *Famous shapes*

Variation: Have the children create a set of cards showing the seven wonders of the modern world and discuss what 2D and 3D shapes they can see. Pictures and names of the seven wonders could be added to a world map. The seven wonders are: Chichén Itza, Mexico; Christ the Redeemer Statue, Brazil; Colosseum, Italy; Taj Mahal, India; Great Wall of China; Petra, Jordan; and Machu Picchu, Peru.

Make a picture

Aim: Developing an awareness of differences

Materials: Pattern blocks or similar

Activity: Give the children a verbal description and have them build a picture using blocks. This description can be written on the whiteboard. For example:

A long straight path led to a small house and above the house was a plane.

After the children have completed their pictures, they can be displayed on their tables. The children can work around the pictures, checking for any picture that does not suit the description. Challenge the children to explain why there are so many different pictures. (The children would have used different colours and sizes of shapes; there would also be differences in how long they made the path and how far they placed the plane above the house.)

Variation: In groups of three, one child makes up a story similar to the above. The second child makes a matching picture. The third child judges whether the picture matches the story. Children rotate roles until everyone has had a turn at being the narrator, the creator and the judge.

Further resources

Books

Bailey, D. and Butterworth, C., *Butterflies*, Steck-Vaughn

Barner, B., *Space Race*, Bantam Books for Young Readers

Dorras, A., *Abuela*, Dutton

Emberley, E., *The Wing on a Flea: A Book about Shapes*, Scholastic

Grifacolini, A., *The Village of Round and Square Houses*, Little, Brown

Hoban, T., *Circles, Triangles and Squares*, Macmillan

Hoban, T., *Shapes and Things*, Macmillan

*Hennessy, B. G. and Joyce, P., *The Once Upon a Time Map Book*, Walker Books

*Lasky, K. and Hawkes, K., *The Librarian Who Measured the Earth*, Little, Brown

McMillan, B., *Beach Ball – Left, Right*, Holiday

McMillan, B., *Mouse Views: What the Class Pet Saw*, Holiday

Mullarkey, L. and Harris, P., *Bent Out of Shape*, Magic Wagon

*Neuschwander, C. and Geehan, W., *Sir Cumference and the First Round Table*, Charlesbridge Publishing

*Neuschwander, C. and Langdo, B., *Patterns in Peru: An Adventure in Patterning*, Henry Holt and Co

Pienskowski, J., *Shapes*, Harvey

Schachner, J., *Skippyjon Jones Shape Up*, Dutton Juvenile

Tompert, A., *Grandfather Tang's Story*, Crown

*Books with complex ideas

Apps

Blocks in the Garden (Aurelio Calegari) (creating with blocks)

Curious about Shapes and Colors (Houghton Mifflin Harcourt) (shapes)

Doodle Buddy (Pinger) (general doodling app)

Doodle Fit (Gamelion Studios) (fitting blocks into a shape)

Doodle Kids (Virtual GS) and Drawing Pad (Darren Murtha Design) (general doodling apps)

Falling Wall (Busythings) (position)

Kids Shapes Fun – Create and Play (ShiXian Li) (creating with geometric shapes)

Let's Make Shapes (Interbots) (picture making with shapes)

Sculptmaster 3D (Volutopia) (3D shapes)

Summary

This chapter has been designed to raise awareness of the spatial perception skills and to provide children with activities to apply these skills and build their spatial sense. Space is a broad concept encompassing two- and three-dimensional shape, location, transformation, problem solving, and geometric and positional vocabulary. Although some of the activities in the early years are similar to activities prior to school, the expectations of children are higher. For example, drawing is commonplace in pre-school settings; however, in the early years of school children can be encouraged to apply their knowledge of space to add interest to their drawings. Exemplars of drawings with indicators of spatial sense are included in the chapter. Children typically enjoy spatial activities and can engage in a large variety of activities to build their spatial capability, including the use of various digital resources. However, due to the three-dimensional component of space, children's engagement in the virtual world should complement, rather than replace, hands-on work in space.

Chapter 9

Chance and data

Overview

In this chapter you will become familiar with:

- activities designed to raise children's awareness of the role of chance in everyday life
- activities focusing on developing children's knowledge and skills in collecting, organising, representing and interpreting data.

Chance and data is a relatively new concept area in mathematics for young children. *Chance* includes ideas of randomness and probability that are relevant to everyday life – for example, in games involving spinners. *Data* includes collecting, organising, representing and interpreting information. For example, data can be collected in a survey, organised in a table and represented on a graph. Someone looking at the graph needs to be able to interpret the information that was collected in the survey. Understanding data is particularly important in the information-rich age of the 21st century. Children's experiences of chance and data in the mathematics program should enrich their understanding of the world around them, so it is important that these experiences have personal relevance. Playing games with dice or reading a television guide and a bus timetable are examples of children interpreting data in meaningful contexts.

Chance and data experiences

Chance. There are many chance events in everyday life. These include playing games that use dice or spinners, the weather, flipping coins, raffles and lotto, and horse and car racing. To consider the role of chance in each of these events, children need to develop an appropriate vocabulary to describe the likelihood of various events occurring (e.g. certain, maybe, possible, impossible, likely, unlikely, fair, unfair).

Data. There are three aspects of understanding data: *collecting data*, *organising and representing data* and *interpreting data*. Children need to develop skills in each of these data processes to explore mathematical aspects of their worlds.

- *Collecting data* involves posing suitable questions to investigate and deciding how to record the information. Teachers should model suitable questions for children and support them in posing questions. For example:

  How did you get to school today?

- *Organising and representing data* includes the use of tally marks (e.g. //// /) for collating the information, and the use of tables and simple graphs, such as picture graphs and bar graphs.
- *Interpreting data* requires children to derive information from a table or graph and to answer questions about the embedded mathematical information. The simplest questions require the children to read information from the display.

  How many children like red M&M's the best? Which colour M&M's did nine children like best? Which colour M&M's did no one choose?

- More complex questions involve comparisons and explanations.

  Which two M&M colours were chosen by the same number of children? Why do you think that there are only a couple of green M&M's in most boxes?

Chance

Word watch

Aim: Developing a vocabulary of chance words

Materials: A wall chart with three columns

YES	NOT SURE	NO
I'm certain.	*It's possible.*	*It's impossible.*

Activity: During everyday activities, write on the chart chance words and statements that are used in class to illustrate how certain the children can be about a particular event – for example, if it is raining. *I'm certain* and *certainly* would be placed under 'yes'.

Variation: The children could search for chance words in books to add to the chart.

Maybe, maybe not

Aim: Identifying chance words in everyday situations

Materials: Magazine pictures and manilla folders

Activity: Prepare several manilla folders of everyday chance situations. Glue a picture on one side of the folder and write a question on the other side of the folder. The children select a folder, choose some correct responses from a selection of chance words and explain their answers. Some examples are given below.

PICTURE	QUESTION	APPROPRIATE VOCABULARY	INAPPROPRIATE VOCABULARY
Cloudy sky	Will it rain tomorrow?	possible, maybe, likely	certainly, impossible
Game dice	Can I roll a 7?	impossible	possible
Children at the beach	Will the children get wet?	maybe, possible	impossible

Variation: Children could make up new questions for the pictures or make their own folders.

Figure 9.1: *Rain tomorrow?*

Weather forecasting

Aim: Using chance words to predict the weather

Materials: A calendar with space near each date

Activity: Each day, the child predicts the weather for the coming day. She draws a picture and writes a simple sentence. The following day the accuracy of the prediction is checked. This can be done as an individual or a whole-class activity.

Figure 9.2: *When will it rain?*

Variation: The weather forecast on the television or radio can be discussed.

If the forecast says it *might* rain, does that mean it definitely will rain? Should I take an umbrella *in case* it rains?

Heads and tails game

Aim: Investigating the variation of outcomes from two coin tosses

Materials: Two large, identical coins

Activity: Using one coin, ask each child to put a hand on her head if she thinks it will be heads or a hand on her hip if she thinks it will be tails. After a couple of turns, explain that if the children are wrong this time they need to sit down and are out of the game. Continue with the game until there is a winner. Once the game is understood, use two coins and ask the children to choose where each hand will go. They can choose two heads, two tails or a head and a tail. Play the game as above. Discuss with the children which choice is the most likely to occur. The possible outcomes of two coin tosses are: heads, heads; tails, tails; head, tails; or tails, heads. Each of these outcomes has a one in four chance of occurring.

Figure 9.3: *Heads and tails*

Variation 1: Vary the game by using marked lines or rope to make a series of lines on the ground and placing the children behind the first line (like a race). Each time a child is correct, she walks forward to the next line. Each time a child is incorrect, she stays still on the line. The winner is the child who finishes first.

Variation 2: Use flipping a coin as opportunities arise, such as when the children want two different books read or when deciding whether boys or girls should go to lunch first. Discuss whether flipping a coin is a fair way of making decisions. Ask what would be a fairer way. (Children might suggest voting, which provides an opportunity to talk about what happens when more people want a particular decision.)

Weather predicting: true or false?

Aim: Exploring chance combinations of numbers to 12

Materials: Two large dice for a small group. Die 1 is a word die and has the terms *possible, impossible, certain, likely, unlikely* and *might* recorded on each face of the die. Die 2 has pictures of different types of weather – 'rain', 'snow', 'wind', 'sun', 'cloud' and 'lightning' – on each face of the die.

Activity: The children sit in a circle with the two dice in the middle. Rotate each die and 'read' the six faces one at a time. Check the children understand the terms 'true' and 'false'. The first child then follows the three-step process below after modelling by the teacher.

1. Child says: 'Today it is (*describe the weather, e.g. sunny*) in (*suburb name*)'.
2. Child throws the word die and reads what it says: 'Possible'. Child says: 'It is (*possible*) that ... (*pause*).'
3. Child throws the weather die and uses the weather term to describe the picture in the following sentence: 'Tomorrow will be (*rainy*) here.'

The other children take it in turns to say whether the 'Tomorrow' statement is true or false. If the children agree, one child is asked to explain her thinking. If the children disagree, one child who states it is false and another who states it is true explain their reasoning. The children should be encouraged to reach a consensus. The other children then have a turn, moving clockwise around the circle. The game continues until each child has had a turn.

Variation: One child could be the recorder and use tally marks to record how many times each word and each weather picture are rolled. After the game is finished, discuss the tally marks, highlighting anything unexpected, such as one word being rolled many times or one weather picture never being rolled.

Chance outcomes

Aim: Exploring the possibilities in everyday chance events

Materials: A large wall chart as shown on the opposite page

Activity: Have children draw or use cut-out pictures to show the possibilities for each of the chance events shown on the chart and record the total number of different possibilities. Ask questions about the likelihood of particular events that encourage the use of chance words. For example:

Is it certain that the spinner will land on a red segment?

How possible is it that the spinner will land on a black segment? (*impossible*) Is it impossible or possible that the coin will land on a head or tail? (*possible*)

CHANCE SITUATION	POSSIBILITIES	HOW MANY DIFFERENT POSSIBILITIES?
Flipping a coin		**2**
Arrival of a new baby (boy or girl)		
Spinning a spinner		
Rolling two dice		
Colours of M&M's in the box		
Drawing a card from a pack		

Variation: For students with advanced understanding, model the mathematical description of chance. For example:

The baby could be a boy or a girl. There is a one in two chance the baby will be a girl.

Encourage the children to create their own mathematical statements of chance.

Dancing dice

Aim: Exploring chance combinations of numbers to 12

Materials: Pair of dice per child and a recording sheet

Activity: Have the child throw a pair of dice. The total of these dice is the target number. If a 6 and a 4 were thrown, the target would be 10. The child then throws the first die (e.g. a 7 is thrown) and records the number in the 'first die' column on the sheet. The second die is thrown until the target is achieved (e.g. a 3 is needed if a 7 was thrown first). If the number on the first die has already been used, the first die is thrown again. After all combinations have been recorded, a new target is set.

FIRST DIE	SECOND DIE	TARGET
6	**4**	**10**
7	**3**	**10**

Figure 9.4: *Rolling dice*

Lucky dip

Aim: Exploring the outcomes in a chance situation

Materials: Various small treats so there is enough for everyone in the class (for example, stickers, pencils, novelty rubbers, notepads), newspaper, container, sticky tape, scissors, whiteboard, whiteboard markers

Activity: Discuss with the children objects that they might get in a lucky dip at a fete or show. Show the children one of each object for the class lucky dip. Have the children do the counting themselves to determine how many objects will be needed so that each child will get a prize. The children list the objects for the lucky dip and the quantity of each object (e.g. seven erasers, two pencils). Have each child wrap one object and place it in a container.

Ask each child to predict and record what she thinks she will pull out. Check her selections are limited to the objects that are in the lucky dip. One by one, ask each child what she thinks she will pull out. Each child then chooses a lucky dip item, unwraps it and adds a tally mark beside the items on the board, showing the item she pulled out. For example, if there were seven erasers to begin with and three have been pulled out, the recording would be 'seven erasers I I I (tally marks)'. Discuss why this activity is called a 'lucky dip'. What does it mean to be lucky?

Figure 9.5: *Class lucky dip*

Variation: Ask the children to make a lucky dip (without wrapping items) using pattern blocks. Ask them to think about how they could guarantee that they will get a particular result, such as pulling out a red block (only put in red blocks). Ask them to think about how to have the best chance of getting the colour they want, such as red, if they have to put in two different colours. (Put one blue block in and make all the rest red.) Have them draw out the blocks to see what happens. (All children except one will get red blocks.) This activity starts to explore the chance or likelihood of something happening. Encourage the children to conduct their own investigations about chance with pattern blocks and pose problems about what would happen if different colours or numbers of blocks were placed in the lucky dip box.

Data

Questions, questions, questions

Aim: Matching questions with people who might ask them

Materials: Pictures of people in different occupations, and questions written on cards

Activity: Children choose a person and find the question that this particular person might need investigated.

OCCUPATION	QUESTION
Teacher	What is the most popular sport?
Shopkeeper	Which drinks sell the best?
Children	Which day do children watch the most television?

Variation: Children write their own questions.

Teeth tally

Aim: Using tallying to record data on a table

Materials: A piece of chart paper and a marker pen

Activity: Make a table with two columns. Label the columns 'Top Teeth' and 'Bottom Teeth'. Each time someone in the class loses a tooth, ask the child to put a tally mark in the correct column. At the end of each week, month, term and year, discuss the results with the children.

How many top and bottom teeth were lost this week/month/term/year?

How many teeth were lost altogether this week/month/term/year?

Have more top teeth or more bottom teeth been lost in total?

Weather data

Aim: Exploring weather data and representation

Materials: A calendar with space for a drawing on each day, coloured marker pens, scissors, glue and chart paper

Activity: Record the weather with a drawing (e.g. sunny, cloudy, rainy) on a calendar every day for a month. At the end of the month, cut up the calendar and sort the days into groups based on the weather picture. Make a vertical bar graph from the pieces of the calendar and glue them onto a chart. Add labels for the x and y axes and a title. Ask the children to pose some questions for each other that can be answered about the bar graph. For example:

How many days did it rain in June?

Variation: The weather on the graphs for different months could be compared.

Extension: Have children record the maximum temperatures on a calendar. Help the children to create a bar graph for the month on squared paper to show these temperatures by colouring in the correct number of blocks. Ask the children to look at what has happened over the month (e.g. the temperature dropped). Ask them whether this is what they expected to happen in that season. Encourage the children to think about the next season and ask them to predict what will happen to the temperature in the next month. Temperature graphs could be made for each month and then grouped on a display board and labelled with the seasons.

Loads of lunch boxes

Aim: Using a grid to investigate the variety of lunch boxes

Materials: Shower curtain or roller blind or large piece of plastic, thick marker pen, and children's lunch boxes

Activity: Draw a grid on the plastic, ensuring that a large lunch box will fit in a cell. Have the children sort their lunch boxes into the different colours and place them in the correct columns. Only one box should be placed in each cell. Add labels for the colours and the numbers of the boxes.

3			
2			
1			
	red	yellow	blue

Variation: Use this grid for graphs of other everyday objects, such as shoes or toys.

Car colours

Aim: Representing information on a bar graph

Materials: Coloured pegs and wooden rulers

Activity: Label each ruler with a different car colour (e.g. red, blue, green). Ask each child to collect a peg that matches her car colour. Have the children attach their pegs to the ruler labelled with the matching colour. Arrange the pegs so that the first peg is at one end of the ruler and so that there are no spaces between the pegs. The rulers can then be lined up to make a horizontal or vertical bar graph. The rulers can be rearranged so that they are in ascending or descending order. Discuss which car colours are the most popular and least popular.

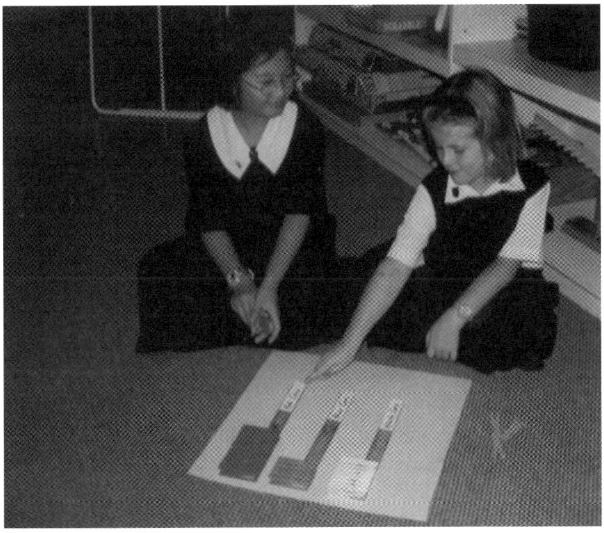

Figure 9.6: *Car colours*

Pet graph

Aim: Constructing and reading a vertical bar graph

Materials: Large sheet of cardboard, small paper squares of equal size (Post-its), pencils and marker pen

Activity: Survey the class to determine the types of pet children would like to have at home. (This avoids leaving out children who do not have a pet.) Each child draws a picture on a coloured square of the pet she would like to have.

Ask one child what she has and start a vertical bar for that pet, recording below what the pet is – e.g. 'Dog'. Then ask any other children who want the same pet to add their papers above the first one. The papers should be placed one above the other. As each child adds a paper, record the number of dogs on the left-hand side of the graph. Once the first kind of pet has been represented, ask a child for another kind of pet. Start a second bar for that pet and proceed in a similar way. There is no need to add more numbers unless there is more of the second pet than the first pet. When the vertical bar graph is finished, add labels to the vertical ('Number of pets') and horizontal axes ('Types of pet'). Ask the children how to show that no one wants a type of pet not shown, such as a rabbit. Add the label 'Rabbit' to the right of the other pets. Ask the children how to show that there would be no rabbits. Add a zero (0) to the vertical axis below the number 1. Finally, add a title to the graph: 'The Pets that Year 2 Would Like'. Once the graph is finished, ask the following questions:

What is this graph showing?

Name the different animals. How many types of animal are there?

How many birds are there? Which pet is the most/least popular?

Which pets are equal in popularity?

How many pets altogether?

How many pets have fur?

How many pets have two legs?

How many children have no pets? How can we work this out?

Would our results look the same on a horizontal bar graph?

Encourage the children to generate some of their own questions.

Finding out about families

Aim: Comparing the composition of families

Materials: Unifix cubes (interlocking cubes)

Activity: Identify all the people that might be in a family (e.g. self, mother, father, sister, brother, grandma, grandpa). Choose a colour for each of these people (e.g. mother is a red cube). List the family members and their colours on the blackboard. Have each child build her family using unifix cubes. Label the family with the child's name. Sort the families by size. The children work in a group with others who have the same-sized family. The children check to see if others in their group have the same combination of family members (e.g. self, mother, grandma). Discuss the variation in family size and composition.

Variation: Children could explore all the different combinations of family members in a certain size of family.

Figure 9.7: *Using unifix cubes*

Problem solving with chance and data

Red or blue?

Aim: Exploring expectation and variation in chance

Materials: A piece of chart paper, a thick pen and glue per group; one container and one blindfold per group; one empty egg carton, six blue counters, six red counters, three pieces of paper and a pencil per child

Activity: Have children work in groups of three. One child puts an egg carton in front of her with 12 spaces. The second child counts six red counters into the container, randomly placing one counter in each space. The third child counts the six blue counters into the remaining spaces. Explain that each child will have a turn to choose six counters from the container without looking. These counters will then be returned for the next child's turn. Ask the children to record on paper what colours they *expect* to select (e.g. 3 red, 3 blue). Discuss any differences in the children's expectations.

The first child places her predicted colours in the flat section of the egg carton lid. She is then blindfolded. She chooses six counters from the container, placing them in front of her. She removes the blindfold, sorts the selected counters by colour and puts these colours into the egg carton, making a red row and a blue row. She then compares her prediction recorded on the paper with what is shown in the egg carton. If the numbers on the paper match the number of counters in the carton, she does nothing. However, if the numbers on the paper do not match the number of red and blue counters in the carton, the child puts a line through the expected number (it should still be readable) and writes the result to the left of the previous number (see Figure 9.8). The other children then have a turn. The children repeat the process twice more so they have three recordings showing what they expected and what actually happened.

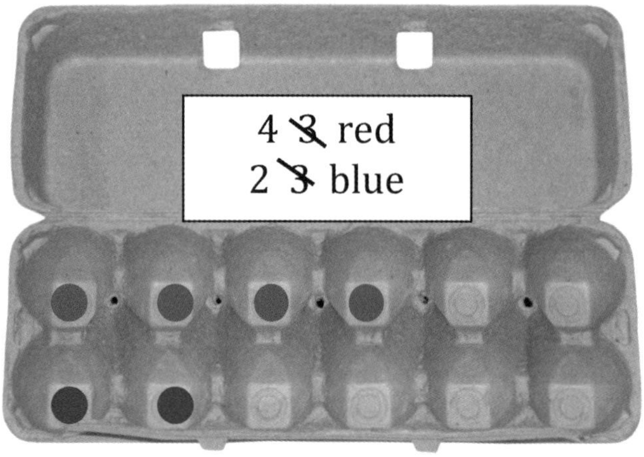

Figure 9.8: *Reds and blues*

Remove all materials except the three recordings of each child. Invite the children to glue these on the top half of the blank chart. Challenge the children to explain why there are differences between what they expected to happen and what actually happened using chance words (e.g. possible, certain). The group should come up with a joint statement about expectation – for example:

It is possible that the result will be the same as what we expected, but it is not certain.

Record this statement on the bottom of the chart.

Ask the children to look at all the different results and verbally list them one colour at a time from the chart. For example, starting at the lowest number:

There were 0 red, 1 red, 2 red, 3 red, 4 red and 6 red. No one had 5 red.

Do the same with blue counters.

Record on the bottom-left of the chart all the possible combinations of six red and blue counters (e.g. 0 red and 6 blue; 1 red and 5 blue). Count the number of possible combinations that were selected across all the turns. Then challenge the children to create a group statement using chance words that explain the different results:

Each time you choose 6 counters, you might get a different combination of red and blue counters. We found 7 possible combinations of red and blue counters.

Record this statement to the right of the list of combinations on the chart.

Variation: Repeat the activity using coins flips (heads and tails) instead of choosing red and blue counters.

The readers

Aim: Organising and interpreting data

Materials: A chart to record students' preferences (see below)

Activity: Provide some data about a group of children who like to read. For example:

Jodi likes books about animals and hobbies, but she doesn't like poetry or joke books.

Ashley only reads joke books and animal books.

Kris only likes to read animal books.

Jade enjoys reading all types of books.

The children represent the information in a table and decide which type of book all the readers would enjoy. The completed table is shown below.

	ANIMALS	JOKE	HOBBIES	POETRY
Jodi	√	X	√	X
Ashley	√	√	X	X
Kris	√	X	X	X
Jade	√	√	√	√

Variation: The children can create their own problems by collecting data about another topic and writing statements about the data.

Which foods do children like?

Aim: Investigating children's food choices

Materials: Pencils and paper

Activity: Pose the problem:

You have been asked by the local shop owner to find out which new food your class would like the shop to sell.

The children need to decide how to collect, organise and represent the information for the shopkeeper.

Variation: Discuss whether or not the foods selected are healthy. Use the information collected to compare the selection of healthy foods and the selection of unhealthy foods.

Further resources

Books (chance)

Axelrod, A. and McGinley-Nally, S., *Pigs at Odds: Fun with Math and Games*, Aladdin (chance)

Cushman, J. and Westman, M., *Do You Wanna Bet?: Your Chance to Find Out about Probability*, Sandpiper (chance)

Einhorn, E., *A Very Improbable Story*, Charlesbridge (chance and probability)

Herman, G. and Roth, S., *Bad Luck Brad*, Kane Press (chance)

Leedy, L., *It's Probably Penny*, Henry Holt and Co (probability)

Murphy, S. J., *Probably Pistachio*, HarperCollins (probability, vocabulary)

Books (data)

Base, G., *Uno's Garden*, Penguin Viking (graphs)

Gréverand, G., *Tell Me If You Like*, Pavilion Children's Books (data, survey)

Harris, T. and Harris, A. N., *Tally Cat Keeps Track*, Lerner Pub Group (tallying)

Leedy, L., *The Great Graph Contest*, Holiday House (bar graphs)

Murphy, S. J. and Tusa, T., *Lemonade for Sale*, HarperCollins (bar graphs)

Apps (data)

Graphs by Tap to Learn (TapToLearn Software) (bar graphs)

Hands-On Math Graph Cubes (Ventura Educational Systems) (bar graphs)

Probability: Grade 3 (Electrokite) (probability)

Summary

Chance is often associated with luck. However, the activities in this chapter have been designed to highlight the mathematical aspects of chance to children. For example, if you use a six-sided die, you can only throw a 1, 2, 3, 4, 5 or 6. It is not possible to throw a 7. To support the mathematics of chance, various activities are included to build students' chance vocabulary and raise their awareness of the role of chance in everyday life. The other part of this chapter focused on data. In recent years, due to technological advances, there has been a massive surge in available data. The data activities in this chapter have been designed to assist children in developing foundational skills in data collection, organisation, representation and interpretation. These skills will have wide applicability beyond mathematics. The problem-solving activities for chance and data provide the opportunity for children to apply their knowledge in novel situations.

Chapter 10

Contexts and connections

Overview

In this chapter you will become familiar with:

- the ways in which mathematical understandings can be used in everyday life and in projects designed by teachers or instigated by young children
- the importance of using mathematics in our everyday lives
- the need to challenge, extend and build children's capacities for posing and solving problems in realistic contexts.

Working with topics or on projects that derive from young children's spontaneous interests is an excellent way to create *contexts* for learning that are meaningful and enable learners to *connect* mathematics to their personal, cultural and everyday lives. In this chapter three topics are illustrated. The first topic, *Ourselves*, focuses on the child. The second topic, *Celebrations*, considers traditional events in an integrated approach to the curriculum. It is a very useful topic for those living in multicultural communities, as it enables different cultures to understand some of the main ideas inherent in a particular culture or community group. The final topic, *Out and About*, explores mathematical ideas in everyday community life. The activities related to these topics are intended as starting points for investigations.

Ourselves

Children enjoy activities that relate to themselves and the people around them. They enjoy finding out their height, shoe size and eye colour, how many friends and family are included in their lives and generating data about what they do. In fact, who we are, and how we relate to the world, is one of the fundamental concerns of the human race, beginning the investigation in the early years can only be an advantage. Some curricula are arranged around broad themes of relevance to children. For example, the Primary Years Programme (PYP) in the Primary International Baccalaureate (IB) curriculum (http://www.ibo.org/pyp/) is organised around six trans-disciplinary themes:

- who we are
- where we are in place and time
- how we express ourselves
- how the world works
- how we organise ourselves
- sharing the planet.

All of these themes have their origin in a topic that with very young children could be called *Ourselves*. In the context of this book, this topic lends itself to a variety of mathematical possibilities. They include data collection and analysis – for example, deciding what foods are favoured by the children and constructing a graph to determine the most popular food. An overview of the potential of this topic to be extended across the curriculum is shown in a curriculum web below (Figure 10.1). Activities and explorations can be designed so that the children are afforded the opportunity to use their mathematical skills and demonstrate their understanding of concepts in a variety of contexts. By taking a topical approach to these activities, mathematical concepts and processes are introduced and extended in a meaningful and enjoyable way. As well, the topic of *Ourselves* connects with other curriculum areas and enables learners to apply their mathematical knowledge and skills in everyday situations.

The activities suggested in the *Ourselves* curriculum web give an overview of the potential range of the topic. What follows are examples of specific activities that are primarily mathematical in origin.

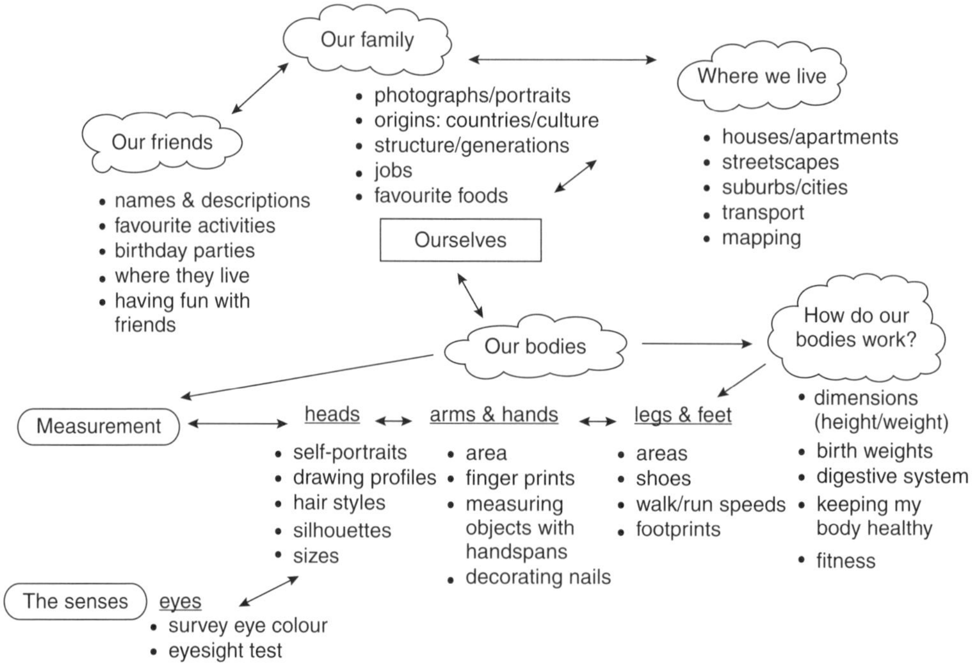

Figure 10.1: *'Ourselves' curriculum web*

Self-portrait

Aim: Classifying features by facial characteristics

Materials: Paper and coloured pens

Activity: On large sheets of paper children draw and make a self-portrait using coloured markers and collage materials (e.g. wool, coloured paper, scrap material). The self-portraits are sorted according to hair type. The different groupings are discussed. They can be sorted into eye colours, gender groups, based on clothing – the children can sort and explain their 'sorting rule'.

Four children with curly hair. Six children with brown hair.

Variation: Look closely at the faces of the group. Classify them according to their shape (e.g. square, round, oval, heart shaped, oblong). Collect baby pictures and discuss the ways in which the faces have changed.

Figure 10.2: *Self-portrait*

My family

Aim: Classifying by number

Materials: Paper and coloured pens

Activity: Each child draws a picture of his family. Sort the families according to the number of people in the family.

Five children have 3 people in their family. Seven children have 4 people in their family.

Look at me

Aim: Using a range of positional language

Materials: Everyday classroom objects

Activity: The children can discuss and explore things that they could hide in or behind; stand on, in or under; or jump over or climb under.

Fancy foot

Aim: Ordering (longest to shortest)

Materials: Paper and coloured pens

Activity: Each child traces around his foot and decorates the shape. Small groups of children order their feet from longest to shortest.

Which group?

Aim: Sorting into groups

Materials: Children in the group

Activity: Children are sorted according to different criteria (e.g. eye colour, height, type of hair, clothing). Create a mystery set of children (e.g. children wearing red shirts). Ask the children wearing red shirts to stand together. The other children can then guess the mystery sorting rule. Encourage the children to devise their own sorting rules. The following song can be used to add interest to the sorting process:

Here is my choice,
What can you see?
Is there a rule?
Can you tell me?

Figure 10.3: *Which group?*

My day

Aim: Ordering events

Materials: Paper and coloured pens

Activity: Children illustrate their day chronologically and present it to the class as if they were a news reporter.

In the morning I catch the bus to school. In the afternoon I play with my dog. In the evening I have dinner with my family.

Figure 10.4: *My day*

Handspans

Aim: Measuring length

Materials: Paper and coloured pens

Activity: Each child traces around his hand, decorates the shape and cuts it out. He then searches for things that are longer or shorter than his handspan. The child can repeat this activity with a tracing of his foot.

Variation: Use the outline of the hand to measure the distance of each finger.

Is finger number two always the longest? Does anyone have some fingers the same length as one another? What is the width of a handspan?

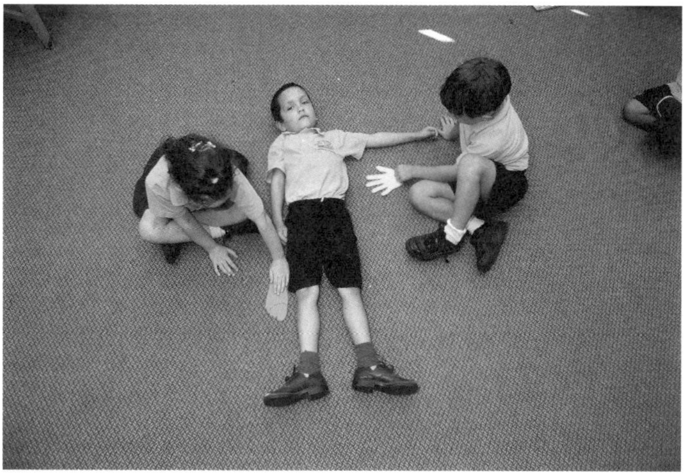

Figure 10.5: *Measuring with handspans*

Measuring heads

Aim: Measuring in centimetres

Materials: Prepare a matrix so that the children can easily enter their data – this can be on paper or on the computer in the form of a table

Activity: Children take it in turns to measure each other's heads with a tape measure. They record and compare the results.

Variation: Cut a piece of string to the size of each person's head. Display the string in graph form to compare the different lengths.

How big is your hand?

Aim: Exploring volume

Materials: A clear jug, big enough to put a hand in and mark off the height of the water with a non-permanent pen

Activity: Put some water in a clear, tall jug. Mark the level of the water on the side of the jug. Have a volunteer make a fist, place his hand in the water and note how high the water rises. Repeat this with the second hand.

Who has the biggest or smallest hand? Is your hand bigger if you open it out instead of keeping it as a fist?

Discuss what we mean by 'the biggest' in relation to the amount of water that is displaced. Read the book *Who Sank the Boat?* (Pamela Allen, Scholastic).

People graphs

Aim: Creating picture graphs

Materials: Masking tape on the floor in a grid pattern

Activity: Make a large floor grid out of masking tape. Children stand in the appropriate columns in response to a set criteria (e.g. footwear). The group then responds to questions such as:

Are there more children wearing sports shoes or sandals? What is the most popular type of footwear?

Variation: Other graphing ideas include eye colour, hair type or colour, age, number in the family, favourite food, favourite book.

Silhouette

Aim: Measuring surface area

Materials: Large sheets of squared paper, pens and scissors

Activity: Ask a friend to lie down on the squared paper. Draw around him. Count the squares to find the area of his body. There may be some partially covered squares. Include those squares that are at least half-covered in the count. Do not count those squares that are less than half-covered.

Variation: Repeat this activity using the outline of a hand or foot.

Silhouette profile

Aim: Matching shapes

Materials: Data projector, large sheets of paper (stuck onto wall) and pens

Activity: Using the beam of light from a projector, draw a silhouette of the profile of each child in the class. Mix them up and have the group try to guess the owner of each silhouette.

My body

Aim: Estimating, measuring and comparing lengths

Materials: Large sheets of paper and pens

Activity: In pairs, children take it in turns to trace around each other's body shape. To make the shape more realistic, add facial features, such as hair colour. Estimate, measure and compare body parts using arbitrary units (e.g. blocks, handspans, iceblock sticks).

My arm is 5 blocks long. My leg is 8 blocks long. My leg is longer than my arm.

Figure 10.6: *My body*

How high can you jump?

Aim: Measuring height

Materials: Large sheets of paper, paint and pens

Activity: Stick a large sheet of white paper on a wall. Ask each child to dab his fingers in some paint. The child stands facing the sheet of paper with his heels flat on the ground and an arm held as high as possible above his head. Ask the child to make a mark on the paper to show how high he can reach. The child then jumps up and makes a second mark on the wall to show how high he can jump. Label both marks with the child's name and record the distance between the two marks.

Maths Olympics

Aim: Collecting and comparing data

Materials: During physical education time, include activities and materials that will enable comparison questions to be asked.

Activity: Link maths to physical education by devising a series of activities in which the emphasis is on measuring, counting, timing and comparing.

Do the children with the longest legs jump further? How far can you jump with both feet together? How long did it take you to climb through or over the tunnel? How many sit-ups can you do in a minute?

Figure 10.7: *Maths Olympics*

First in line

Aim: Using and exploring ordinal numbers

Activity: Children are located in various positions in different places around the school or centre. As the children form lines to move around the school, emphasise ordinal positions (e.g. first, second, third). Establish each child's position in a line by giving them ordinal number cards (e.g. 1st, 2nd, 3rd) and ask them to stand in the correct position.

Where do you live?

Aim: Exploring everyday uses for numbers

Materials: Cards with children's house numbers written on them

Activity: Collect the children's house numbers. Arrange the numbers into groups (e.g. under 10, between 10 and 20, over 50). Talk about odd and even numbers. Order the selected numbers, starting with the largest.

Personal diaries

Aim: Making graphs to use for describing and comparing features

Materials: Exercise book or tablet.

Activity: Each child makes a personal diary about herself. Include relevant data, such as eye colour, hair colour and shoe size. Use the information to make class graphs and charts. Make comparisons and look for trends and relationships.

Which is the most common eye colour? Which is the most common shoe size? Do the tallest children have the biggest feet? Is the longest foot also the widest?

The topic of *Ourselves* is endless. This section has made just some suggestions about the mathematical potential of studying various aspects of ourselves. The curriculum web shown in Figure 10.1 shows how this topic might be extended into a family study that could link to where we live and what types of housing styles and designs our cities have. There is the potential to explore types of job, countries of origin, and many more aspects of our lives that can be photographed, mapped or documented, all of which require an understanding and application of mathematical concepts. These activities will all form the basis of an extended conversation which will require the children to use mathematical language in diverse ways. This in turn will enrich their vocabulary and enable them to feel more confident and competent with school mathematics.

Celebrations

The topic of *Celebrations* also provides a rich context for integrating all areas of the curriculum, including mathematics. The topic might start with birthdays but also affords the opportunity to celebrate community diversity by considering cultural events, such as Easter, Christmas, Diwali, Passover, Rosh Hashanah, Ramadan, harvest festivals, May Day, Arbor Day and Kwanzaa. There are so many to choose from, whether or not you have a child in your class who celebrates that particular festival. The topic might be introduced on a particular festival day or with the birthday of one of the children. An internet search for each event will result in a wide range of options to choose from.

Birthdays

For young children, birthdays are wonderful celebrations. They are always excited about their own and others', and view the occasion as a time of joy and fun. Birthdays can also be the stimulus for using mathematics in context. The ideas contained in Figure 10.9 can form the basis for planning a topic around birthdays. You might start with reading stories about a birthday or planning a birthday party. There is a great deal of potential for using mathematics in birthday planning, as well as in collecting data about birth dates and the items and activities associated with party fun. Once the activities have taken place and the activities completed they can be compiled into a birthday activity centre (Figure 10.10) for ongoing explorations.

Figure 10.8: *Birthday parties are mathematical moments*

When is your birthday?

Aim: To consider and collate all the class birthdays

Materials: Children's literature, for example:

Carle, E., *The Secret Birthday Message*, Hamish Hamilton

Keller, H., *Lizzie's Invitation*, Franklin Watts

Oxenbury, H., *The Birthday Party*, Walker Books

Activity: Ask the children:

How old are you? When is your birthday? What presents did you get on your last birthday?

There are many ways to represent the birthdays of the children. For example, you can make a graph for each month or within a particular month sequence the birthdays from first to last. With any of the representations there are plenty of opportunities to ask questions to support learning:

Whose birthday is the first one for the year? Whose is the last?

Which month has the most birthdays for the children in our class?

Is anyone born on a special festival day and if so which festival?

Let's find out who has a birthday on weekdays and who has one on a weekend.

If we look at September, how many birthday are there? How many days are there between each birthday?

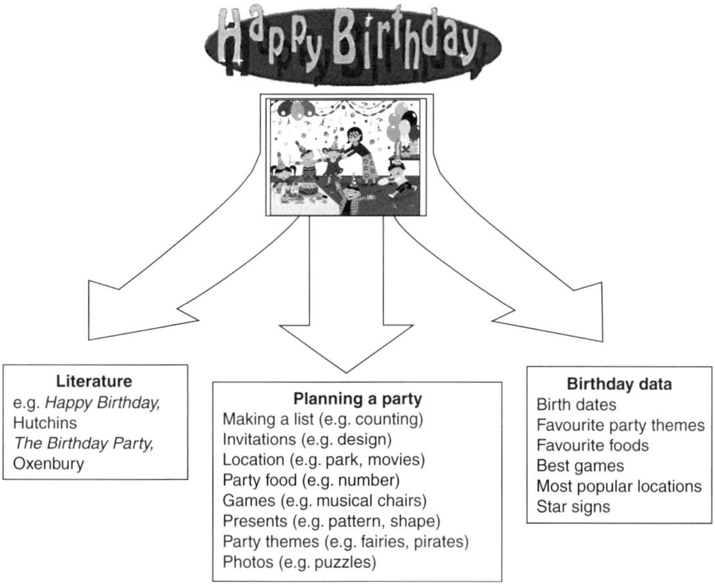

Figure 10.9: *Birthday ideas*

Birthday display

Aims: To explore the range of birthdays and birthday traditions of the children in the group, and to use number and various representations to document the information gathered

Materials: Display board covered with dark backing paper and a contrasting coloured border, pens, pencils, felt pens, crayons, scissors, coloured paper, string, fabric remnants, scales, glue, sticky tape, five boxes (wrapped as presents and containing different amounts of sand)

Activity:

1. Ask each child to draw and colour his own birthday cake. Tell the children to put any number of candles on the cake and request that some be lit and others not. The difference between the lit and unlit candles is the basis of a subtraction sentence that is written on the cake (e.g. 5 – 2 = 3). These cakes are glued on the border of the birthday display.
2. Make a big HAPPY BIRTHDAY sign for the display.
3. Create 12 balloon shapes and label them with each month of the year. These are stapled to the board.

Figure 10.10: *Birthday display and activity centre*

4. Ask the children to draw pictures of themselves. Attach each child's picture to the balloon corresponding to his birthday month.
5. Each month could be labelled to show how many children have birthdays in that month.
6. Make wrapping paper by cutting out different shapes (e.g. circles, squares, triangles) and using them to make decorative patterns.
7. Place the present boxes on a table in front of the display board. Label each present with a number (e.g. Present 1)
8. Estimate the mass of the presents and put them in order. Check the order by weighing each present on the balance scale.

The topic of 'Birthdays' can lead to an investigation of the concept of time (e.g. months, the year, past and future).

Months of the year

Aim: To link the months of the year with actions and events

Materials: Paper, scissors, glue, coloured pens, a large circular wall chart divided into 12 sections and labelled with each month of the year

Activity: The children say the months of the year. Discuss the important events that occur in each month.

We start school in January.

Christmas is in December.

Encourage the children to think about things such as the month each season starts, the timing of the longest school holidays, Easter and other festivals. Ask the children to draw an event that is special to them. Each child pastes his picture onto the chart and tells the class about it. The chart can be added to at any time of the year.

The year

Aim: To be able to sort children by birthdays or by age

Materials: Wall chart, Blu Tack

Activity: Ask the children to bring photographs of themselves. Sort the photographs according to age. Attach the photographs to a chart labelled with a particular age (e.g. six years old). When the child has a birthday, move his photograph to the next age group.

Past and future

Aim: To be able to sequence events

Materials: Paper, coloured pens and pencils, glue and scissors

Activity 1: Ask the children to draw pictures or bring photographs that represent the different stages in their lives (e.g. the child as a sleeping baby, a crawling baby, a toddler, going to preschool). Put each picture in sequence and display them in the classroom.

Activity 2: With parents' help, the children can create personal timelines. Each significant event in a child's life can be recorded in pictures with a short description (e.g. winning my first race, starting school).

Activity 3: Create a diagram of family members and sequence them by age.

Further resources – birthdays

Books

Bruna, D., *Miffy's Birthday*, Methuen

Claret, M., *Melissa Mouse's Birthday Surprise*, Metheun

Hill, D., *Spot's Birthday Party*, Heinemann

Hughes, S., *Alfie Gives a Hand*, Bodley Head

Hutchins, P., *The Best Train Set Ever*, Bodley Head

Pragoff, F., *The Birthday Party*, Dent

Stevenson, J., *Barbara's Birthday*, Bodley Head

Zolotow, C. and Sendak, M., *Mister Rabbit and the Lovely Present*, Bodley Head

Cultural celebrations

In addition to personal celebrations, children can develop cultural understanding by learning about festivals, such as Chinese New Year. Figure 10.11 shows some of the festivals and events that are recognised throughout the world. Children can be introduced to festivals in other cultures using background information. For example:

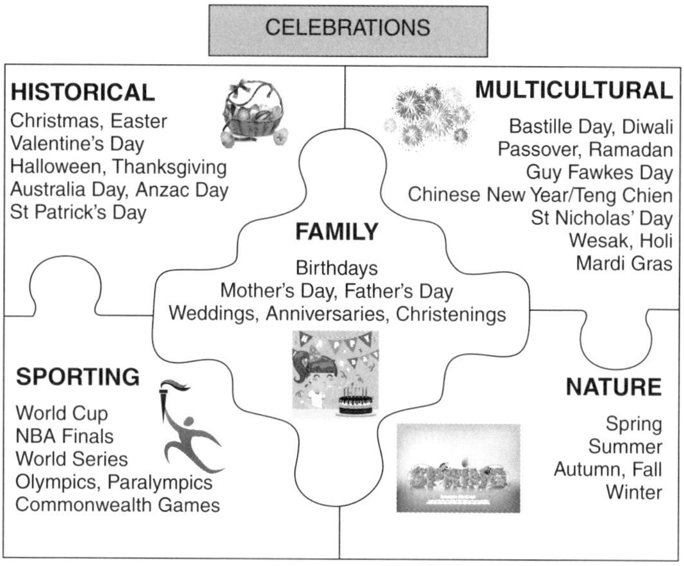

Figure 10.11: *Celebrations*

Here we focus on Chinese New Year, which occurs on the first day of the lunar calendar. Therefore, it is on a different day each year. It generally occurs between mid January and mid February. Chinese New Year is the most important festival for Chinese communities all over the world. It is celebrated with festivities in the home and in the streets. The origins of Chinese New Year are religious and the celebrations contain rituals that honour the gods of the people. However, most of the festivities today are secular. Each year, one of the animals that ran in the Jade Emperor's race is honoured. The Year of the Rat is the beginning of the sequence. Just before the New Year begins, people clean their homes to wash away any bad luck that may have befallen them. Red decorations are hung on doors and the windows are decorated with messages such as 'longevity, prosperity, happiness and harmony'. Families often decorate their homes with the blossom from peach trees, which flower in mainland China around this time. The front doors of people's houses are kept open and it is a time for visiting relatives and friends. Children often receive gifts of money in small red envelopes that have gold inscriptions on them. The special food of the festival is a pastry filled with nuts and fruits, such as oranges and tangerines, which are symbols of longevity.

Lucky money envelopes

Aim: To understand the value of different amounts of money

Background: To celebrate Chinese New Year, people create *Hung Pao* envelopes which contain gifts of money. In creating these traditional envelopes, children are exploring two- and three-dimensional shapes and are engaged in the processes of representing, measuring, analysing and estimating.

Materials: Red paper (A4), gold paper, crayons or pens, scissors, glue, pencils and copies of the envelopes (see Appendix 1)

Activity: Use the stencil to create a pattern for the envelope with the red paper. Fold and stick the sides together as shown. Fold the bottom flap over and stick it. Do the same with the top flap. The Chinese greeting 'Kung Hei Fat Choy' (Happy New Year) can be written in gold or cut out using gold paper.

Paper weaving

Aim: To help develop spatial sense, to consider length, and to engage in measuring, predicting, analysing and designing

Materials: Red paper (A4 or 30 square centimetres), thin strips of white, yellow or gold paper (two centimetres wide)

Activity: Use the red sheet of paper as the loom. Fold this in half from top to bottom. From the centre, draw parallel lines that are about two centimetres apart. The lines should go from the folded edge to about two centimetres away from the edge of the paper. Cut along the lines and open the paper out. Weave the strips in and out of the loom, sticking the ends down when each has been completed.

Chinese addition

Aim: To become aware of different number systems, as well as engaging in calculating, predicting, estimating, and recording in symbolic forms

Materials: Copies of the Chinese addition sheet (see Appendix 2)

Activity: Ask the group to solve the problems on the sheet and then have them try to create some of their own.

There are many traditional activities that take place for Chinese New Year (see e.g. http://www.chinesenewyears.info/chinese-new-year-traditions.php). Look for videos of celebrations of Chinese New Year on the internet and you will find the lion dance (e.g. http://www.youtube.com/watch?v=Mc4eKooZ9Bk), as well as the dragon dance (e.g. http://www.youtube.com/watch?v=J3MIv69C38Q) on YouTube. There is a lot of information about the various traditions of food and the meaning of each of the animals associated with the various years in the Chinese calendar (e.g. http://www.travelchinaguide.com/intro/social_customs/zodiac/).

These resources can all be incorporated in an e-book and a collection can be established in the library corner. If using a tablet, store the webpages on the tablet and read in the same way as a traditional book.

Out and about

There are many opportunities to extend children's mathematical understandings when they are '*Out and About*' in their local environment or in a broader context. Figure 10.12 provides examples of questions that might be a catalyst for discussion or inquiry. For example, visiting a new baby provides an opportunity for children to explore the concept of mass.

How much did the baby weigh? How much did you weigh when you were born? How much do you weigh now? What things are the same weight as you? What is heavier or lighter than you?

Further questions can be linked to different mathematical concepts, such as length and time:

How long was the baby when she was born? What time and date was she born?

Questioning serves to focus children's attention on the mathematics in a situation and can provide the stimulus for meaningful interaction with mathematical concepts.

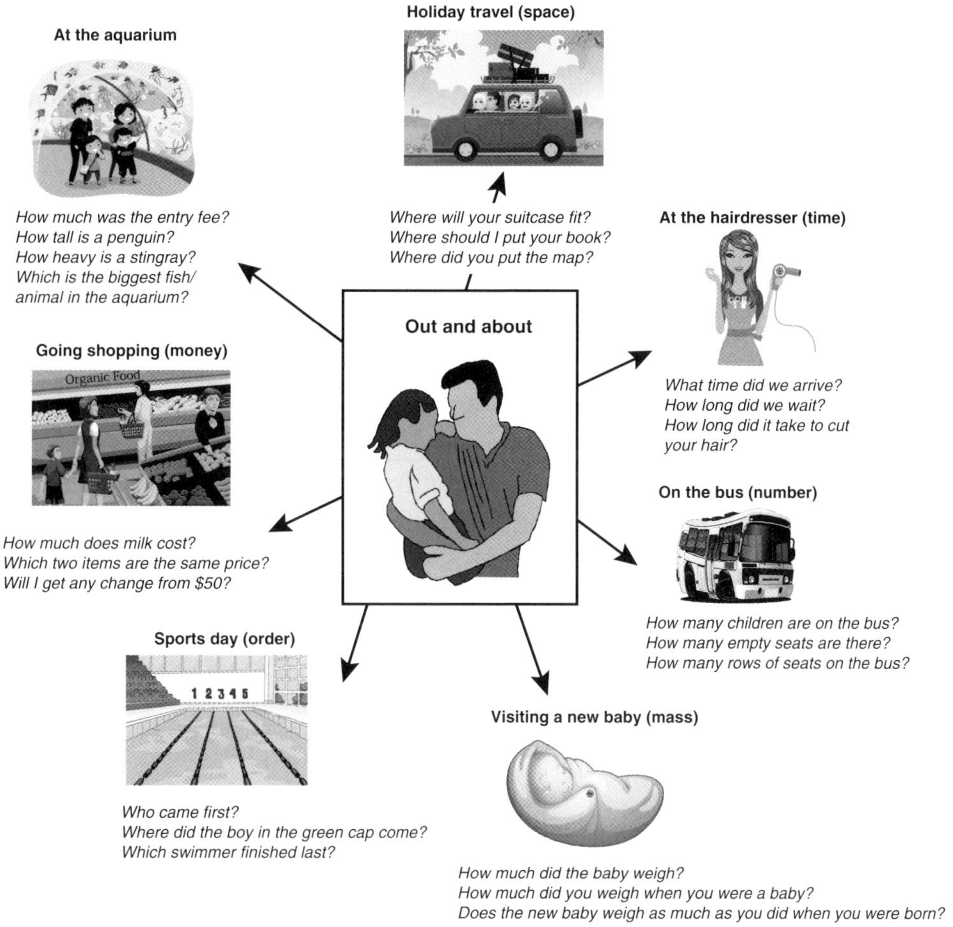

Figure 10.12: *Out and about*

As well as asking about events taking place in everyday life, you can investigate happenings that occur in the school grounds or nearby. You might make a new garden in the school grounds, watch the plants and vegetables grow and then use them for recipes. There is a wide range of events that provide contexts for using mathematics in everyday practices, the basis of numeracy. Many teachers now use an inquiry-based approach in which the children's questions form the basis of an investigation that has meaning to the whole group.

In one Year 2 class in Australia (consisting of seven- and eight-year-olds) the children participated in designing the garden area for their new early years classroom area. They used a program called Appleworks to measure, map and draw their garden design to scale, using rulers, protractors, measuring tapes and orienteering compasses to ensure their measurements were accurate. At present there are many such drawing programs that may be used in a similar way. Figure 10.13 shows a bird garden planned by one of the students, Gwendolyn.

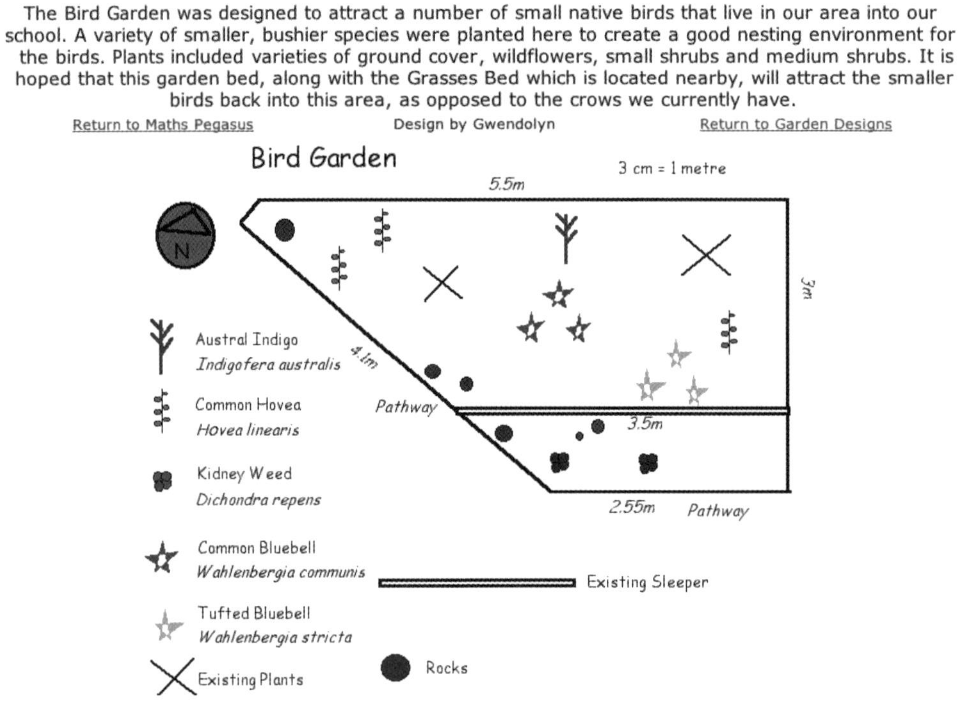

Figure 10.13: *The bird garden*
Source: Yelland 2007

The 'design a garden' task enabled the young children to apply various mathematical concepts and processes to create and design a functional garden based on a theme of their choice. In creating her garden, Gwendolyn was provided with the time and resources to investigate the problem of how to create a new garden, and in particular what plants the native birds would prefer. She represented her ideas using new technologies and was then able to share this with a wide audience beyond the classroom since her plans were uploaded to the school's website. The varied learning outcomes – for example, the different gardens the students created and the ways in which they approached the task – were broad, as were the multiple opportunities for exploration provided by the task. Gwendolyn was able to create her own plant key, represent the scale of the garden within the software, and add to this when required – all this resulted in multiple opportunities for learning and showing her own initiative. This task was not completed within one mathematics class, but rather it was completed within a series of classes over an extended period, allowing for ample time to achieve a worthwhile outcome and satisfying results.

Summary

In this book we have focused on the mathematical concepts and processes that are essential for a good start to learning. We have contended that mathematics is an integral part of our lives and the ideas and processes inherent in mathematics enable us to make meaning and understand our lives in coherent ways. Knowing how to 'do' mathematics enables us to use it in our everyday lives so that we become numerate. This chapter has brought together many of the ideas contained in this book to illustrate the ways in which the early concepts and processes of mathematics can be used in topics to investigate ideas that are important and interesting to know. A topic can act as a framework for explorations in other topics. The topics can be initiated by the teacher or the child, and will only be sustained as long as the children find their investigations relevant and meaningful. They might lead to new topics and explorations, but in every case they will require the application of mathematical skills and processes in new and dynamic ways each time they are encountered. Such flexibility and innovation demonstrates why we need to champion mathematics in the 21st century.

References

Yelland, N. J., 2007, *Shift to the Future: Rethinking Learning with New Technologies in Education*, New York: Routledge

Chapter 11

Designing mathematical experiences for numeracy in the 21st century

Overview

In this chapter you will become familiar with:

- the ways in which mathematical understandings support numeracy in the 21st century
- the elements in the design cycle that can be used to create effective teaching and learning contexts for numeracy
- using child-centred assessment to maximise individual learning potential.

Chapter 11 Designing mathematical experiences

The chapters in this book have considered the foundational concepts and processes of mathematics that are fundamental in establishing confidence and competence in the early years. The book has considered some of the ways in which these concepts and processes can be incorporated into learning activities designed by teachers and caregivers, and encountered and experienced in the early years of a child's life. It has explored the concepts of number, measurement, space, chance and data, and patterns and algebra, since these form the basis of the mathematics curriculum in many countries, and shown how they might be incorporated into early childhood learning experiences. A critical link has been made between the acquisition of confidence and competence in mathematics and becoming numerate in the 21st century. That is, we need to be able to *understand* and *use* mathematical concepts and processes in order to function effectively in the 21st century. Throughout a child's life, she will encounter problems, challenges and technologies that require the application and successful use of mathematical concepts and processes.

This chapter discusses and describes the pedagogical decision making that underpins the design of successful and relevant mathematical experiences for young children.

Mathematics is an essential part of any school curriculum and learning opportunities should be characterised by:

- experiences in problem solving and problem posing
- discovering patterns and relationships
- using inquiry and intuition in explorations
- using spontaneity and imagination in mathematical investigations
- sharing, documenting and communicating ideas and findings with others.

In the early years, effective teachers facilitate children's understanding of mathematics and create opportunities for them to become numerate by:

- exploring mathematics in different contexts (classroom, outside, on visits, in the children's homes)
- providing materials and resources that help children to make sense of ideas (this includes the use of new technologies)
- being explicit about the ways in which mathematics is used to solve everyday problems
- encouraging children to discuss and document their experiences and activities
- integrating mathematical concepts and processes across the curriculum
- valuing the contribution of all children.

Mathematics and numeracy

Yelland (2007) has suggested that the goal of using and understanding mathematical concepts and processes is to become numerate. This means that learners will be able to function effectively using mathematical concepts and processes in their everyday lives. Yelland (2007) proposed a model consisting of the processes that enable learners to become numerate in the 21st century. The model, shown in Figure 11.1, features three main tasks: to *inquire, create* and *communicate*. In thinking about *inquiries* that might warrant investigation, teachers and children will generate ideas and work collaboratively in active learning contexts that require them to use existing knowledge and skills in order to make sense of their world. Additionally, they will *create* new knowledge that can be shared with a variety of appropriate audiences. This approach involves the generation of new ideas via designing, planning, problem solving and problem posing, and then *communicating* strategies, ideas and findings in an effective way to promote new understandings.

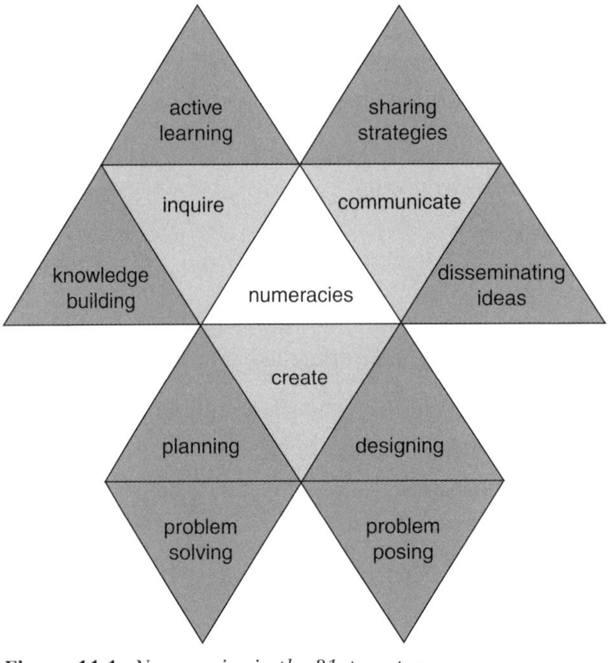

Figure 11.1: *Numeracies in the 21st century*
Source: Yelland 2007.

The *contexts* in which mathematical thinking occurs need to be carefully considered and designed, and the learner can be encouraged to use the mathematical concepts and skills in both teacher-designed and spontaneous learning experiences. From a teacher's perspective, creating a supportive mathematical learning environment can be viewed as a cyclic process that involves the three phases of *designing*, *teaching* and *evaluating*. The specific features that need to be addressed within each of the phases of the design cycle are shown in Figure 11.2.

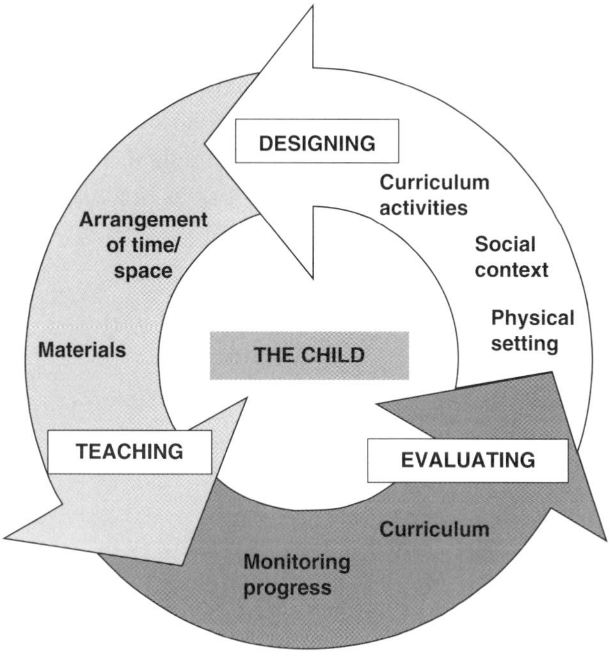

Figure 11.2: *The design cycle*

Designing

The social context

Communication and collaboration are key in mathematical learning and problem solving. Throughout this book we have provided examples of the ways in which teachers, parents and caregivers can encourage young children to explain how they explore ideas and represent their discoveries. We have focused on using language in a variety of contexts, since discussion is integral to collaborative learning. When children collaborate on tasks, they benefit from the ideas of others and from having the opportunity to express and reflect on their own ideas. The process of collaboration enables children to become competent and confident in their mathematical abilities. Additionally, by collaborating with their peers, children learn from each other.

In everyday life, young children often learn by mirroring the behaviours and actions of adults. Adults can support children's mathematical understandings and dispositions by involving children in everyday mathematical tasks, and by explaining the ways in which using mathematical ideas and processes can be relevant and exciting. For example, a child can help count the money for a school lunch or she might go on a visit to a restaurant. Children can also benefit from seeing adults engaged in, and persisting with, challenging mathematical activities when a solution is not immediately apparent or, more importantly, when there are several possible solutions. For example, an adult can collaborate with a child on a problem or puzzle and talk about how to overcome obstacles in the solution process. They might embark on designing an enclosure for a pet rabbit or think about how to cook a favourite food. There are so many examples that not only require the use of concepts and skills but also need the learner to be creative in their pathways to solutions.

Figure 11.3: *Children explore and talk during play*

Physical spaces and resources

When planning for mathematics, it is important to create a physical environment that is conducive to learning and stimulates thinking. The physical environment includes the arrangement of the physical space and places for displaying children's work.

Various resources can be used to facilitate mathematical understandings. These resources include everyday items, 'junk' materials, specific mathematical resources and manipulatives (see Appendix 3 for a list of suggestions). Many resources that were used in the preschool years continue to be appropriate. For example, children can investigate volume with cups and jugs, and make patterns with materials from the collage trolley. When children are engaged in mathematical tasks, they require access to mathematical resources, such as calculators and measuring devices, and manipulatives, such as counters and base 10 arithmetic blocks.

Figure 11.4: *Materials should be readily available for children*

The use of new technologies, including computers, tablets, cameras and other devices, is becoming increasingly important for learning. In Chapter 3 we discussed how new technologies have the potential to encourage deep learning because they afford opportunities for multimodal learning. It is essential that they be accessible and that they complement the use of traditional three-dimensional learning materials. *All* learning resources should be organised and stored so that they are easily accessible for children to use in their learning.

The physical space in a room should provide opportunities for children to work in different ways. In Chapter 2 we discussed the ways in which young children's playful explorations need to be encouraged. This means that the physical space has to support their needs and interests, and so materials should be located where they can be accessed and used. Children need to be able to work independently and in groups. Ideally, they will have access to floor space and tables for working. The furniture arrangement needs to allow for flexibility in working arrangements. For example, in a particular activity the children may participate in a group discussion on the floor and then proceed to table work, or use a laptop or tablet in either location. Children can be involved in designing the physical layout of the room.

Displays convey the character of the occupants of a room and indicate what is valued. Children enjoy seeing their work displayed and can learn from observing the work of others. Think carefully about interesting ways to display the children's work and encourage them to express their ideas about the displays. Displays can also form the basis of teaching by providing information or the stimulus for an activity. A good display can create opportunities for children to communicate their ideas to each other and can motivate children to engage with ideas and materials. We showed one way that this might be achieved in Chapter 10: having a 'birthday table'.

Figure 11.5: *Display children's mathematical discoveries*

Curriculum

The content of any early childhood mathematics program is influenced by local and national curriculum documents, existing school-based programs and the needs of individual children. Curriculum documents provide frameworks and suggestions for teaching and evaluating mathematics. The examples provided in this book are aligned with the foundational stages of mathematical curricula. They are labelled differently in various countries but the content is essentially the same.

Many schools use national curriculum documents to develop school-based programs that provide additional guidance for teachers and meet the needs of children in a particular locality. In a school-based program, consideration should be given to how the program will:

- provide opportunities for concept development in number, measurement, space, and chance and data, and patterns and algebra
- support the use of mathematical processes
- address the central role of problem solving
- facilitate the development of positive attitudes
- emphasise activities that are cognitively challenging
- promote the use of authentic tasks and problems
- incorporate representations that are commonly used in mathematics
- address children's preferred modes of learning.

Children are more likely to build on their mathematical understandings and develop an appreciation for mathematics when they encounter the subject within meaningful contexts. Working with topics is one way to provide opportunities for children to see the relevance of mathematical thinking in their everyday lives. The previous chapter provided examples of how topics such as 'Ourselves', 'Celebrations' and 'Out and About' can provide contexts for mathematical thinking. Encouraging children to solve problems equips them with the knowledge and skills to pose problems and conduct their own investigations highlighting the personal relevance of mathematics. Possible topics for investigation can be identified from children's questions and from their interests.

Mathematical opportunities should include variable tasks that support learning. Teachers often present children with closed tasks, such as calculating how many items are in a specified group. However, there is also a need to include open-ended tasks in which children are encouraged to explore, reason about and reflect on mathematical ideas. For example, the child may be asked to generate a list of equations that have the common answer of 10 (e.g. $6 + 4$; $14 - 4$). Open-ended tasks provide opportunities for children to:

- generate their own solution methods rather than apply a given method
- justify the strategies that they have chosen
- work at their own level
- use different modes of representation
- develop an awareness of multiple solutions for a problem
- work collaboratively and reach a consensus.

Figure 11.6: *There were 4 people on the beach and 3 more came: 4 + 3 = 7*

In Chapter 4 we presented the Mathematical Tasks Continuum, which can act as a pedagogical prompt to assist a teacher in designing a series of balanced activities ranging in complexity from unidimensional to multidimensional. Over time and through experience, children can understand concepts to varying degrees of depth. When they are able to apply and analyse a concept, they have a deeper understanding of it than if they just demonstrate their capacity to use it in simple tasks.

Teaching

Arrangement of time, space and materials

Successful teaching in mathematics requires an understanding of how the teacher can support children's learning and effectively manage the learning environment. This entails knowing the interests and needs of the children, selecting appropriate tasks and resources, creating a supportive social context, and making optimal use of the available time and physical space. The role of the teacher is to facilitate the learning of mathematics by providing the appropriate support and guidance for individual children. This involves:

- providing tasks that are engaging and that extend children's thinking
- broadening the children's range of experiences
- providing opportunities for the development and use of mathematical processes in a variety of contexts
- encouraging children to persevere and overcome obstacles

- developing an acceptance of alternative solution methods and multiple solutions
- empowering the children to take responsibility for their own learning
- organising sufficient time for mathematical activities, including the communication of findings
- designing activities of different time lengths (e.g. long-term investigations).

Pedagogies as knowledge processes

We suggested in Chapter 1 that our approach resonates with constructivism, since we believe that young children learn by *doing*. However, they need to have a broad base of experience and conceptual understandings before they are able to extend what they can *do* and build on it. Further, they do not do this in a vacuum, and thus we believe that learning takes place in a social context with support from others, before it is individualised.

These beliefs are important for teachers of young children who need to support this type of active learning. Kalantzis and Cope (2012) and Yelland, Cope and Kalantzis (2008) have suggested that pedagogies can be viewed as knowledge processes that incorporate *experiencing, conceptualising, analysing,* and *applying*.

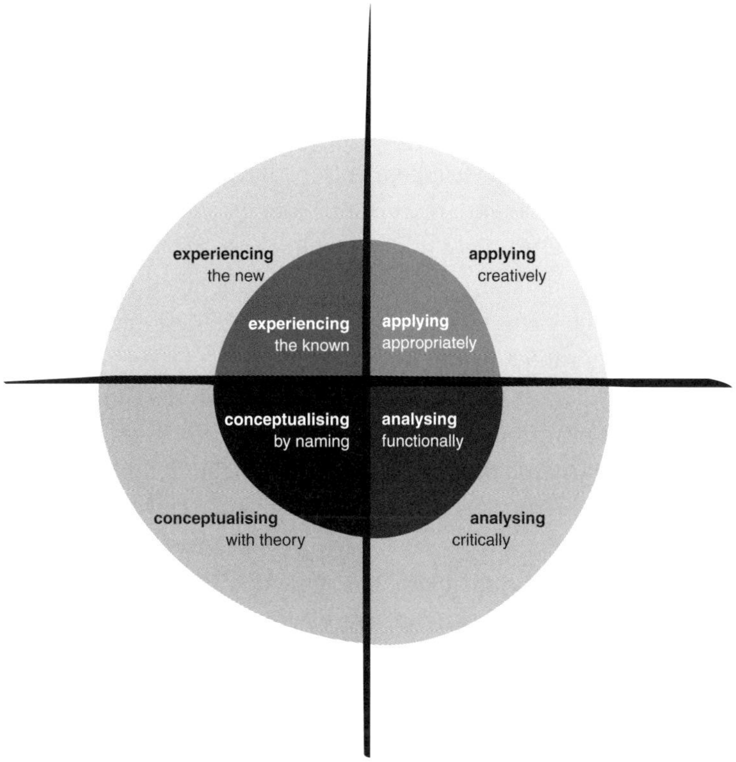

Figure 11.7: *Learning by Design*
Source: Kalantzis & Cope 2012

Experiencing is regarded as immersion in the everyday lifeworld of the learner and involves the teacher in creating two different kinds of experience for learners: the *known* and the *new*. In order for learning to be meaningful there needs to be a link between what is already known and what will be experienced. In experiencing the known, teachers afford opportunities for children to make links with their prior knowledge and experiences (e.g. personal, community) which they can then use to make connections to the new learning that is planned to occur. *Conceptualising* enables learners to make meaning from their experiences and build ideas (concepts) about the nature of things and how the world works. In the Learning by Design model conceptualising occurs via *naming* when learners are able to label and characterise ideas or objects in order to make generalisations (theories) about them. In this way, a learner can recognise and *name* various two-dimensional shapes, and then build up a *theory* about how they might fit together to make a tiling pattern or how they are used in buildings that they see every day. The knowledge process of *analysing* requires that learners be able to examine a context, event or piece of information, and articulate in a systematic and *critical* way the underlying assumptions and implications of its application or function. In analysing functionally, learners consider what an idea means and how it might impact on themselves, the community or the world. When critically analysing knowledge, learners are required to ask questions about the ramifications of its application and realise the ramifications of its impact in diverse situations. Finally, in *applying* what we know in diverse ways, especially in authentic contexts, we are extending learning so that it has a purpose and can add value to our lives and the lives of others. In applying *appropriately*, we often follow traditional ways of doing things, such as using objects for the purpose for which they were designed. However, there are always opportunities to extend such applications when people use things in innovative ways and are able to create contexts in which they redesign or transform objects and ideas. If this notion is taken further, it represents applying *creatively*, since the transformation has generated a new idea or product that is original or a hybrid of a combination of ideas.

The focus of learning by design is on *meaning* and *action* as *ways of knowing*, and the four knowledge processes are the constituent parts of this. The ways of knowing are sensitive to learners, cultures, knowledge domains and pedagogies, so that they will have different emphases depending on the context for which they are planned. Making the knowledge processes explicit enables teachers to consider which elements they regard as being most effective depending on their context and content and enables them to use the most effective elements to support or scaffold the deep learning of the students in their classes. It also ensures that teachers and learners are fluent in their use – this has a profound impact on children not only on their learning outcomes but also on creating a positive learning climate in which they become confident about being lifelong learners.

Evaluating

Monitoring progress

Teachers should monitor children's progress by *observing* them as they engage in mathematical activities. As observation provides the basis for future teaching, evaluation is integral to the teaching–learning process. Each country or jurisdiction will have different reporting schedules for mathematics curricula. There are also some broad principles which can be considered. While observing the children, consider the following questions:

- What do the children know now and what can they do confidently?
- What types of activity will help children build on what they know?
- What difficulties are children experiencing and how can their mathematical understanding be developed?
- How can mathematics be incorporated into other curriculum areas?

Observations should be conducted regularly. When monitoring children's progress in mathematics teachers should:

- observe children performing a range of mathematical tasks and in a variety of contexts
- record observations systematically
- note which modes of representation children prefer
- annotate and collect work samples over time to complement observations.

In addition to observations, teachers are often required to complete *checklists* of mathematical behaviours and skills and to conduct *tests* to determine their mathematical levels and progression. Although assessment has become more formalised in recent times, observation continues to be the most appropriate method for evaluating the progress of young children.

However, with the advent of new technologies, using *e-portfolios* to document children's progress over a school year is a powerful way to show their progressive and cumulative learning. Observations can be recorded and artefacts of learning can be collected over time. There are many new *apps* coming onto the market every day, but in fact children are also able to create their own learning stories with simple software like PowerPoint. Buddying up young children in the first years of compulsory schooling with a partner in the final years of primary school can result in wonderful collaborative work. In the following example, Sean, five years of age and in his first year of school, worked with a buddy in Year 6 (11 years of age) to create a portfolio of his learning in his early years class. They used a digital video and still cameras, recording devices and PowerPoint (for importing pictures, movies and sound) to create what Sean regarded as the most important examples of his learning, within a framework that was designed by his teacher.

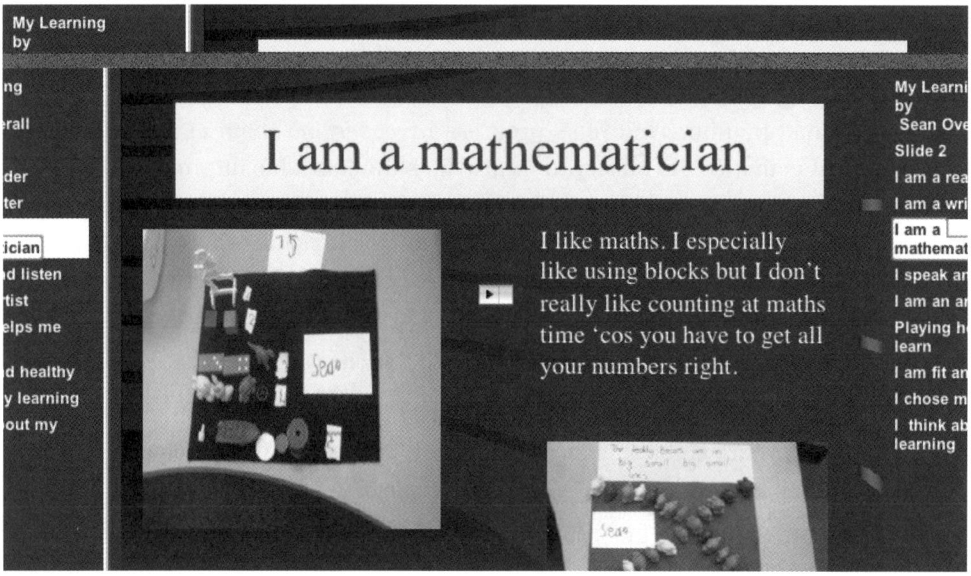

Figure 11.8: *'I am a mathematician', by Sean*

Sean's portfolio (Figure 11.8) summarised his views on his first year at school:

I am a reader
I am a writer
I am a mathematician
I speak and listen
I am an artist
Playing helps me learn
I am fit and healthy
I chose my learning
I think about my learning

This form of documentation about an individual's learning goes beyond knowledge acquisition to facilitate his reflections about the experience of learning itself and enables him to build a strong identity of self as a learner who is engaged and interested in the process. Having a permanent and electronic version of these experiences then enables the learner to see his growth over time. This powerful record of their progress builds the children's confidence and provides a catalyst for sharing their achievements with their families.

Authentic assessment that is part of the ongoing education process has become much more important in the early years. Yelland et al. (2008) created a multiliteracies *portrait, pedagogies* and *pathways* framework (Appendix 4) in order to locate their *observations* of young children engaged in learning in positive and productive ways. They believed that their documentation could create a multilayered framework of portraits, pedagogies and pathways that would allow them to better *document* and *understand* how to create effective contexts for learning. This framework was focused on the children's strengths rather than on what they *did not* know. It formed the basis for their observations and evaluations of what the children were capable of and how they, as their teachers, could build on the knowledge.

The multiliteracies *portrait* documents the interests, capabilities and preferences of a child and considers what they *can* do and enjoy doing. It provides an opportunity for parents and teachers to share information on home practices and discuss how they might contribute to the child's learning. The portrait thus provides a starting point for teachers and enables them to make connections between school and home practices so that children realise that their existing skills and knowledge are *valued*. The multiliteracies portrait constructs an image of the child as competent and capable in her world. Teachers can send home a digital camera, or voice recorder, and provide 'prompts' that would enable a family to help their child to structure a portrait. Table 11.1 presents a portrait of four-year-old George, who loved to build major constructions in his preschool class.

Each child's portrait began with a consideration of her interests and her natural inclinations. What sort of things did she show interest in at home, with her extended family and in her community? When did she seem most engaged, interested and curious? Families were encouraged to take or select photos that represented these particular interests of their child. The photos could have been of people, activities, objects or games. Thus families, who knew the most about the children, were recruited to assist in creating a visual and linguistic portrait of each child. The children were encouraged to take their own photos of their world and interests as part of portrait making. This was valuable data for the portrait.

The portrait was complemented by observations from teachers at school who watched the children at play and noted their preferences. A teacher could focus on the activities that a child enjoyed the most, document choices she made and note how the child made use of available resources. In particular, teachers looked for evidence as to how children chose to represent their ideas and make meaning. They could also take photographs and make anecdotal notes about the various activities the child completed. The provision of time for preschool teachers and primary school teachers to co-construct a child's portrait with parents was valued (Yelland et al. 2008).

Table 11.1: *The multiliteracies portrait*

PORTRAIT PROMPTS	EXAMPLE OF GEORGE
What does the child like and show interest in?	Building, drawing, making things Photo of card construction Photo of block construction Photo of house plan
When and how is she most engaged, interested and curious?	Investigating, creating, making things. Generally engaged, interested and curious.

Table 11.1: *cont.*

PORTRAIT PROMPTS	EXAMPLE OF GEORGE
What can the child do and how does she represent his ideas and make meaning?	Intricate drawings and buildings in particular.
What choices does she make and how does he choose to communicate and make sense of things?	Builds or makes reconstructions of experiences or ideas.
What resources can/does he choose to use?	Blocks, cardboard shapes, boxes, cards, tape, paper, scrap materials.
What evidence is there of the child actively designing, inquiring and initiating?	See anecdotes and learning stories.
What does he wonder about?	How things in the world work.

Source: Yelland et al. 2008

Teachers translated the questions into activities that they believed enabled them to construct a useful profile of each child and her learning preferences. Some ideas they tried were:

- Sending home a camera for the child to use or asking the parents to take digital photos of the things their child most likes doing at home or in the community. The children were also asked to take photos of the three things they most like doing at school.
- Having the parents and their child create a collection of things they wanted to share with the teacher (e.g. photos, objects).
- Providing the children with an opportunity to specifically articulate what they like to do and the things they regard as being important for them.
- Creating a 'digital suitcase' of items that reflected the interests of the child.
- Creating a portfolio or learning story of each child's learning journey over the period of the year that the child was in the group.

Some teachers used the portrait process to map out a range of ways to identify the obvious modes of learning for which children demonstrated a preference. They arranged for opportunities to:

- talk to a parent or the child about what the child likes or loves
- give the child an enlarged photo of herself on which she was to record 'things I like to see/watch, things I like to do, things I like to think about, what I like to talk about, what I like to play, things I like to design or build, things I like to listen to, places I like to be, people I like to be with, things I can do'

- send home with the child a blank A3 piece of paper – everyone who met the child was to trace his or her hand and write something about the child within the hand.

Applying the multiliteracies portrait, pedagogies and pathways framework

Yelland et al.'s (2008) project focused on pedagogy. A teacher's pedagogical approach – how he or she planned for learning in the classroom, and responded reflexively to the strengths and needs of each child – was guided by the pedagogy of multiliteracies (New London Group 1996). This maps directly onto the components of Learning by Design (Kalantzis & Cope 2012) whereby *experiencing, conceptualising, analysing* and *applying* correspond respectively with *situated practice, overt instruction, critical framing* and *transformed practice.*

Constructing and documenting this framework with examples of young children's entry-level and advanced practices constituted one way of organising children's learning. It helped teachers to plan more effectively and richly for each learner in the Yelland et al. (2008) study. By compiling examples of children's practices within the Multiliteracies Pedagogical Framework, teachers were able to see more options for learning and subsequently construct creative pathways to print literacy as required by the traditional school curriculum.

The observations were very detailed and were only used for those students who were identified as being at risk. The Multiliteracies Pedagogical Framework enabled teachers to think more precisely and systematically about what strategies were needed to advance the learning of particular children. For many teachers, creating a portrait was enough for them to design appropriate learning activities. The Multiliteracies Pedagogical Framework then provided teachers with a way in which to better understand the learning needs of the children.

The Multiliteracies Pedagogical Framework was designed to allow teachers to make decisions about the best entry points for children's literacy and numeracy learning. It identifies the complexities and sophistication of children's practices that are not often visible in traditional testing techniques.

In the Yelland et al. (2008) project, the framework was constructed across four dimensions of learning and four communication modalities (visual, spatial, aural and gestural) – the linguistic mode that is more commonly associated exclusively with literacy learning was omitted. Each modality was mapped across the relational, foundational, critical and creative dimensions of learning. As teachers observed evidence of a child operating in a particular mode, they simply marked (by shading) the degree to which this evidence has been demonstrated. In the teaching and learning context, teachers planned for and were alert to the emergence of foundation skills and knowledge, as well as being aware of the children's relational understandings, insight and connections. They actively fostered and encouraged the children to critically analyse or question the way things are, and provided diverse opportunities for children to explore and realise their ideas through creative collaborations and actions.

The pedagogical framework could be used to construct learning *pathways* that provided children with personalised learning approaches – these were built on strengths initially and were later expanded to a full repertoire of communication modalities. The pathways planner (Appendix 5) was designed to help teachers to think through how they might best provide new learning experiences for a learner. Consideration of the Multiliteracies Pedagogical Framework and subsequent learning pathways was regarded as a practical way to plan for responsive learning opportunities for children, with explicit examples provided to illustrate a continuum of learning.

Summary

This chapter has highlighted some important issues in the design of teaching and learning experiences in mathematics. In the teaching–learning process, the three phases of designing, teaching and evaluating are cyclic. These phases are constantly revisited in the daily practice of teaching in order to facilitate young children's learning.

Throughout this book we have suggested activities and materials that support and encourage the development of mathematical thinking. A teacher's beliefs about teaching and learning mathematics and the availability of resources also influence the type of classroom activities chosen and how time and space are organised.

Finally, teachers should reflect on the relationship between teaching and learning in mathematics and ask themselves and, if appropriate, their colleagues:

- What was the purpose of this activity?
- What did the children learn while they were engaged in this activity?
- Did the learning outcomes match the purpose?
- How could this activity be implemented more effectively?
- Which activities would provide an appropriate follow-up to this activity?

References

Kalantzis, Mary and Bill Cope, 2012, *New Learning: Elements of a Science of Education*, 2nd edn, Melbourne, Australia: Cambridge University Press

New London Group, 1996, 'A Pedagogy of Multiliteracies', *Harvard Educational Review*, 60(1), 66–92

Yelland, N. J, 2007, *Shift to the Future: Rethinking Learning with New Technologies in Education*, New York: Routledge

Yelland, N., Cope, W. and Kalantzis, M., 2008, 'Learning by Design: Creating Pedagogical Frameworks for Knowledge Building in the 21st Century' (Special Invited Issue), *Asia Pacific Journal of Teacher Education*, 36(3), 197–213

Yelland, N. J., O'Rourke, M., Lee, L. and Harrison, C., 2008, *Rethinking Learning in Early Childhood Education*, Buckingham, UK: Oxford University Press

Lucky money envelope for Chinese New Year

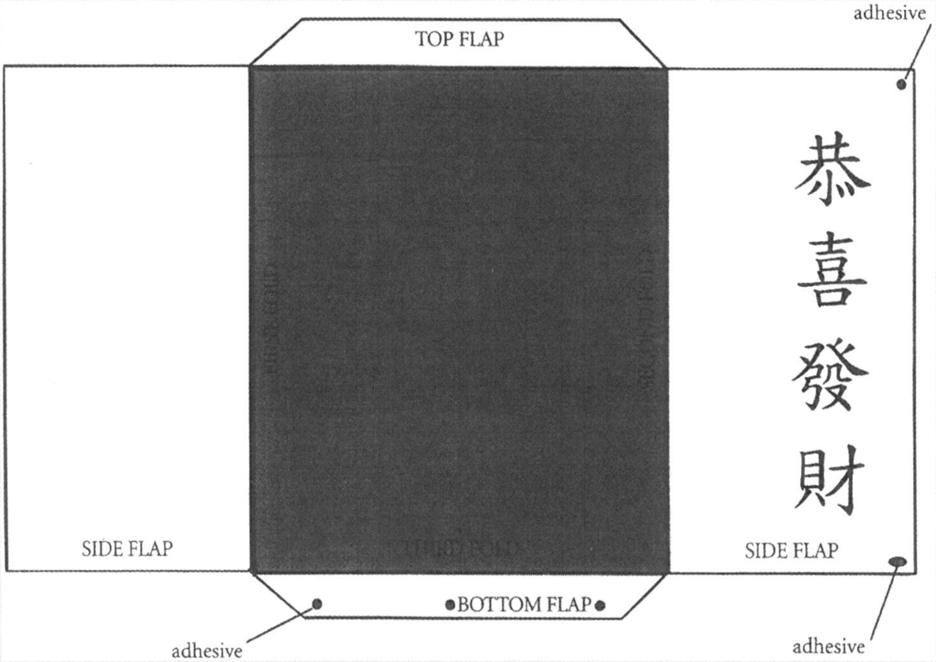

Chinese addition sheet

1 = 一	6 = 六
2 = 二	7 = 七
3 = 三	8 = 八
4 = 四	9 = 九
5 = 五	10 = 十

Try these:

二 + 八 =　　　　一 + 七 =

六 + 一 =　　　　九 + 九 =

四 + 五 =　　　　十 + 三 =

七 + 四 =　　　　二 + 六 =

Now make up some of your own for your friend to calculate!

What do you think these numerals are?

十一
十六
二十三
八十五

Materials for early mathematical explorations

acorns

bags – paper and plastic
balance scale
balloons
beads
bolts
bottle tops
boxes
bread tags
buttons

calculators
calendars
cards for collage
cocktail sticks
clay
clipboards
clocks
clothes pegs
coloured paper
containers
corks
cotton reels
counters
cubes
cups

diaries
dice
dominoes
dowling rods

egg cartons
egg timers

fabrics
feathers
felt pieces
foil
funnels

glitter
glue

hooks

keys

Lego
lids

magazines
marbles
margarine tubs
milk cartons
mirrors

newspaper
number lines
nuts and bolts

paddle pop sticks
paints
paper
paper plates
pasta
pebbles
pipe cleaners
plastic cups

ribbons
rubber bands
rulers

scissors
scrapbooks
seed pods
shells
shoe boxes
sorting trays
spinners
straws
string

tape measures
tape recorder
thread
toothbrushes
toothpicks
toys of all kinds

zips

Multiliteracies Pedagogical Framework

DIMENSIONS OF LITERACY	VISUAL MODE: DRAWINGS, PAINTINGS, PHOTOS, GRAPHICS, VIDEO	
Foundational Direct teaching of skills and knowledge – i.e. what visuals mean and how you might use them.	**Entry** Responds to visual cues, such as photos or graphics, to direct to routines – e.g. washing hands, snack time, a sequence of activities. Successfully completes repetitive tasks such as jigsaw puzzles. Recognises and responds to road signs.	**Advanced** Able to make sense of and interpret the visual world symbolically with diagrammatic representation. Able to use symbols to communicate abstract concepts, such as speed or other movements.
Meaning making Makes connections and uses visual cues for his/her own purposes.	**Entry** Able to make choices from visual cues to decide what to do. Creates a link between visual cues and a sequence of actions. Able to make a connection between colours and feelings. Sequences a series of visual cues to tell a story.	**Advanced** Able to interpret feelings and emotions from photos and drawings. Can respond to such questions as 'how does the photo make you feel?' Able to construct a mind map with multiple connections. Can use colours to communicate a mood.
Critical Analyses contextual cues and relationships to weigh up possible meanings and courses of action.	**Entry** Distinguishes between alternative choices for a particular situation and able to decide on an appropriate course of action. Uses contextual knowledge to assist evaluation and decision making.	**Advanced** Able to analyse why visual advertising shapes people's behaviour. Can 'read' possible intentions of those communicating through visual representations.
Creative Uses visuals to construct his/her own meaning and translate ideas.	**Entry** Able to construct a photo story using props. Creates a 2D design and uses in 3D construction – e.g. for block and sandpit play.	**Advanced** Uses an intricate visual design to map out an idea or experience. Translates intentions into a design.

DIMENSIONS OF LITERACY	SPATIAL MODE: CONSTRUCTION, DESIGN	
Foundational Developing a sense of own space and interpersonal space. A repertoire of skills and knowledge for objects in space.	**Entry** Realisation of 'fit' in space: • Bodies – personal and community space. • Objects in space – e.g. jigsaws. • Activities in space. Can distinguish different shapes, such as 'straight' bits, to assist in completing puzzles.	**Advanced** Understands terms such as *length*, *perimeter* and *area*. Knows spatial symbols and can construct a story map. Uses symbols and space to represent 3D constructions.
Meaning making Sees links and connections between different spatial representations and constructions.	**Entry** Cause and effect – understands why/how space is taken up. Realises components of objects/bodies in space. Sees connections between representations of constructions.	**Advanced** Able to follow meaning of maps. Can see links between a 2D design and 3D construction. Records details of own constructions in a 2D drawing.
Critical	**Entry** Uses strategic thinking to work out a puzzle. Works out an order to progress in a puzzle. Uses guess and check. Goes beyond trial and error.	**Advanced** Engages in problem solving when boundaries and limits are given – e.g. create a structure with newspaper and tape that is one metre tall, which the group could sit inside.
Creative Designing, developing, making, acting on and realising ideas.	**Entry** Builds detailed constructions that include order, pattern and form.	**Advanced** Builds intricate constructions and can talk in detail about them. Creates a design from an idea and makes a 3D construction.

DIMENSIONS OF LITERACY	AURAL MODE: MUSIC, VOICE TONES, SOUND EFFECTS	
Foundational Knowledge of vocabulary to describe sounds and music.	**Entry** Identifying sounds and rhythms. Following sound patterns. Recognising voice tones.	**Advanced** Reads with expression. Modulates voice to mood of story.
Meaning making Using prior knowledge and life experience to make sense of different sounds, tones and music.	**Entry** Demonstrates understanding of the meaning of different voice tones. Knows when to use loud and soft voices. Recognises meaning of different sound cues – e.g. bells. Can put a sound to a visual – e.g. car skidding.	**Advanced** Changes tone and speed of voice to add a layer of meaning. Interprets mood from music. Communicates via music.
Critical Engages in feedback, analysis and comparison.	**Entry** Discriminates between different types of music and can comment on cause and effect. Can comment on how sounds convey meaning.	**Advanced** Able to discuss musical interpretations and responses. Able to identify music preferences and explain why. Reflects on what works in a musical composition or soundscape.
Creative Takes a risk and steps into the unknown to compose.	**Entry** Experiments with voice tones and modulations. Creates a sound to communicate a mood, object or person.	**Advanced** Creates a soundscape as background to a story which includes a sequence of changes. Recognisable beginning, middle and end.

DIMENSIONS OF LITERACY	GESTURAL: BODY LANGUAGE, FACIAL EXPRESSIONS, SOCIAL CONNECTION	
Foundational Developing a repertoire of gestural communication forms.	**Entry** Follows gestural indicators – e.g. pointing, mimicking, facial expressions. Uses gestures to make social contact and interact. Uses eye contact signals. Successfully engages in games requiring gestures to indicate turn taking.	**Advanced** Knows, understands and uses the basics of body language and gestural communications. Has developed a vocabulary in relation to gestural communication.
Meaning making Communicating through and interpreting gestural communication forms.	**Entry** Can 'read' the meaning behind gestures. Able to role play various emotions and communicates needs via gestures. 'Reads' feelings from an image.	**Advanced** Interprets meaning of a dance or mime. Reads different levels of intensity related to body language. Aware of cultural differences for social norms of gestures.
Critical Critiquing, analysing and revising actions on receiving feedback about effectiveness.	**Entry** Acts out a scenario – e.g. from a playground incident – then revises actions using feedback. Works out what is needed to communicate such things as friendship, welcome and acceptance. Can make suggestions about another child's body language in order to assist social relationships.	**Advanced** Uses contextual knowledge to understand meaning of gestures and expressions in different situations.
Creative Designing, developing, making, acting on and realising ideas.	**Entry** Can plan and design a simple sequence of actions that tell a story.	**Advanced** Can design (plan, negotiate) and organise a complex sequence that tells a story – e.g. mime, dance.

Planning the multiliteracies pathway

Name of child

Preferred modes of communication (i.e. visual, aural, gestural, spatial)
To build on his/her strengths in these modes, I will:
Interests, knowledge and experience the child brings that could provide a foundation for literacy learning
Foundational skills that are a priority for development
Ideas for development that utilise strengths and interests
How the child responded
Implications for my practice and approach, based on the child's response
Meaning making skills that are a priority for development
Ideas for development that utilise strengths and interests
How the child responded
Implications for my practice and approach, based on the child's response
Critical-thinking skills that are a priority for development
Ideas for development that utilise strengths and interests
How the child responded
Implications for my practice and approach, based on the child's response
Priorities for fostering the child's creativity and applying multiliteracies learning to pursue his/her own ideas
Ideas for development that utilise strengths and interests
How the child responded
Implications for my practice and approach, based on the child's response

Index